Population, Resources and Development

Jane Chrispin

Geography Co-ordinator, South East Derbyshire College

Dr Francis Jegede

Lecturer in Geography, University of Derby

Collins Educational

An imprint of HarperCollins*Publishers*

Contents

Skills matrix
(distribution of numbered tasks)

Chapter	Understanding text: newspapers, classification	Graphical/mapping methods, annotated diagrams	Analysis of data: tables, graphs, diagrams	Analysis of photographs	Analysis of maps	Statistical analysis, calculations	Values enquiry	Project work: library research, fieldwork	Writing: essays, reports, speeches, creative
1	4, 14, 15, 16, 19, 23	11, 20, 21	7, 8, 10	2	1, 6, 7, 8, 12, 15, 18	9	4, 13, 21, 23	3, 5, 17	22
2	3, 4, 5, 6, 8, 9, 12, 13, 17, 18	7	11	4			13	1, 2, 14, 15	10, 16, 19
3	1, 3, 4, 8, 13, 15, 18, 28, 31	7, 9, 12, 23, 29, 30	6, 8, 10, 16, 21, 24, 25, 26	11, 18	5, 11, 13, 14, 27	2, 17, 19, 22	28	20	20, 28, 32
4	2, 3, 7, 11, 12, 16, 18, 19, 21, 22, 25	6, 14, 15, 17, 20, 24, 26	7, 9, 10, 13, 14, 15, 16, 22	21	1, 4, 10, 13	5	3, 27, 28	4, 5	23, 29
5	5, 7, 8, 13, 14, 16, 26, 28, 32, 33, 34, 37, 38, 39, 40	2, 6, 20, 36	3, 4, 10, 11, 15, 22, 23, 27, 30, 31, 35	21	10, 12, 27	25	14, 19	1, 12, 17	5, 7, 9, 10, 24
6	4, 5, 6, 17, 18, 19, 23, 27, 28, 30, 33, 34, 35	7, 12, 15, 21, 29, 37	1, 2, 3, 4, 8, 9, 13, 14, 16, 22, 24, 25, 26, 32, 33	1, 10, 11	31	20	6, 11		21, 36
7	2, 3, 6, 10, 20, 23, 24, 25, 26, 27, 30, 31	3	1, 7, 11, 12, 16, 17, 19, 31		4, 5, 13, 14, 15, 17		28	8, 9, 21, 29	5, 18, 22
8	5, 6, 7, 12, 13, 15, 16, 17	9	3, 4, 7, 8	11	1, 10, 3		11	1, 2	14, 18
9	1, 2, 4, 7, 13, 18, 19	8, 10, 16	2, 4, 14	2, 4, 18	3, 9, 11	12		5, 15	6, 20
10	6, 7, 8, 9, 10, 14, 15, 19, 20	16	1, 2, 3, 4, 7, 13, 16, 17, 19			2	21	5, 11, 18	12, 18, 21, 22
11	1, 3, 4, 5		2, 3	2, 3		5	5		5

To the student

In this book we have tried to illustrate how the uneven global distributions of population and resources lead to different levels of development throughout the world. We are constantly being reminded, on our televisions and through other forms of media, that there are many people who are underprivileged and who lack the basic essentials which others take for granted. Quality of life varies enormously throughout the world and we have written this book in order to help you understand why some of these inequalities exist.

The main theme of each chapter is outlined in a chapter plan. This plan shows how each section in the chapter is linked. We hope that this helps simplify the otherwise very complex nature of the subject-matter of the book.

We have included a variety of activities, in the form of questions and tasks, to help you work either on your own, or in groups, on the issues raised in the book. These, we hope, will help you to understand the whole nature of development and to put it into a real life context.

Most chapters include case studies which range across a variety of countries from all over the world. The case studies help reinforce theories about development and we hope will help you to understand the rather abstract nature of some of these theories. In the text, both theories and case studies are clearly identified to make it easier for you to follow. In order to succeed at A-level, it is advisable to supply a variety of examples and include detailed information in your answers to questions. We hope that the numerous case studies provided will help you do this.

Words with which we thought you might not be familiar are printed in bold where they first appear in each chapter. This indicates that they are included in the glossary. At the end of each chapter, there is a summary bringing together important points and which may be useful for revision purposes.

We hope that the contents of this book will prompt you to investigate further aspects of development and encourage you to take an interest in matters which affect the global community. As one of the authors is a Nigerian, and the other British, we have pooled our wealth of experience with the intention of helping students appreciate the complex nature of development. A number of the issues covered by this book show that there are almost always varied opinions towards the same topic. We would therefore encourage you to consider as many different viewpoints as possible. This may involve you in your own research and we hope it will stimulate you to hold your own, lasting interest in themes about development. Ultimately, it may be that you could contribute something worthwhile towards making the world a better and fairer place in which to live.

Jane Chrispin and Francis Jegede

1 Growth, wealth and happiness

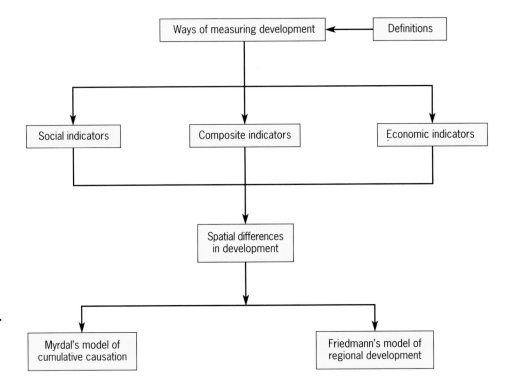

?

1 Study Figure 1.1. The aim of the Peters projection is to show the correct size of continents in relation to each other.

a Compare Figure 1.1 with map projections used in an atlas and state how the Peters projection is different.

b Explain why the Peters projection has been used here to show the North-South divide.

2 Look at Figures 1.2–1.4.

a Would you say that the people shown are happy or unhappy in their situations?

b In your opinion, is there anything that they are lacking or have, that affects their happiness?

c Using one image, write a letter expressing how you would feel in a similar situation.

3a Identify those areas in your country which may be regarded as either 'rich' or 'poor'. Describe the main features of these areas which make you classify them in this way.

b On a smaller scale (such as your local government area or nearest city), identify the places which could be regarded as rich or poor. Suggest reasons for the differences.

1.1 Introduction

Wealth is not evenly distributed among countries and people throughout the world. We live in a world where inequality is a fact of life. In spite of the advances in technology, which have made many rich countries even richer, the vast majority of the world's population still lives in poverty.

Inequalities exist at different scales. On a global scale, the rich countries of Western Europe, North America, Australasia and Japan are often grouped together and referred to as the **developed countries**. The term the rich 'North' is also used to describe them because most of these countries, except those in Australasia, are in the northern hemisphere (Fig. 1.1). Other countries, located mainly in the southern hemisphere, are generally poorer and are often referred to as the poor 'South'. The term **developing countries** has been used to describe these countries which are relatively poor. The **North-South divide** is also used to express the spatial patterns of inequalities on this global scale.

Even on a national scale, within each country, whether more developed or less developed, we can see areas or regions which are wealthier than others. This inequality of wealth within a country is just as extreme as the inequality which exists between different nations, and this is particularly so for the developing countries. Here, the poor regions tend to be so lacking in resources that it is highly unlikely that they could ever attract any development or investment without active government policies aimed at diverting resources to such areas. The poor areas therefore tend to become even poorer, while the comparably wealthier areas become richer (see section 1.4). Even at the local level in any country, there exists an uneven distribution of wealth and resources (Figs 1.2–1.4).

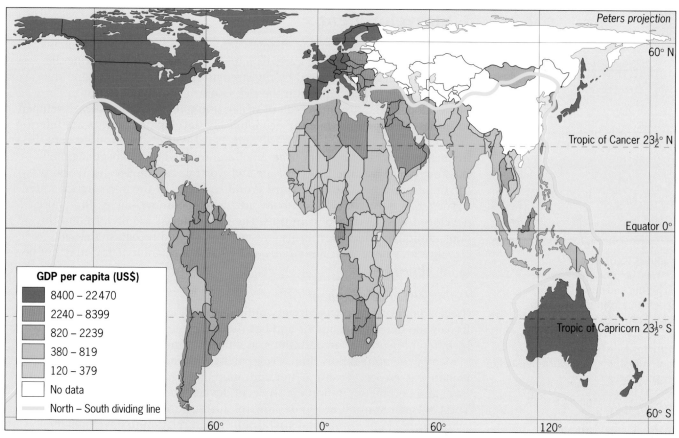

Figure 1.1 The 'developed' North and the 'developing' South as identified in the Brandt report, 17 December 1979, with the global distribution of GDP, 1992 (*Source: World Factbook*, CIA)

GDP per capita (US$)
- 8400 – 22 470
- 2240 – 8399
- 820 – 2239
- 380 – 819
- 120 – 379
- No data
- North – South dividing line

Peters projection

60° N

Tropic of Cancer 23½° N

Equator 0°

Tropic of Capricorn 23½° S

60° S

60°   0°   60°   120°

Figure 1.2 Homeless, London

Figure 1.3 Waiting for food distribution, southern Sudan

Figure 1.4 Ladakh village school, Kashmir, India

1.2 Development

The meaning of 'development' changes according to the value judgements we make about other countries. Early examples of terms used to describe the poorer countries (as measured by the strength of their economies and the nature of their relationship with the rich countries) include 'colony', 'undeveloped' and 'primitive', all of which imply that economically developed countries are superior while the economically developing counties are inferior. Similarly, terms such as 'First World' and 'Third World' are not used very frequently now, as they stem from a definition based on political alignment – the First World was the USA, Europe and Australasia, the Second World was the Communist bloc, and the Third World consisted of the non-aligned states.

The terms most widely used today are 'developed/developing' and 'more developed/less developed' countries. The former terms are preferred in this book, although whichever terms you use, you should recognise that all classifications have their limitations and what is acceptable today, may not be so in the future.

Definitions of development

'Development' as a concept is very difficult to define. The term 'development' has a wide range of meanings and has therefore been used in a variety of ways, by different people or organisations, at different times.

Many geographers now link development with improvements in human welfare e.g. greater wealth, better education and health. Environmental issues have also become an important aspect of development throughout the world. The UN Earth Summit in Rio de Janeiro, during June 1992, examined the whole issue of environmental **sustainability** in relation to development (Fig. 1.5). Conservation and the sustainable use of the environment, rather than just the economic factors, are now important considerations in all debates about development (Fig. 1.6).

?

4   Read Figure 1.6.
a   List the possible responses, including your own, to development in the Amazon rainforest.
b   Identify a range of values and attitudes which influence responses to development in environmentally sensitive areas.

5   Make a newspaper search for articles which deal with environmental issues in development. Summarise the issues involved.

Brazil to drive road through rainforest

The Brazilian government is to accelerate plans for a far-reaching development programme in the Amazon rainforest, including driving paved highways hundreds of miles through one of the last great wildernesses on Earth.

President Fernando Henrique Cardoso wound up a visit to the Amazon by pledging to extend the Trans-Amazonian highway system, begun under the military regime in the 1960s, which has already enormously damaged the environment.

The new paved road will link Brazil to Peru and the Pacific, giving it an important outlet to the Far East. 'We're making economic studies of the viability of this highway, and I think the road will happen,' Mr Cardoso said. 'The road to the Pacific is an old dream of Brazilians.'

Existing unpaved routes will also be surfaced to the north to Venezuela, and to the south to Cuiabá, in the Mato Grosso, joining the Amazon road system to the industrial heartland.

Referring specifically to the Trans-Pacific link-up, Fernando Gabeira, a Green Party deputy, warned: 'This highway poses a great danger not only to plant and animal species in the Amazon but would also endanger the survival of Indian tribes living on its proposed route.'

The pledge came after the president promised a new attitude to the rainforest that would allow development while preserving the environment.

During his high-profile tour, he also met Indian and community leaders and promised to step up the effort to create protected areas for Indians of the region.

Announcing plans to expand environmental tourism, he said: 'Nothing generates more jobs than tourism, nothing generates more foreign exchange than tourism.'

While the advanced countries are pushing hard for conservation in the Amazon, an indication of the domestic pressures on Mr Cardoso came from Amazonino Mendes, governor of Amazon state.

Refusing even to shake the hands of visiting G7 ambassadors in Manaus, he said: 'We don't need these outsiders telling us what to do. If they want to help, they can give us technology.'

Figure 1.6 Development and the environment (*Source*: Noll Scott, *The Guardian*, 4 April 1994)

Figure 1.5 The Earth Summit, Rio de Janeiro, 7 June 1992: children sign a giant quilt called the Earth Flag supporting pro-environmental measures. At the same time, 178 UN member states agree to a commission on sustainable development to oversee nations' efforts to develop without harming the environment.

Table 1.1 GNP for selected countries, 1992 (*Source:* World Development Report, 1992)

Country	Per capita GNP (US$)
Brazil	2 770
The Gambia	390
Italy	20 510
Nigeria	320
USA	23 120
Japan	28 220

We shall use the term 'development' to mean improvement in people's quality of life and general well-being. It is essential to note that economic growth both leads to, and results from, an increase in output or income of a nation – but economic growth does not necessarily mean that the country is developing. It is possible therefore to have economic growth without development. In other words, development needs economic growth, but economic growth does not necessarily lead to development.

1.3 How do we measure development?

There are several methods of measuring development – some focus on economic indicators, others on the quality of life. The common indices of development and the problems associated with the use of each of these indices are discussed below.

Economic indicators of development: GNP and GDP

Gross National Product (GNP) and **Gross Domestic Product (GDP)** are the most widely used economic measures (indices) of development. GNP may be defined as the total value, or output, of goods and services which become available during a period of time (usually a year) for consumption or saving within a country, plus income from foreign investments. This is usually expressed per head of population (per capita) i.e. the value of GNP divided by the total population. GNP/capita is therefore a measure of average national income.

GNP, as an indicator of development, does have its weaknesses. First, it is often very difficult to obtain accurate information about the economy of a country. Second, what is actually produced in many economically developing countries does not always have a monetary value, so in this respect GNP could be very misleading. For example, **subsistence agriculture** is still extremely important in developing countries. Most of this agricultural produce is used for domestic consumption, and does not count towards the GNP. Third, GNP and GDP are always given in US dollars, so there is a problem of currency conversion – some countries have artifically high or low currencies. Fourth, apart from showing the monetary value of goods and services produced in a country, the GNP alone tells us nothing about the quality of life experienced by the majority of the population (Table 1.1). Fifth, although an increase in GNP is necessary for improvements in living standards to occur, it does not always follow that economic growth automatically produces better living conditions. GNP does not show the *actual* distribution of wealth or the levels of inequality.

Another economic indicator of development is GDP (Figs 1.1 and 1.7). Gross domestic product is defined as the total monetary value of all goods and services produced by a nation during a year (excluding any income from foreign investments).

The major weakness of GNP and GDP as indices of development is that they define a country's economy (rather than its well-being) in monetary terms. They are quantitative rather than qualitative measures and therefore give no indication of the distribution of wealth in each country. Although it is easy to assess the growth of the economy through the GNP figures, GNP does not show if the increase in wealth has been used to improve living standards across the population as a whole.

Social indicators of development

Other non-monetary indicators have been used to measure the levels of social development and standards of living for different countries. Many of these, unlike the strictly economic measures, reveal information about general living

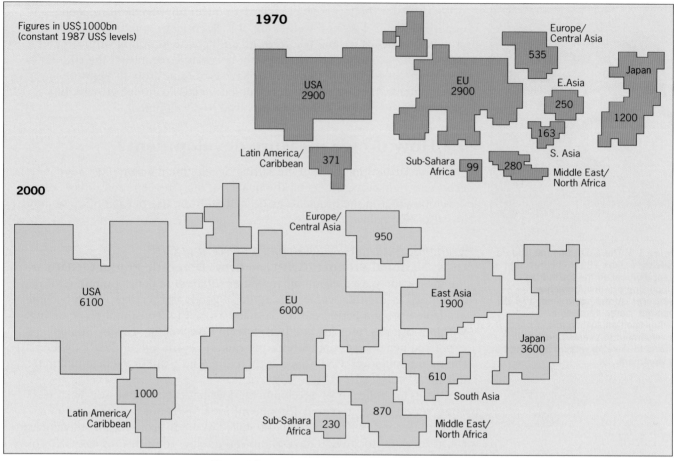

Figure 1.7 Cartograms of global GDP: the size of each country is drawn in proportion to the size of its GDP (*Source: The Financial Times*, 9 March 1994)

standards in each country. Some of these social and demographic indices emphasise quality of life and include measures, or a combination of measures, such as those shown in Table 1.2. We can use a selection of these social indicators to show differences in levels of development between countries (Table 1.3).

In recent years, some of these individual social indicators have been combined and used as composite measures of development. Generally, the latter examples below recognise that economic, social and demographic indicators are closely inter-related.

Physical Quality of Life Index

Life expectancy, infant mortality and adult literacy rates have been combined to produce a useful measure of development known as the Physical Quality of Life Index (PQLI). The PQLI was devised in 1977 by the Overseas Development Council.

Table 1.2 Social indicators of development

- Labour force in agriculture (%)
- Literacy rates (%)
- Life expectancy (years)
- School enrolments as a percentage of the relevant age group
- Infant mortality (deaths per 1000)
- Number of people per doctor
- Calorie supply (per capita)

- Energy consumption (kJ per capita)
- Ownership of consumer durables e.g. washing machines (per capita)
- Ownership of telephones (per capita)
- Quantity of letters sent (per capita)
- Real income (per capita)
- Growth of labour force (%)
- Urban population growth (%)

6a Describe the global variations in levels of GDP per capita in Figure 1.1.
b Say, giving reasons, whether you agree with the division between the rich North and the poor South.

7 Study Figure 1.7.
a Using the figures for 1970 and the estimated GDP figures for the year 2000, calculate the rates of change over the 30-year period.
b Comment on the areas with:
• the greatest rates of change and
• the smallest rates of change.

8a Study Figure 1.1 and Tables 1.1 and 1.3. For those countries listed, compare the levels of GDP per capita with the other indicators of development.
b Which of the indicators best reflect the level of development of the countries selected? Give reasons for your answer.

9a Using Table 1.4, calculate the Spearman's rank correlation (see Appendix A1) between: • GNP per capita and energy consumption, • GNP per capita and average annual population growth.
b Comment on the level of significance of your results.

Table 1.3 Social indicators of development for selected countries (*Source:* CIA, World Bank, WHO, FAO, UNDP)

	Adult literacy (% of total population >15 yrs), 1992	Life expectancy at birth (average year, M and F), 1992	Number of doctors per 10 000 population, 1992	Telephone main lines per 1 000 persons, 1990	Total calories per capita per day, 1991	Human Development Index (HDI), 1990
Brazil	81	66	9.3	63	2 730	0.730
The Gambia	27	45	—	—	2 290	0.086
Italy	97	78	42.4	388	3 498	0.924
Nigeria	51	52	1.3	3	2 200	0.246
USA	98	76	21.4	545	3 642	0.976
Japan	99	79	15.1	441	2 921	0.983

Table 1.4 Social indicators of development for 15 selected countries

	GNP per capita, 1992 (US$)	Energy consumption per capita, 1991 (kg oil equivalent)	Average annual population growth, 1991–2000 (%)
Switzerland	36 080	3 694	0.7
Germany	23 030	4 358	0.0
Norway	25 820	4 925	0.4
France	22 260	4 034	0.4
Japan	28 190	3 586	0.3
New Zealand	12 300	4 284	0.8
Poland	1 910	2 407	0.3
Hungary	2 970	2 392	0.4
Argentina	6 050	1 351	1.0
Turkey	1 980	948	1.9
Colombia	1 330	670	1.5
Egypt	640	580	2.1
Sri Lanka	540	101	1.1
Kenya	310	92	3.5
India	310	235	1.8

The PQLI values range from 0 to 100, and a country with an index greater than 77 suggests that the minimum requirements for well-being are satisfied in that country. One advantage of the PQLI is that the index is simple to use. However, its use is limited because it only takes account of three variables: income levels or purchasing power are not included in the calculation.

Human Development Index
Similar to the PQLI is the Human Development Index (HDI). In 1990, the United Nations Development Programme (UNDP) argued that income growth alone was not a good indication of development and that human development should lead to greater and more sustainable economic growth.

This is a reflection of the current emphasis on human welfare in development, as against the economic priorities of the 1950s and the 1960s. Consequently, the UNDP devised the HDI in an attempt to measure development.

The HDI consists of three aspects of development:

• real income per capita, i.e. taking into account what a person is actually able to buy with a given income;

• adult literacy combined with the mean number of years of schooling, which gives a measure of educational attainment;

• life expectancy at birth.

The HDI is expressed as a value between 0 and 1. The closer to 1 the score is, the higher the level of human development. The variations in levels of human development in West Africa are illustrated in Table 1.6.

?

10a Study the PQLI values in Table 1.5 and group the countries into those that are developing and those that are developed.

b Using Table 1.5, list the countries which have a low PQLI and a high GNP, and those which have a high PQLI and a low GNP. Suggest reasons for these differences.

11 Study Table 1.6.

a Using an appropriate graphical technique, compare life expectancy at birth with levels of adult literacy for the selected countries.

b Comment on your results.

Table 1.5 Physical quality of life index and GNP (*Source:* UN, CIA, World Bank)

	Male and female life expectancy at birth, 1994	Infant mortality (per 1 000 live births 1994	Adult literacy (%), 1992	PQLI (index from 0–100)	GNP per capita, 1992
Afghanistan	43	163	29	20	—
Bangladesh	56	108	35	41	220
Brazil	66	58	81	74	2 770
Brunei	74	8	77	87	—
Cambodia	52	116	35	36	—
Cameroon	56	63	54	49	820
China	68	44	73	80	470
Egypt	64	67	48	60	640
Ethiopia	47	119	62	29	110
Hong Kong	79	7	77	93	15 360
India	60	82	48	48	310
Jamaica	74	14	98	92	1 340
Japan	79	4	99	100	28 190
Kenya	56	69	69	61	310
Kuwait	75	18	74	84	—
Nigeria	50	84	51	49	320
Peru	66	64	85	64	950
Philippines	66	44	90	81	770
S Korea	71	11	96	88	6 790
Saudi Arabia	70	29	62	49	7 510
Sri Lanka	72	18	86	87	540
Sweden	78	5	99	100	27 010
Tunisia	68	43	65	54	1 720
UAE	74	19	68	76	22 020
UK	76	7	99	98	17 790
USA	76	9	98	98	23 240
Venezuela	72	23	88	83	2 910
Yugoslavia	72	20	—	89	—

Table 1.6 Human development index for West Africa (*Source: World Development Report 1994*, World Bank)

HDI Rank		Life expectancy at birth (years), 1990	Adult literacy rate (%), 1990	Mean years schooling, 1990	Real GDP per capita (PPP[1]$), 1990	Human development index, 1990	GNP per capita rank minus HDI rank[2]
131	Ghana	55.0	60.3	3.5	1 016	0.311	9
136	Cote d'Ivoire	53.4	53.8	1.9	1 324	0.286	−23
142	Nigeria	51.5	50.7	1.2	1 215	0.246	11
144	Liberia	54.2	39.5	2.0	857	0.222	−17
145	Togo	54.0	43.3	1.6	734	0.28	−10
150	Senegal	48.3	38.3	0.8	1 248	0.182	−35
161	Mauritania	47.0	23.4	0.7	1 043	0.113	−17
162	Benin	47.0	23.4	0.7	1 043	0.113	−17
164	Guinea Bissau	42.5	36.5	0.3	841	0.090	1
167	The Gambia	44.0	27.2	0.6	913	0.086	−19
168	Mali	45.0	32.0	0.3	572	0.082	−14
169	Niger	45.5	28.4	0.1	645	0.080	−19
170	Burkina-Faso	48.2	18.2	0.1	618	0.074	−21
172	Sierra Leone	42.0	20.7	0.9	1 086	0.065	−17
173	Guinea	43.5	24.0	0.8	501	0.045	−41

[1] PPP = purchasing power parity
[2] A positive number shows that HDI rank is higher than the GNP rank, a negative the opposite

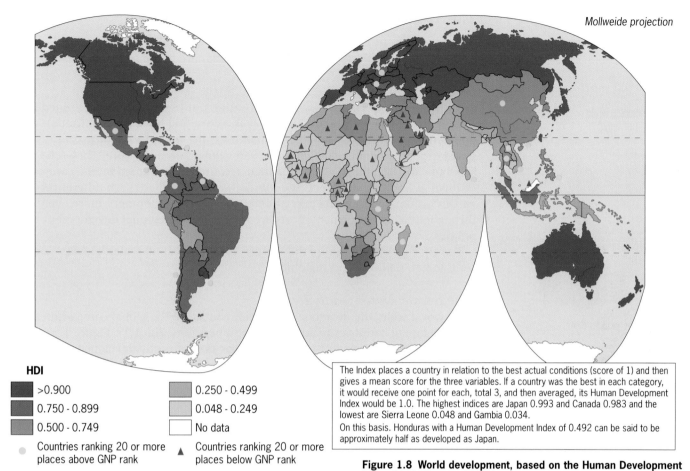

Mollweide projection

HDI

- ■ >0.900
- ■ 0.750 - 0.899
- ■ 0.500 - 0.749
- ■ 0.250 - 0.499
- ■ 0.048 - 0.249
- □ No data

● Countries ranking 20 or more places above GNP rank

▲ Countries ranking 20 or more places below GNP rank

The Index places a country in relation to the best actual conditions (score of 1) and then gives a mean score for the three variables. If a country was the best in each category, it would receive one point for each, total 3, and then averaged, its Human Development Index would be 1.0. The highest indices are Japan 0.993 and Canada 0.983 and the lowest are Sierra Leone 0.048 and Gambia 0.034.

On this basis. Honduras with a Human Development Index of 0.492 can be said to be approximately half as developed as Japan.

Figure 1.8 World development, based on the Human Development Index 1991 (*Source:* NEAB)

12 Study Figure 1.8.
a Give examples of countries which have an HDI ranking 20 or more places *above* their GNP rank.
b Give examples of those countries which have an HDI ranking 20 or more places *below* their GNP rank.
c Suggest reasons why some countries have low GNPs yet high HDIs.

13 Devise your own Human Suffering Index selecting social indicators which you think are important for measuring development.

International Human Suffering Index

The International Human Suffering Index (IHSI) was developed in 1987 by the Population Crisis Committee of Washington, DC. The index measures development based on the following variables: • GNP per capita; • rate of inflation; • growth of the labour force; • urban population growth rate; • infant mortality rate; • daily calorie supply as a percentage of requirements; • access to clean drinking water; • energy consumption per capita; • adult literacy; • personal freedom.

Based on the IHSI index (low indicating good, high indicating bad), Switzerland scored 4, the USA 8 and Mozambique 95 – the worst in Africa according to the 1991 figures. Of the ten highest scores of the IHSI in the world, nine are in Africa.

General problems with indicators of social development
There are other social indicators of development, some of which are under constant review as definitions and concepts of the term 'development' change. Certain aspects of daily life, such as freedom of speech, the right to vote, freedom from discrimination and from subservience to others, and the role of women in society are some of the issues which are considered important in measures of development.

Whichever index you choose, many social indicators of development unfortunately do not reflect inequalities in income distribution. This is in spite of education, health care, and infant mortality being commonly associated with income patterns. Another problem is the lack of agreement for a universal system of measuring social aspects of development.

1.4 Spatial aspects of development

Great contrasts in development often exist between different parts of a country, and it is these contrasts which give rise to what are called 'regional problems'.

Core and periphery

Wealth is never spread evenly over a country, but tends to be concentrated in certain areas. These areas are known as the **core** and have a concentration of population, wealth and resources. In contrast, the **periphery** consists of sparsely populated areas which are less developed than the core. They tend to lack both wealth and resources, or their resources are drained by the core (known as **backwash effect**, see Myrdal's model). Where such differences of wealth occur, governments may attempt to spread development more evenly throughout a country. Such efforts are referred to as regional development policies.

The concept of core and periphery can be applied at all scales: global, continental, national and regional.

Global scale: North-South divide

On a world scale, the developed countries constitute the global core, whereas the developing countries make up the periphery (see Fig. 1.1). Figure 1.9 illustrates the development gap between the economically developed core (rich North) and the economically developing countries of the periphery (poor South).

Continental scale: Western Europe

The west European core (Fig. 1.10) is more attractive to industries than its periphery. This is because the core:

• is near to a large wealthy market;

• has skilled labour available;

• has higher-quality infrastructures;

• has facilities for research and development.

In contrast, the peripheral areas are a long way from the largest industrial markets and the other advantages of the core.

A significant proportion of the UK lies outside the main European core. It may be that the creation of the Channel Tunnel, a fixed all-weather link between Great Britain and mainland Europe, will reduce Great Britain's peripherality. It is important to do this, because the creation of the single European market at the beginning of 1993 gave greater freedom to industry to invest anywhere in Europe, and it is likely that the core will attract even more capital at the expense of the periphery. One of the main responsibilities of the European Commission is to formulate policies which aim at restricting industrial growth in the core areas and diverting it towards more peripheral areas, which might otherwise suffer from continuing decline and rising unemployment.

National scale: Nigeria

Nigeria is a typical example of a country which has wide regional variations in development. Like so many countries in the world, Nigeria is characterised by wide spatial and social inequalities that in some cases have increased in recent years. According to the 1991 census, the official population figure for Nigeria then stood at 88.5 million. The 1991 census gives the mainly Muslim (Hausa-Fulani) northern states a 5 million majority over the southern (mainly Ibo and Yoruba dominated) states. The population throughout the whole of Nigeria is unevenly distributed (Fig. 1.11).

The developing world has 75% of the world's people, but only...

15% of the world's energy consumption

17% of the world's GNP

30% of the world's food grains

18% of world export earnings

11% of world education spending

6% of the world's health expenditure

5% of world science and technology

8% of world industry

Figure 1.9 A world divided (*After:* Trocaire, *Dialogue for Development,* Catholic Agency for World Development, 1984)

Figure 1.10 The core and peripheral areas of Western Europe. Even within the core, wealth is not spread evenly: some areas will attract more investment than others and these wealthier areas are known as the inner core. Areas with a lower concentration of wealth are known as the outer core.

14 What economic advantages could the UK and Ireland derive from developing transport and communication links with the European core?

15a Refer to Figure 1.10 and identify three countries that are within the European core and three countries within the periphery.
b For the three countries in the periphery, explain how their locations relative to the core may affect the future development of each country.

16 What problems may result from a growing concentration of wealth, population and resources in the core area of Europe?

17 Investigate what steps have been, or could be, taken by the European Union (EU) in order to reduce the concentration of wealth in the core and spread it more evenly throughout the member states of the EU?

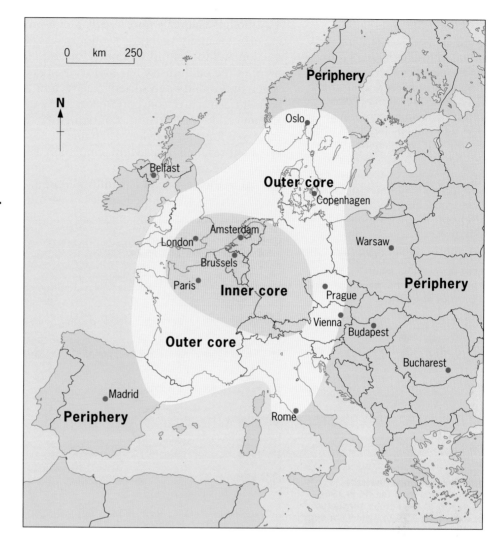

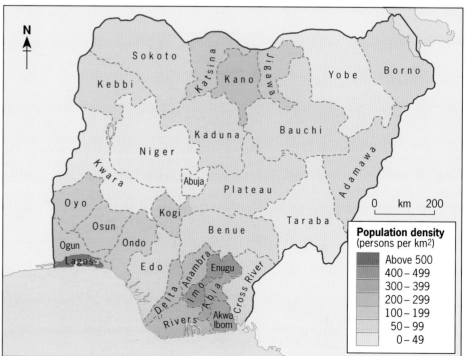

Figure 1.11 Nigeria: population density, 1991 (*Source*: Binns, *Teaching Geography*, vol. 18, no. 2, 1993)

18 Study Figures 1.11–1.13.
a Suggest where Nigeria's core and the peripheral areas might be, and give reasons for your answer.
b The new capital city of Abuja was given planning approval in 1979, and building for Phase 1 of the plan was complete by 1993 (see Fig. 3.1). Do you think that the construction of Abuja will help the Nigerian authorities to reduce these spatial inequalities of development? Give reasons for your answer.

19 Describe the problems facing those developing countries, such as Nigeria, which have wide regional disparities of wealth.

Although Nigeria is now largely a one-product economy (oil production and export), for many years the economy was geared towards agricultural production and the export of a range of cash crops (Fig. 1.12). The rapid development of the oil industry has had widespread repercussions throughout the Nigerian economy and society (see section 7.5). There has been investment in basic infrastructure concentrated in a few urban centres, such as Lagos, Kano, Kaduna and Port Harcourt. Consequently, the output of manufacturing industry increased fourfold between 1970 and 1980. The regional concentration of investment resulted in a steady population drift away from the rural areas to the growing urban centres (Fig. 1.13, see section 4.6). The rural-urban migration has led to the decline of agricultural output. This pattern of development has created greater spatial inequalities of wealth throughout Nigeria.

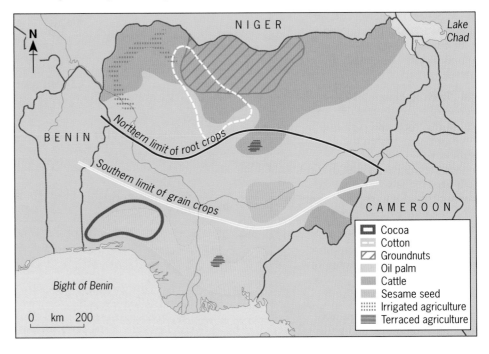

Figure 1.12 Nigeria: main agricultural regions. Before independence from the UK in 1960, the export of cash crops accounted for more than 75% of export earnings and the country was generally self-sufficient in basic foodstuffs.

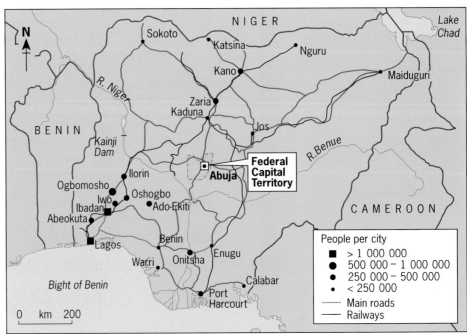

Figure 1.13 Nigeria: cities and communications (*Source:* Binns, in *Teaching Geography*, Vol. 18, no. 2, 1993)

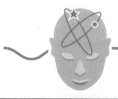

Myrdal's model of cumulative causation

Within individual countries, economic development is likely to take place more rapidly in some areas than in others (Fig. 1.14). The processes which lead to this uneven spread of development were first outlined in a model by Gunnar Myrdal in 1956. This is now known as the model of **cumulative causation** (Fig. 1.15). Essentially, this spatial model attempts to explain why some areas become more economically developed than others. Myrdal's model sets out the following main stages of regional development.

Stage 1

Early economic growth takes place where there are natural advantages. This may be a sheltered coastline where a natural harbour could lead to the development of a major port. Similarly, industries may develop where there is an abundance of natural resources, such as coal mining or iron and steel. Once growth in a region is under way, the area develops more rapidly than its surroundings as the process of cumulative causation takes place. Gradually, acquired advantages, such as skilled labour, improved infrastructure, more efficient services and sizeable markets, reinforce the natural advantages. This area, with both natural and acquired advantages, constitutes the core. As job opportunities arise within the core, people continue to migrate from the periphery. Original industries prosper and the demand for labour increases as further industrial growth occurs. This is the **multiplier effect** which takes place as linked industries become established. As the original growth area continues to develop, this then becomes a **growth pole** (see section 9.3). A chain reaction is set in motion producing self-sustaining economic growth.

Stage 2

The concentration of economic activity leads to a backwash effect as the core region develops at the expense of the periphery. **Downward spirals** in the periphery then occur as people leave in order to find work in the core. Growth in the core is therefore sustained by a constant supply of labour, as well as

Figure 1.14 London's Docklands: In 1980 the Docklands were among the most run-down parts of the capital. Within 10 years, public and private investment had transformed the economy and physical environment of this core region; 1981–90 saw the location of more than 600 new companies and employment boosted from 27 000 to 42 500.

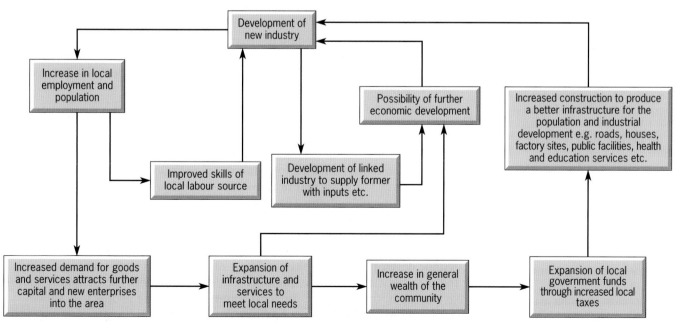

Figure 1.15 Myrdal's model of cumulative causation

Myrdal's model of cumulative causation

COMPANIES FROM
ALL OVER THE WORLD ARE
FLYING INTO WARRINGTON

YOU'D BE BEST
ADVISED TO JOIN THEM

Figure 1.16 Local government advertisement designed to attract investment into an area in England's North-West. This was part of a core region in the late 19th century, but suffered from a downward spiral during de-industrialisation.

?

20 Using the example of Nigeria (see pages 15–16), produce a flow diagram similar to Myrdal's model (Fig. 1.15) for:
a the development of the oil industry,
b the creation of the Federal Capital Territory of Abuja.

21a Draw an annotated diagram to show how a cycle of decline can affect the periphery.
b Around your diagram list the possible responses to regional decline.
c What range of values and attitudes have influenced these?

resources, from the periphery. The loss of valuable labour and resources seriously reduces further industrial development in the periphery.

Stage 3

As core areas flood the periphery with cheap products, the poor areas have little necessity to develop any industry. The result is the industrially expanding region of the core on the one hand, and the stagnating or declining periphery on the other.

In theory, once the process of cumulative causation is under way, it becomes self-sustaining and the core region continues to grow. This process may also work in reverse, however. A factory may close as happened in many parts of Britain during the **de-industrialisation** of the 1980s and 1990s. This creates an overall regional depression, since other industries dependent on the factory will also close. A downward spiral in the core is therefore established, and it may only be possible to reverse this trend through government intervention.

Using Myrdal's model

The cumulative causation model helps to explain the regional variations in the UK's industrial development and the government policies aimed at promoting economic growth in the depressed peripheral areas (Fig. 1.16).

In the UK, both Labour and Conservative governments have used regional development policies to address the problem of regional inequalities – with varying degrees of success. It is important to note that each of the main political parties has its own view on the long-term effectiveness of regional development policies.

The free market viewpoint

One political viewpoint is that inequalities of wealth and development will eventually disappear as a matter of course. According to this view, **spread effects** (opposite to backwash effects) will eventually lead to the spread of wealth throughout the periphery, often along growth poles or along growth axes. This spread of wealth will result from an increasing demand from the core for the raw materials found in the periphery, in order to help sustain the growth of the core. Increased activities in the periphery will lead to an increase in wealth so expansion of industries in this area is eventually made possible.

This view suggests that in a free market, imbalances of wealth are temporary and will ultimately be reduced by the market forces. The Conservative governments of the UK, since 1979, have followed this school of thought: their policies assume that growth will eventually happen even in peripheral areas, without much need for government intervention.

The interventionist viewpoint

Another political viewpoint is that government policies are needed to stimulate economic development in the otherwise peripheral areas. In post-war Britain, successive Labour governments introduced strong regional policies in the form of tax incentives or infrastructure provision to encourage companies to locate in areas of high unemployment. These policies are intended to stimulate economic growth in the periphery, and so increase the likelihood of future industrial investment in these areas.

Whichever political viewpoint is followed, continuing regional imbalances in economic development will have an effect on human development, especially in the periphery. For example, prolonged unemployment in the periphery may have a demoralising effect on the local community. Young people may move away in search of employment elsewhere and leave an ageing population. There is then often a shortage of service provision, as industries moving out, or

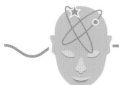

closing down, result in lower tax revenues to pay for services. The productivity of the periphery declines as a result of the loss of the bright and best educated members of the community who may not wish to return to the area.

Friedmann's model of regional development

A more complex model or theory of regional development was proposed by a regional planner, John Friedmann, in 1963. This model is evolutionary, because it shows that spatial inequalities change over time. It is also a spatial model: Friedmann identified four types of areas, each at different stages of development (Fig. 1.17).

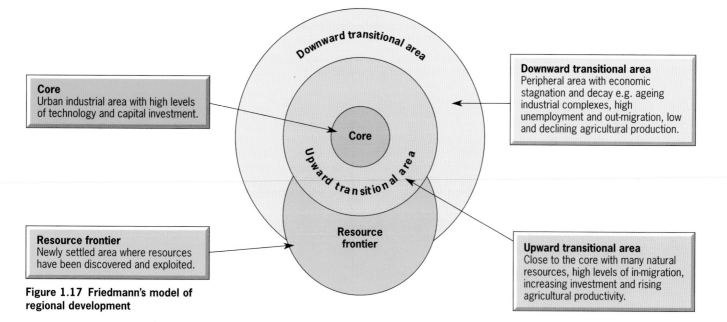

Core
Urban industrial area with high levels of technology and capital investment.

Downward transitional area
Peripheral area with economic stagnation and decay e.g. ageing industrial complexes, high unemployment and out-migration, low and declining agricultural production.

Resource frontier
Newly settled area where resources have been discovered and exploited.

Upward transitional area
Close to the core with many natural resources, high levels of in-migration, increasing investment and rising agricultural productivity.

Figure 1.17 Friedmann's model of regional development

Figure 1.18 Cambridge Science Park: High-tech activitites tend to cluster in areas where they can recruit and keep highly-skilled researchers and technicians. The enterprises need suppliers and services and so reinforce existing centres of production. This then attracts other industries.

The core regions

Core regions are concentrated metropolitan economies with a high potential for economic growth and innovation. These are the centres of the national or international markets with large-scale industry, commercial services and high levels of technology. The core regions present a positive image, and have a concentration of resources, professional and highly skilled workers and a well-developed infrastructure. The growth of the core is often at the expense of the periphery because labour and resources from the periphery move to the core to sustain economic growth. In this respect, the core may be described as parasitic in relation to the rest of the country.

On a national level, we can see this pattern in the urban hierarchy with the country's capital as the national metropolis and other large cities as secondary cores. On an international level, metropolitan areas such as the Paris-London-Amsterdam-Berlin cluster constitute the European core (see Fig. 1.10).

Upward transitional areas

These are growth regions within the periphery and are relatively close to the core. In these areas, the availability of natural resources promotes greatly intensified use of these resources. They are characterised by high immigration rates and industrial and economic growth (Fig. 1.18). These areas also benefit from high levels of investment in industry as well as in agriculture.

Friedmann's model of regional development

22 Essay:
a With reference to any one named country, identify those areas which may be regarded as
• core areas, • resource frontiers and • peripheral areas.
b Describe why and how the economic circumstances of these areas might change in the future.

Downward transitional areas

These are peripheral areas characterised by declining or stagnant economies, often with low agricultural productivity or the loss of a primary resource base, caused by a reduction in the demand for minerals such as coal. These areas may also have old and declining industries, a negative image, and be unfavourably located in relation to the core. Other characteristics of such areas are low rates of innovation, low productivity and an inability to adapt to new economic circumstances due partly to an ageing population as a result of young people moving out of the area. Usually, labour and resources are drained from this area by the core.

Resource frontiers

These areas also lie outside the core regions. They are zones where new development is taking place, for example as a result of newly discovered mineral resources. Other examples of resource frontiers include mountains, deserts and island areas which could be used for recreational purposes. Along with the core regions, these areas perform a major role in generating economic growth throughout the nation.

'Development will never be, and can never be defined to universal satisfaction. It refers, broadly speaking, to desirable social and economic progress, and people will always have different views about what is desirable. Certainly, development must mean improvement in living conditions, for which economic growth and industrialisation are essential. But if there is no attention to the quality of growth and to the social change one cannot speak of development.'

Brandt Report, 1980

'A country, or a village, or a community, cannot be developed: it can only develop itself. For real development means the development of people. Every country in Africa can show examples of modern facilities which have been provided for the people – and which are now rotting unused. If real development is to take place, the people have to be involved… Roads, buildings, increase in crop output… are not development; they are only the tools of development.'

Julius Nyerere, 1973

'Development represents a re-definition of a country's international relations. It involves a shift from an outward-oriented, dependent status to a self-centred, self-reliant position with regard not only to the process of decision making, but more importantly, the pattern and style of production and consumption.'

Marxist/socialist concept of development

Figure 1.19 Selected definitions of development

23 Read Figure 1.19.
a Which of the definitions do you agree with most? Explain why.
b Write your own definition of development.

Summary

- The concept of development has changed over the years, and so have the methods of measuring levels of development.

- Economic development is often expressed in terms of GDP and GNP, which are indicators of national wealth.

- There is a wide 'development gap' between countries mostly in the northern hemisphere and those mostly in the southern hemisphere; a situation often described as the North-South divide.

- Increasingly, development is becoming associated with improvements in human welfare rather than just economic gain.

- Concern for the environment has become a major issue in matters of development.

- Some regions develop more rapidly than others, leading to spatial inequalities in the distribution of resources and wealth.

- Regional development policies are aimed at reducing such variations in levels of development.

- Myrdal's model of cumulative causation and Friedmann's model of regional development help to explain how regional inequalities occur.

2 Colonialism, dependency and aid

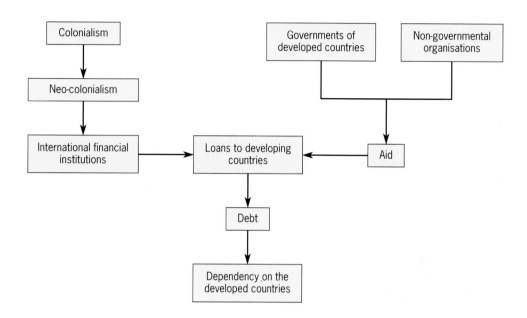

2.1 Introduction

We have to understand the nature and influence of colonialism before we can understand the inequalities which exist between the rich and the poor nations today. Although many countries have gained independence from their colonisers, they have now become dependent on such international financial institutions as the World Bank and the International Monetary Fund (IMF). Increasing amounts of aid given to the **developing countries** by the rich nations, and high interest rates on loan repayments, have plunged many of the poorer countries into a debt crisis. This in itself is a form of dependency. This chapter focuses on some of the economic and social consequences of past colonial control and looks at attempts to ease dependency through aid.

2.2 Colonialism and development

From the mid-fifteenth century onwards, and particularly after about AD1500, powerful European countries began to explore, and expand, into the rest of the world. There were three main motives behind this expansion. First was the exploration motive, the desire to discover places and peoples that were unknown to the explorers. Second was the desire to take Christianity to other people across the world. Third was exploitation: the craving to gain wealth and/or territory through trade or possession.

Europeans 'discovered' new lands in Asia, Africa and the Americas and settled, traded and took possession of them either by treaty or force (Fig. 2.1). By the end of the nineteenth century, much of the world was controlled by the European countries either directly, as part of their empires, or indirectly through the power held by colonial settlers from the home nations (Fig. 2.2). In the twentieth century, **neo-colonialism**, or economic control, over some former colonies still exists through **transnational corporations** (**TNCs**) (see section 6.8).

Figure 2.1 Spaniards in Peru force Indians to carry their loot, *circa* 1532

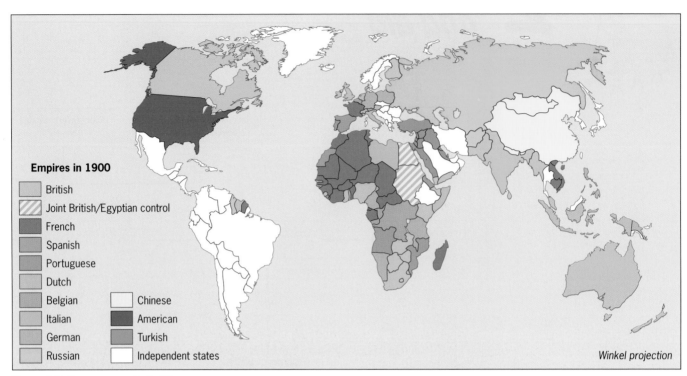

Empires in 1900

- British
- Joint British/Egyptian control
- French
- Spanish
- Portuguese
- Dutch
- Belgian
- Italian
- German
- Russian
- Chinese
- American
- Turkish
- Independent states

Winkel projection

Figure 2.2 European control of the world, 1900

Colonialism in South America

After Christopher Columbus had 'discovered' the 'New World' in 1492, other Spanish and Portuguese sailors set out to claim land for their countries and to spread the Christian faith. At the Treaty of Tordesillas, in 1494, the two colonising nations agreed to the 'Pope's line', which was a boundary between the Portuguese dominated eastern part of South America and the Spanish controlled regions to the west (Fig. 2.3).

The Spanish moved into Mexico during the 1520s and began exploring the west coast of South America. The indigenous people known as the Incas controlled a huge area, including part of the Andes, and stretching from what is now known as Ecuador to as far as northern Chile. Inca society was very complex and organised. The people were cared for by the state when ill, as well as when they reached old age. Most occupations were hereditary, with important skills passed down from one generation to another. The Incas governed a large empire but did not over-exploit it. They needed the resources of their mountain environment to live on, so they **sustained** those resources as best they could within the limits of the farming practices and technology of the time.

Led by Francisco Pizarro, the Spanish army landed on the South American coast in January 1530. During the following two years, the army slaughtered thousands of indigenous people, took possession of large areas of land, and finally executed the Inca leader for refusing to become a Christian. Huge sums of gold, collected as ransom, were sent back to Spain. Between 1500 and 1650, 180–200 tonnes of American gold were added to the European treasury, worth an estimated US$2.8 billion in today's terms.

Most Spanish and Portuguese colonies had gained their independence by the year 1900 (Fig. 2.2). However, it was not until many decades later that the majority of countries in Africa and Asia became independent from European rule. Although some countries show certain gains from foreign domination, such as the institution of democratic government systems, others still suffer from their colonial experience. This is because their economies and political administrations had mainly served not their own needs, but the needs of the colonising power.

Figure 2.3 South America's colonial heritage: countries, their dominant languages and religions

?

1 Select five developing countries and carry out a library search to find out:
a whether these countries were ever colonised,
b who were the colonisers,
c the duration of the colonial period,
d some of the gains and losses resulting from the colonial experience.

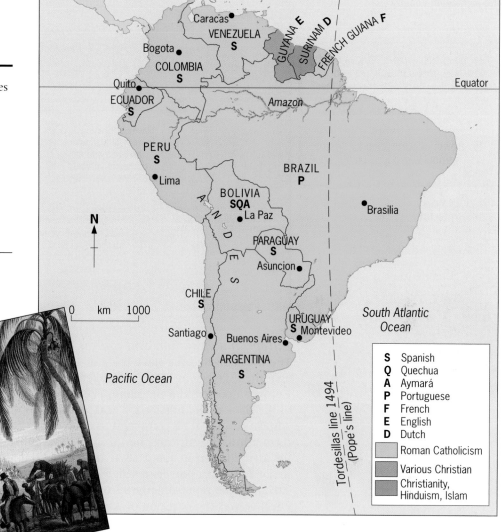

S Spanish
Q Quechua
A Aymará
P Portuguese
F French
E English
D Dutch

Roman Catholicism

Various Christian

Christianity, Hinduism, Islam

Figure 2.4 African slaves felling ripe sugar cane, Antigua, 1823

Colonialism in Africa and the effects of slavery

During the time of the Spanish and Portuguese colonisation of South America, other Europeans were exploring the western coast of Africa and making the first contacts with the well-developed settlements along the west African coast.

With the extension of their influence in Africa by the mid-sixteenth century, Europeans began forcefully taking West Africans across the Atlantic. They then sold them as slaves to work on the new sugar and cotton plantations of South and Central America and the Caribbean (Fig. 2.4). Although trading in slaves was not new (the Greeks and Romans had done it, and Arab traders had for centuries traded in African slaves), the European slave trade was more systematic and on a greater scale than had ever been seen before (Fig. 2.5).

It was usually the most able men and women, often well-skilled in local crafts, who were taken as slaves. Although impossible to calculate, it has been estimated that traders shipped over 12 million slaves from Africa to the Americas between about 1650 and 1850. It is unknown how many millions of these died, as a result of ill treatment or disease, in either Africa or on the apalling 'middle passage' journey on the slave ships. The impact of this on Africa had disastrous and long-term effects: the export of slaves, combined with the many lives lost in the slave wars, meant that the size of the African population probably remained static for over two centuries.

Figure 2.5 The 'triangular trade' of the eighteenth century

European ship owners, African chiefs, slave and goods merchants and plantation owners all increased their wealth

The growth of ports such as Bristol and Liverpool was based on the slave trade

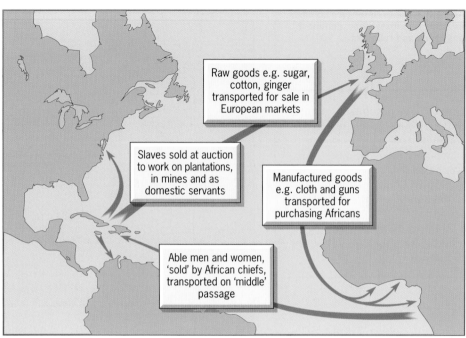

Raw goods e.g. sugar, cotton, ginger transported for sale in European markets

Slaves sold at auction to work on plantations, in mines and as domestic servants

Manufactured goods e.g. cloth and guns transported for purchasing Africans

Able men and women, 'sold' by African chiefs, transported on 'middle' passage

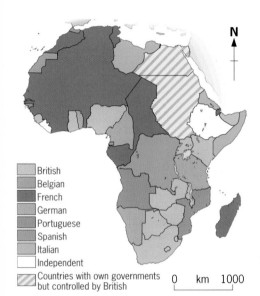

N

British
Belgian
French
German
Portuguese
Spanish
Italian
Independent
Countries with own governments but controlled by British

0   km   1000

Figure 2.6 Sharing out the wealth: Africa in 1914, after partition by the European powers

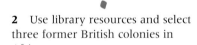

2 Use library resources and select three former British colonies in Africa.
a List the different ways in which the African continent was exploited by the British.
b Assess the impact this exploitation has had on the present-day economic situation in Africa.

European domination and control in Africa

The UK abolished the slave trade in 1807 and slavery in 1833 (the Danes had abolished slavery in 1804), and over the next twenty years the USA and most European powers did the same. The decline in trade as a result of the abolition of the slave trade, missionary zeal, and optimism regarding the riches of the African continent all combined to encourage the European powers to explore further into the African interior in the mid-nineteenth century. The 'scramble for Africa' began in about 1870, and at the Conference of Berlin in 1884–5 the major European powers decided among themselves how they would divide Africa up (no representatives from Africa were invited to the conference). So effective was the partition of Africa that, by 1914, only Liberia and Ethiopia remained independent (Fig. 2.6).

The European powers controlled these artificially created African countries by military force. Their motives for such control were mainly political (reflecting the struggle for power and influence between the European countries) and economic (colonies provided a source of raw materials and a market for manufactured goods, see section 8.2). A great deal of European wealth originates from this time in colonial history.

Different people have viewed the European colonial influence in Africa in different ways. One view is that, as a result of European involvement in Africa, many social and economic improvements were made. These included commercial farms, large-scale plantations, mines, roads and railways. Another view, held by most Africans, is that Africa and its people lost far more than they gained from this period of European domination.

2.3 International financial institutions

Western influence on the developing countries is not just limited to the period of colonisation. Even after their independence, many poor countries still depend on financial aid, credits and support from their ex-colonisers and political allies to help with their development programmes.

Such reliance on foreign capital has consequently increased the economic dependency, and the debt burden of the poor countries on the rich. This is sometimes referred to as neo-colonialism. Several international financial institutions, such as the World Bank and the International Monetary Fund (IMF) now play a key role in the development process of the developing countries.

World Bank and the International Monetary Fund

The World Bank and the IMF are two international financial institutions that were set up following the Bretton Woods Conference of 1944. Their original aim was to help rebuild the economies of Europe devastated by World War 2 and the effects of recession. The conference members believed that global economic problems could be solved if international trade were encouraged. This meant greater economic co-operation among countries, free movement of capital and goods and the establishment of the US dollar as the international currency. Consequently, the World Bank aims to assist countries developing their economies by providing aid. This takes the form of loans and technical assistance. In turn, the IMF promotes the expansion of international trade by, e.g., providing borrowing facilities and easing exchange rate controls.

Part of this overall strategy to solve global economic problems included the General Agreement on Tariffs and Trade (GATT). This was established to encourage **free trade** and commerce between countries (see section 8.5).

The Marshall Plan and the rebuilding of Europe

After World War 2, European countries lacked the resources for reconstruction. They needed to use World Bank and IMF facilities but refused to accept the strict conditions imposed by these international financial institutions. Had they done so, such measures could have resulted in the European countries losing control over their own economies and thus their sovereignty.

As a result of the European rejection of IMF conditions, the much looser and less stringent Marshall Plan was established. The Marshall Plan aimed at providing finance to Europe through grants rather than loans (though the then Soviet Union and its satellites refused to participate in the Plan).

Unlike the European nations, which receive concessions from the IMF and the World Bank when using their loan facilities, the developing countries are obliged to follow strictly the Bank's conditions (Fig. 2.7). For example, the developing countries are obliged to keep their economies completely 'open' to international market forces. To use the World Bank facilites, therefore, these countries must also import foreign goods, capital and services. Each borrowing country then has to pay for its imports through increased exports.

The World Bank's economic principles

The World Bank follows five major economic principles:

1   Poor countries need cash to develop their economies. To get this, they have to borrow money, mostly from Western creditors and international financial institutions.

2   For their economies to be competitive, the poor countries need to buy technology from the rich nations. With the technology, they can produce goods and services which they could sell back to the rich nations to generate the foreign exchange necessary for development and help pay back their debts. According to the World Bank, this is one way in which the developing countries can be integrated into the global market.

3   Government spending on social services, such as health, education, transport, etc., needs to be cut to save money, and more money needs to be earned through exports so as to make the economy 'efficient' and competitive.

4   Efficiency in the economy can only be achieved through the adoption of what the Bank regards as the policy of **structural adjustment** (see below).

Zaire debt 'shame'

The World Bank has suspended its existing projects in Zaire until the country settles the $25m arrears it owes. Reliable sources say the deadline for the payment had been set for November 15. They added that if this deadline was not met various projects being funded by the World Bank, which amount to a total of $175m could be cancelled outright.

Zaire had apparently been notified for the past six months that it should pay its arrears. The World Bank had been funding more than 10 projects in Zaire, mostly in road and social sectors and in the Water and Power Distribution Administration, a public company which supplies drinking water to Kinshasa and other towns in the interior.

Meanwhile, the Zairean government has decided to put in circulation new currency notes and is urging those in possession of old Zaire notes to deposit them in their bank accounts or simply exchange them for new notes. 'Those who are unfortunate enough still to be in possession of the old notes on November 23 can only blame themselves,' said Luwowo Ngongo, Zaire's Communications Minister.

Figure 2.7 Unable to pay for World Bank 'support' (*Source: West Africa*, 29 Nov.–5 Dec. 1993)

3   Read Figure 2.8.
a   Identify arguments for and against the Arun III dam project.
b   What is the long-term benefit of this project to Nepal?

World Bank test of credibility

World Bank president Lewis Preston recently replied to each of 26 congressmen who signed a letter condemning the Arun III dam in Nepal project as an example of 'uneconomic, massive, destructive engineering investment.' Mr Preston has also lobbied to defuse American opposition to Arun.

Joseph Wood, the Bank's vice-president for South Asia, spelled out what was at stake. If the Bank failed to win approval of the project he said, 'We will lack credibility as a financing partner for controversial power and infrastructure projects.'

Bank officials say they have bent over backwards to make sure that the project is environmentally and economically sound, but the Bank will be tried anew today when the United States presents its misgivings to bank officials.

Only 155 families are affected by the project in Arun, a remote valley 200 kilometres east of Katmandu inhabited by endangered species such as the Asiatic black bear, the clouded leopard and the Annamese macaque.

Arun, estimated to cost at least $1 billion over eight years, would provide more than 400 megawatts for a country in desperate need for electricity. So far, Nepal has developed only 241 megawatts of hydro-electric power, accessible to barely 10 per cent of the population.

The Bank would provide a loan of $140.7 million through its soft loan arm, the International Development Association, $473 million would come from countries such as Japan and France, and Nepal would put up $473 million.

Arun has been criticised by a coalition of local groups as unnecessarily large and expensive, diverting resources away from social programmes like health and education. The coalition favours small- and medium-scale projects that would not gobble up so much of the Nepalese budget.

Nepalese groups have accused the Bank of failing to follow its policies on environment, indigenous people and energy and for not honouring requests for information, in violation of the Bank's new policy of openness.

Figure 2.8 World Bank under question (*Source*: Mark Tran, *The Guardian*, 7 Nov. 1994)

5   Poor countries should strive to compete with the rich nations on the world market and embrace the philosophy of a free market. This aims to be characterised by completely deregulated trade and a free flow of foreign investments.

World Bank projects

Since their foundation, the World Bank and the IMF have played a leading role in the development of the developing countries. The World Bank has provided long-term loan facilities to the poor countries in order to finance development projects such as building dams, road construction, hydro-electric power schemes and water supply, among many others. Up until 1995, these projects were usually large scale (called mega-projects) and mostly aimed at bringing about the economic development of the nations concerned.

Examples of World Bank assistance include US$304 million lent to Brazil in 1980 to build an iron mine at Carajas, an 890-km railway to transport the ore and a deep-water port at Ponte de Madeira. In 1985, US$156 million was lent to Indonesia for the Kedung Ombo Dam in central Java. In the early 1980s, India received a loan of nearly US$200 million for **social forestry**. Many other countries have received funds at one stage or another from the World Bank's loan facility for development (Table 2.1, see section 9.5).

By 1995, many large-scale development projects were wholly or partly financed by the World Bank and other Western creditors. This has given the international financial institutions and the rich Western creditors greater control over the economies of these poor nations.

Table 2.1   Supply of IMF credits (millions US$) to selected developing countries (*Source: World Development Report*, 1994)

	IMF credit (1980)	IMF credit (1992)	Total external debt (1980)	Total external debt (1992)
Tanzania	171	221	2 476	67 15
Bangladesh	424	732	4 053	13 189
India	977	4 799	20 582	76 983
Kenya	254	393	3 394	6 367
Pakistan	674	1 127	9 936	24 072
Ghana	105	740	1 407	4 275
Sudan	431	924	5 163	16 193
Philippines	1 044	1 100	17 417	32 498
Mexico	0	5 950	57 378	113 378

Impacts of World Bank projects

Investments in large-scale projects financed by World Bank loans are not always completely beneficial to the poor nations. In fact, critics of the Bank believe that many World Bank sponsored projects in the developing countries are unsuccessful. This is because, while such projects may help to increase the **Gross Domestic Product (GDP)** through more exports, the majority of the people in the developing countries do not receive the benefits of this increased wealth. More often than not, these mega-projects financed by the World Bank result in the displacement of indigenous poor people and can cause serious damage to the environment (Figs 2.8–2.11).

Structural Adjustment Programmes

Another major criticism of the Bank is the terms and conditions under which poor countries can benefit from the Bank's credit facilities, alongside the requirements for the repayment of loans. These are the Bank's policies of Structural Adjustment Programmes (SAPs) imposed on the poor countries and which have been a major issue raised by the Bank's critics.

?

4 Study Figures 2.9–2.11 and decide whether each of the mega-projects was a success or a failure. Justify your decisions.

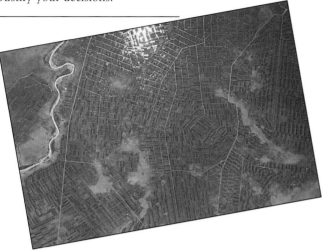

Figure 2.9 Sudan: Gezira Agricultural Project

Figure 2.10 Sri Lanka: Mahaveli Irrigation Programme

Figure 2.11 India: Narmada River Project

El Gezira: The Sudan's prime cotton-producing area covering 2 million ha, accounting for most of the nation's export earnings.
Project: From 1952–62, over 16 000 km of canals were built to control the White Nile and supply irrigation for cotton production. Project aimed to modernise production and reverse falling yields and low productivity.
Costs and donors: World Bank lent Sudan US$50m to purchase pesticides and herbicides for one season. The Bank of Sudan contributed many more dollars for heavy machinery and fuel.
Winners: Multinational chemical companies won the contracts to supply the pesticides and herbicides. (Some of these products were selling poorly on the international market because of health risks.) Farmers in Gezira had at least a temporary boost to their cotton production.
Losers: The government's schemes for alternative pest management were undermined by the heavy promotion of pesticides by the chemical industry. Farmers spent 25–30% of total production costs buying chemical inputs, and have become increasingly dependent on these. The DDT and Malathion dropped on cotton fields by aircraft has drifted into mosquito-breeding habitats, creating strains of malaria-carrying mosquitoes resistant to conventional treatment.

River Mahaveli: 300 km long river in Sri Lanka
Project: 1978 irrigation scheme to supply power; increase food self-sufficiency by modernising agriculture and manufacturing; provide homes; provide a livelihood for 50 000 people. Involved building 3 dams and constructing power stations to triple the country's energy-generating capacity and irrigate 120 000 hectares of new land.
Costs and donors: 60% financed mainly by foreign aid: UK, Sweden and Germany (giving US$100 million each). Sri Lanka also had to borrow large sums on 'soft' commercial terms. However, the budget doubled to nearly US$14 billion, so Sri Lanka had to raise taxes and cut food subsidies to meet the spiralling costs.
Winners: Most construction contracts were awarded to companies in the donor countries who employed expensive foreign personnel and machinery. Most of the newly-irrigated land was leased to foreign companies using imported machinery.
Losers: Little Sri Lankan labour was used. 1.5 million people had to be resettled on small plots of forested land 90 km away from their homelands. To meet expenses, the government had to cut compensation for lost crops, cost of land-clearing and new houses. Habitat of rare animals threatened. Frequent repairs to the dams.

Narmada River valley: interstate (Gujarat, Maharashtra and Rajasthan) valley following the 700 km course of the River Narmada in northern India.
Project: To flood much of the valley using 30 major dams, canals and water from the Narmada River and provide 1450 MW of electricity power, drinking water for 131 urban centres and 4720 villages, irrigation across 1.8 bn ha in a drought-prone area.
Costs and donors: The Narmada Project receives World Bank assistance under two credit/loan agreements of US$450m; machinery, cement, equipment and training supplied by multi-nationals.
Winners: Water supplied to millions of people suffering from a steady decline in available water; people protected against floods in Gujarat; 700 000 workers employed during and post-construction; increased food production.
Losers: 70 000 people displaced; up to 100 000 ha of land sub-merged including 40 000 ha of forest, rare wildlife and heritage sites. Irrigation on such a vast scale will cause waterlogging and a build-up of salt in some of the soils. Dams easily become silted and will then be useless.

Ghana sells seven state companies

The Ghanaian government has sold its stake in seven companies listed in the stock exchange to a number of international investors. The deal, which was priced at approximately $25 m, was equivalent to a quarter of the market capitalisation of the Ghana stock market.

The companies involved are Accra Brewery Ltd (38 per cent); Enterprise Insurance Company (18 per cent); Guinness Ghana Ltd (19 per cent); Kumasi Breweries Ltd (36 per cent); Pioneer Tobacco Company Ltd (19 per cent); Standard Chartered Bank of Ghana Ltd (26 per cent); and Unilever Ghana Ltd (17 per cent).

After gruelling negotiations with a team from the ministry of finance and economic planning, headed by Mr Victor Selormey, the deputy Minister, a deal was struck. The transaction was concluded at $25 m, that is approximately 10 per cent premium on each share, ex-dividend.

Within an hour of trading on February 22, the Ghanaian Stock Exchange emerged as the most progressive in sub-Saharan Africa. The deal has helped the government stabilise the foreign exchange market and also helped it recognise that the capital market and the Ghana stock market have a central role in the on-going privatisation programme.

Figure 2.12 Privatisation (*Source: West Africa*, 13–19 June 1994)

5 Read Figure 2.12. Discuss the view that the imposition of SAPs could be detrimental to individuals in developing countries in the long term.

6 Review the information on SAPs and evaluate how they are affecting development in the countries mentioned.

The World Bank holds the view that the governments of poor countries have mismanaged their economies. As a result, they are not producing sufficient goods to sell or export in order to pay for their expenditure on imports and social services. The Bank's idea, therefore, is that poor countries should adjust their spending in order to pay back their debts. Such SAPs involve cutting back on government spending, especially on 'unproductive' social services, privatising public-sector enterprises (Fig. 2.12) and devaluing currencies so that imports are expensive and exports are cheap. According to the Bank, all these measures will promote domestic investment and increase export earnings for poor countries.

Although the World Bank realises that this process of adjustment might be difficult in the short term, it expects that in the long term SAPs will help the economies of the poor nations. The Bank sees such adjustment as being unavoidable. In fact, millions of people in over 70 countries of the world have been affected by the SAPs and the economic policies of the World Bank and the IMF.

To reduce the hardship initially caused by the SAPs, the World Bank and IMF promises relatively low-interest loans to those countries agreeing to accept the Bank's terms. Loans from other sources, especially from rich Western governments and private banks, have increasingly been made conditional upon the acceptance of World Bank's SAPs. Poor countries in Africa, Asia and Latin America are the most widely affected by the World Bank's economic policies.

Structural Adjustment Programmes in Africa

The SAPs' adverse effects are clearly evident throughout most of Africa. In fact, the effect and influence of the World Bank is extensive. Countries such as Nigeria, Ghana, Mozambique, Liberia, Zimbabwe and Sierra Leone, among others, have adopted the World Bank's imposed SAPs. In Mozambique this led to rising unemployment, which reached 50 per cent in 1992. Reduced government spending, which is part of the SAPs, resulted in fewer jobs in the public formal sector.

There is growing evidence that SAPs are adversely affecting people's lives as well as the economies of developing nations (Fig. 2.13). In fact, many observers blame SAPs for the increasing number of protests and civil disturbances in many African countries. We can see these, in part, as a result of rising unemployment and a drastic reduction in government spending on social services, such as education and health. According to the UN Economic Commission for Africa, expenditures on health in countries where the World Bank has imposed SAPs have declined by 50 per cent during the 1980s and by 25 per cent on education. In Mexico, the wage rate fell by over 75 per cent during the 1980s. Similarly, we can also associate the implementation of SAPs with tribal and regional conflicts in many parts of Africa, together with the spread of disease and growing poverty. If anything, Africa is the World Bank's failure with more poverty than in any other region of the world (see Fig. 1.1, Table 1.6). All these difficulties have led to a progressive weakening of governments' ability to govern. In fact, we need to consider whether people are actually becoming poorer as a result of the Bank's economic policies.

2.4 The growing debt crisis

By the late 1960s, some developing countries had experienced moderately high growth rates in their economies (Table 2.2). This was partly due to the boom in the price of primary commodities, particularly oil. Much of the money earned through oil exports was invested in western banks to generate further income. In turn, these banks lent vast amounts of this money ('petrodollars') at low interest to the poorer non-oil producing countries.

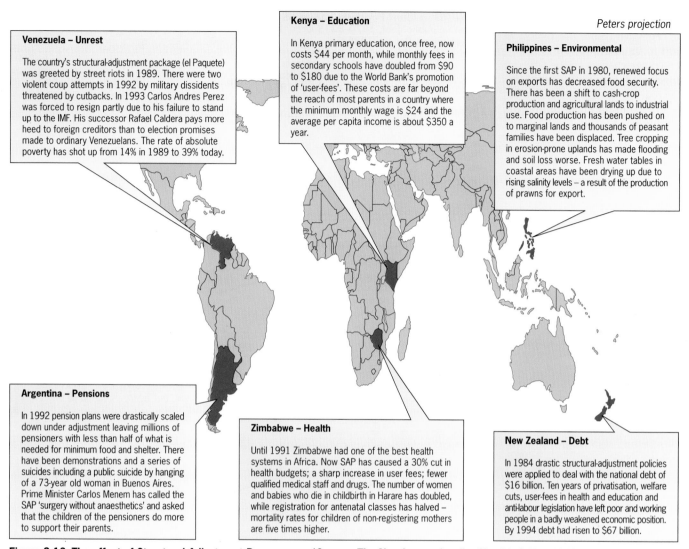

Venezuela – Unrest

The country's structural-adjustment package (el Paquete) was greeted by street riots in 1989. There were two violent coup attempts in 1992 by military dissidents threatened by cutbacks. In 1993 Carlos Andres Perez was forced to resign partly due to his failure to stand up to the IMF. His successor Rafael Caldera pays more heed to foreign creditors than to election promises made to ordinary Venezuelans. The rate of absolute poverty has shot up from 14% in 1989 to 39% today.

Kenya – Education

In Kenya primary education, once free, now costs $44 per month, while monthly fees in secondary schools have doubled from $90 to $180 due to the World Bank's promotion of 'user-fees'. These costs are far beyond the reach of most parents in a country where the minimum monthly wage is $24 and the average per capita income is about $350 a year.

Peters projection

Philippines – Environmental

Since the first SAP in 1980, renewed focus on exports has decreased food security. There has been a shift to cash-crop production and agricultural lands to industrial use. Food production has been pushed on to marginal lands and thousands of peasant families have been displaced. Tree cropping in erosion-prone uplands has made flooding and soil loss worse. Fresh water tables in coastal areas have been drying up due to rising salinity levels – a result of the production of prawns for export.

Argentina – Pensions

In 1992 pension plans were drastically scaled down under adjustment leaving millions of pensioners with less than half of what is needed for minimum food and shelter. There have been demonstrations and a series of suicides including a public suicide by hanging of a 73-year old woman in Buenos Aires. Prime Minister Carlos Menem has called the SAP 'surgery without anaesthetics' and asked that the children of the pensioners do more to support their parents.

Zimbabwe – Health

Until 1991 Zimbabwe had one of the best health systems in Africa. Now SAP has caused a 30% cut in health budgets; a sharp increase in user fees; fewer qualified medical staff and drugs. The number of women and babies who die in childbirth in Harare has doubled, while registration for antenatal classes has halved – mortality rates for children of non-registering mothers are five times higher.

New Zealand – Debt

In 1984 drastic structural-adjustment policies were applied to deal with the national debt of $16 billion. Ten years of privatisation, welfare cuts, user-fees in health and education and anti-labour legislation have left poor and working people in a badly weakened economic position. By 1994 debt had risen to $67 billion.

Figure 2.13 The effect of Structural Adjustment Programmes (*Source: The New Internationalist*, No. 24, 3 May 1993)

Table 2.2 GDP growth rates (%) for selected developing countries, 1965–92 (*Source: World Development Report*, 1979 and 1994)

	1965–73	1973–83	1980–92
Oman	21.9	6.5	7.7
Libya	7.7	3.0	–
Saudi Arabia	11.2	6.9	0.4
Kuwait	5.1	1.4	–
Nigeria	9.7	1.2	2.3
Morocco	5.7	4.7	4.0
Venezuela	5.1	2.5	1.9
Argentina	4.3	0.4	0.4
Chile	3.4	2.9	4.8
Ecuador	7.2	5.2	2.3

The low interest rates and high inflation of the 1970s therefore made borrowing attractive to many developing countries. Between 1973 and 1982, the total external debt of the non-oil-producing developing countries increased five-fold, reaching the US$612 billion mark. Many poor nations had been desperate to take out more loans to finance their desired 'Western' style of development, agricultural development and the green revolution (see section 5.5). However, the world economic situation was changing and as OPEC forced a rise in oil prices (see Fig. 7.10), so banks were forced to raise interest rates during the mid-1980s – with disastrous results for the developing countries.

The knock-on effect of this rise in interest rates on the debtor developing countries was a substantial rise in the interest paid on their external debts (Table 2.3). This also created the problem of a balance of payments deficit for these countries. (The balance of payments is the difference between what a country pays and what it receives through its international transactions.)

As a result, the value of exports from developing countries fell as governments of the importing (developed) countries imposed **tariffs** to protect their own industries. With less income from exports, higher interest rates and an increase in the cost of imports, it became more and more difficult for developing countries to finance their debts. Some countries even found it difficult to pay the interest on their loans, let alone the capital. In 1982, for instance, Mexico suffered from this

7a For each country in Table 2.2, draw a bar chart to show the percentage changes in the GDP growth rates for the three periods covered.
b Comment on the trend shown by your graph.

Table 2.3 Interest Payments (million US$) on external public debt, 1970–83 (*Source: World Development Report*, 1985

	Interest payments on loan (1970)	Interest payments on loan (1983)
Ethiopia	6	24
India	189	55
Pakistan	76	309
Bolivia	6	165
Indonesia	24	1 256
Nigeria	20	974
Turkey	42	1 169
Brazil	133	5 004
Mexico	216	6 850

Table 2.4 Total external debt ratios for 10 of the world's major debtor nations, 1992 and 1980

	1980	1992
Brazil	63.1	23.1
Mexico	49.5	44.4
Indonesia	13.9	32.1
India	9.3	25.3
Argentina	37.3	34.4
Turkey	28.0	31.9
Republic of Korea	19.7	7.4
Thailand	18.9	14.1
Venezuela	27.2	19.5
Philippines	26.6	27.7

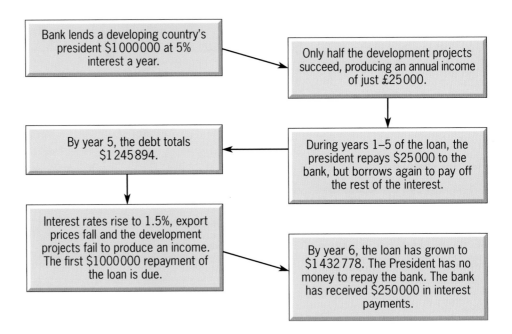

Figure 2.14 The slide into debt

'Corrupt' council

The Accra Metropolitan Authority (AMA) has been accused of corruption and inefficiency. For example, in fraudulent deals involving 40 individual officers, the AMA lost C170 m through falsification of accounts, misappropriation of revenue and other shady dealings, such as financial records going missing, between May 1991 and May 1993. One area accountant is said to have misappropriated over C81 m while two others stole C29 m and C26 m respectively.

Figure 2.15 Lost finances (*Source: West Africa*, 15–21 Nov. 1993)

problem, and so it defaulted. To avoid this trap of not being able to pay their interest, many countries receiving loans use a high percentage of their export income to pay off their debt interest (Table 2.4).

All this marked the beginning of the debt crisis for many developing countries (Fig. 2.14). The total debt owed by the poor nations in the South rose from US$751 billion in 1985 to US$1 355 billion in 1990. Ironically, most of the money borrowed by the developing countries ended up being spent on megaprojects that were sometimes ill-considered and irrelevant to local needs (see Figs 2.9–2.11). Some development experts have suggested that the high level of corruption, especially by the powerful elite and rulers of some of these countries, could mean that some of the loan money ended up in personal accounts, sometimes in the same banks that made the original loan (Fig. 2.15).

Although the World Bank often tries to underplay the growing debt crisis in the developing countries, there is increasing evidence to suggest that the debt burden of the poor nations is hindering the very economic development it was originally supposed to be helping.

Budget and trade deficits now afflict most poor countries in the world, and the debt load on these nations has crippled their capacity to meet all the needs of their citizens. Many of these countries still have to find money to pay off their debts and at the same time find the resources to develop. It is now

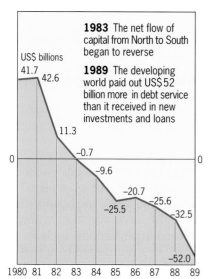

1983 The net flow of capital from North to South began to reverse

1989 The developing world paid out US$52 billion more in debt service than it received in new investments and loans

US$ billions
41.7
42.6
11.3
−0.7
−9.6
−20.7
−25.5
−25.6
−32.5
−52.0

1980 81 82 83 84 85 86 87 88 89

Figure 2.16 Net financial transfer between North and South, 1980–89 (*Source: New Internationalist*, Dec. 1990)

generally believed by development observers that there is a greater flow of money *from* the poorer *to* the richer nations today as a result of the debt situation (Fig. 2.16). In fact, the World Development Movement states that 'for every pound the British public gives for overseas aid, British banks take back eleven pounds in debt repayment'. This has created a 'wealth gap' on a global scale where the rich nations continue to get richer and the poor become ever poorer. However, it should be stressed that both the developed and developing countries are adversely affected by the growing debt crisis (Fig. 2.17).

The six boomerangs

ENVIRONMENT Debt-induced poverty causes people in developing countries to exploit natural resources in the most profitable and least sustainable way. This causes an increase in global warming and a depletion of genetic bio-diversity. This ultimately harms the North too.

DRUGS The illegal drugs trade is the major earner for heavily indebted countries like Peru, Bolivia and Colombia. The social and economic costs of the drug-consuming boom in the North is phenomenal - $60 billion a year in the US alone.

UNEMPLOYMENT Exports from rich countries to the developing countries would be much higher if those countries were not strapped by debt. This would stimulate manufacturing and employment in the North. The loss of jobs due to 'lost exports' is estimated to account for one fifth of total US unemployment.

TAXES Governments in the North have used their tax-payers' money to give banks tax concessions so that they can write off so-called 'bad debts' from developing countries. But in most cases this has not reduced the actual debts of poor countries. By 1991 UK banks had gained from tax credits for more than half their exposure. The eventual total relief will amount to £8.5 billion.

IMMIGRATION The International Labour Organization estimates that there are about 100 million legal or illegal immigrants and refugees in the world today. Many go to the richer countries in the North to flee poverty and the effects of IMF-imposed economic policies.

CONFLICT Debt creates social unrest and war. Iraq invaded Kuwait in 1990 largely in retaliation for the latter's insistence that Saddam's regime repay a $12 billion loan.

Figure 2.17 The impact of debt boomerangs back to the developed countries (*Source: New Internationalist*, May 1993)

Solutions to the debt problem

Four major solutions have been suggested by development experts to solve the growing debt crisis in the developing countries. These are outlined as follows:

Rescheduling Debt rescheduling is the traditional method of debt management. Both the capital and interest repayments are rescheduled to a time agreed between the creditor and the debtor nations.

Debt forgiveness or cancellation This is the idea of 'writing off' the debts owed by poor countries. While debt cancellation may be a practical and compassionate solution to the debt problem in the developing countries, many creditors may be unwilling to do this. However, during the Gulf War (1991–2) American President George Bush granted massive debt forgiveness to Egypt (an allied Arab nation) as a 'reward' for supporting the USA.

Debt-for-nature swaps This is an arrangement whereby a country agrees to preserve an area of rainforest or nature reserve in exchange for a cancellation of debt. Just like the outright forgiveness or cancellation of debt, there is no immediate advantage to the creditors and it is unlikely that many creditors will be keen to accept this solution.

?

8 Use Figure 2.17 to assess the extent to which the developed countries 'suffer' as a result of the growing debt problem.

?

9 In what ways can growing debt in the developing countries hinder economic and social development?

10 You work for a current affairs magazine and have to investigate the policies of the international financial institutions. Write a report assessing the aims and programmes of these institutions and give your own view as to their success.

Table 2.5 Official development assistance (ODA) from members of the Organisation for Economic Co-operation and Development (OECD), 1994 (*Source:* Overseas Development Administration)

	Actual aid 1994 US$ million	Percent of GNP 1994
Australia	1 087	0.38
Austria	561	0.29
Belgium	677	0.30
Canada	2 230	0.42
Denmark	1 450	1.03
Finland	289	0.31
France	8 447	0.64
Germany	6 751	0.33
Ireland	105	0.24
Italy	1 967	0.20
Japan	13 238	0.29
Luxembourg	59	0.40
Netherlands	2 531	0.76
New Zealand	111	0.24
Norway	1 137	1.05
Portugal	(250)	(0.28)
Spain	1 247	0.26
Sweden	1 703	0.90
Switzerland	978	0.36
United Kingdom	3 085	0.31
United States	9 851	0.15

11a Rank the aid-giving countries according to the percentage of aid they contribute (Table 2.5).
b Comment on the methods for measuring aid: is the total figure, or the proportion of GNP, a fairer way of showing aid contributions? Give reasons for your answer.

Debt-for-equity swaps Debt is 'sold' at a discount in order to raise local currency for multinational investors who may be interested in local projects in the debtor nation. Under this arrangement, debt is acquired as a substitute for local currency and then used to make local investments. The proceeds from such investment are used to pay off the country's original debt. Once the debt has been paid off, any further proceeds will be the investors' profits. In economic terms, this is known as *debt equity conversion*.

2.5 Aid and dependency

Aid is the giving of resources from one country to another. When aid is given directly from one country to another, it is called **bilateral aid**. An example of this is the UK's £4.5 million aid package to Angola in June 1995, to support the country's immediate needs and rehabilitation efforts after civil war. Contrastingly, aid is frequently given by and through international organisations, such as the World Bank, which then redistribute the finances to a number of countries. This is known as **multilateral aid**. Funds of about £5 billion for the Narmarda River Project, in northern India, were supplied by the World Bank between 1987 and 1996 (see Fig. 2.11).

Project aid is the term used to refer to aid given by a donor country for special developments, such as road building, water supplies or health and school facilities. In this case, the donor country has some control over the use of the money and some knowledge of the progress of the project. For example, in 1994 the UK contributed £1 million for an environment protection project in China. The three-year project will help prepare effective environmental and social planning to complement existing economic and infrastructure plans. Alternatively, programme aid is given for more general use, and the receiving country can decide how best to allocate the aid. For example, as part of the US government Food Aid Programme, the Bangladeshi government was able to buy tonnes of imported food at very low prices. This was then supposed to alleviate widespread malnutrition across Bangladesh. However, much of the food was distributed in the cities to the urban working class as well as to civil servants – where the government maintains its support. In contrast, only 22 per cent of the rationed food reached the 90 per cent of Bangladesh's population who live in the countryside (including the most malnourished). Clearly, the success of programme aid depends on the aims of the receiving government.

Governments tend to be the main contributors towards development aid, although the contributions made by **non-governmental organisations** (**NGOs**) are also vital (see section 2.7). The United Nations has suggested that each developed country should aim to give 0.7 per cent of its GNP towards helping the development process in the developing countries (Table 2.5). Whether they actually do this is questionable.

Motives for aid

There is a certain amount of controversy surrounding aid, especially when it is 'tied' aid. Donor countries often prefer aid to be 'tied' as this is the type of arrangement which offers the developed countries most benefits. Tied aid means that any goods and services needed during the spending of the aid must be obtained from the donor country. For example, the building of a dam will require construction workers and materials, etc., and these will be acquired from the country providing the money. It is therefore the donor country which benefits in terms of employment and sales of goods.

Some of the aid sent to developing countries, especially during a period of emergency and environmental or natural disaster, such as war, drought, or epidemic, has gone a long way to reducing the suffering and misery of people in those countries. However, a long-term reliance on aid from the rich nations is

EU aid 'damaging' Eastern Europe

THE European Union has been dumping food surpluses in Eastern Europe in the form of food aid, disrupting Eastern Europe's fledgling market economies, according to a report from the EU's financial watchdog.

EU aid to Eastern Europe has in some cases actually hindered reform. Assistance has been poorly administered, poorly thought out and sometimes harmed the people it was intended to help.

In Latvia, for instance, the EU sent rye as food aid from its grain mountains. This led to saturation of the local market, drastically reducing prices and 'sparking off discontent among farmers'. In November 1992 Latvia raised the problem with the EU and in January 1993 asked that the aid either be stopped or converted to a different crop. But a further 32 500 tons were sent in April. After this the government threatened to return food shipments. By December 1993 40 000 tons of rye were still in storage.

The quality of food aid was often poor: five-year-old wheat was sent to Lithuania and substandard meat was sent to Albania. And, in Albania, all the available warehouses in the main port were requisitioned for storage of EU aid. 'There was, in the autumn of 1993, no further capacity for private business', the report says.

It says that EU assistance is 'indispensible' but adds that it is 'sometimes counter productive for the reform process, especially for the newly developing private sector'. In addition to criticism of food aid, the report targets the Phare and Tacis programmes of technical assistance, saying 'no clear strategy' for assistance is apparent and the programme 'still fails sufficiently to take national priorities into consideration'.

The report raises many problems with the use of outside consultants and experts and says that co-ordination of assistance is poor. 'This task should not, in future, be substantially delegated to a group of experts, low-level employees or supply companies.'

In some programmes there has been abuse of internal financial controls, slow implementation, overlapping programmes and irregular charging of expenditure. In some cases, national officials in Eastern Europe were paid directly out of EU funds.

Figure 2.18 Helpful solutions for EU surplus? (*Source:* Andrew Marshall, *The Independent*, 10 Oct. 1994)

12 Read Figure 2.18 and identify five major ways in which food aid could be harmful to the local economy of the recipient nation.

Table 2.6 How British aid has boosted arms customers (*Source: The Observer*, 30 Jan. 1994)

	UK aid growth (%) 1980–92/3	UK arms sales £m
Thailand	625	111
Nigeria	222	50
Jordan	214	54
Indonesia	196	134
Ecuador	157	128
Malaysia	99	52
Oman	95	244
Pakistan	55	105
India	34	694

seen by some development experts as being counter-productive. In some cases, not only has aid discouraged local investment, but it has also caused more harm than good to the recipient nation, as the European Union's aid to some Eastern European countries proves (Fig. 2.18).

It is also sometimes the case that aid is given to countries which share the same political or religious views. In such situations, the giving of aid becomes highly controversial, particularly when linked with the provision of military hardware. A prime example of this is the military aid that was given to Cuba by the former Soviet Union, 1961–2.

2.6 Aid and the arms trade

The need to maintain the defence industry in developed countries such as the UK, Germany, France and the USA, means that these countries may try to link their economic aid to poor nations with sales of armaments (Figs 2.19–2.21). This has increased arms purchases by the poor nations (Table 2.6) and so, as some development experts suggest, may be partly responsible for the increase in military activities in many poor nations. In addition, inter-tribal and domestic conflicts in these countries may also be encouraged by improved access to military hardware – at a time when economic development is being slowed because of the SAPs (see Fig. 2.13).

2.7 Non-governmental organisations

We only need to look at the media to see that governments and other official aid agencies have not succeeded in eradicating poverty, hunger and destitution in many developing countries. This probably explains why many non-governmental organisations (NGOs) are now actively involved in the development programmes of the poor countries. NGOs are non-profit-making organisations, mainly run as charities.

The World Bank defines NGOs as 'groups and institutions that are entirely or largely independent of government and characterised primarily by humanitarian or co-operative, rather than commercial, objectives'. We tend to use the term NGO to describe private organisations that actively try to relieve suffering,

Britain builds on military ties with countries in aid-for-trade programme

Britain is stepping up its defence contacts with many of the countries which receive a big share of the £100 million-a-year aid-for-trade programme, the Foreign Office will disclose in a memorandum to be published next week.

The document summarises Britain's defence arrangements with every country.

Among the big beneficiaries are India, Indonesia, Kenya, Malaysia, Morocco, Mozambique, Turkey and Zimbabwe.

Figure 2.19 UK aid and the sale of arms (*Source:* David Hencke, *The Guardian*, 26 Feb. 1994)

Dam's dark waters

THE GOVERNMENT will come under growing pressure this week to come clean about alleged links between foreign aid and sales of British arms to developing countries.

The row follows the disclosure that £1.3 billion of British defence contracts were linked with £234 million of British aid to the Pergau hydro-electric dam project in Malaysia.

A former Malaysian foreign minister, Rais Yatim, told journalists in Malaysia on Friday that the aid payments were 'undeniably linked' with weapons purchases and military construction contracts, and described them as 'a gross irregularity'.

Similar claims over alleged aid-for-arms deals have been made about Indonesia. Opposition MPs and Third World pressure groups say they believe arms-for-aid deals could have been struck with other developing countries, in breach of guidelines aimed at targeting aid on the poorest nations.

Indonesia agreed last June to buy £500 m worth of British Hawk military training jets, only two months after Douglas Hurd, the Foreign Secretary, visited Jakarta to announce a £65 m 'soft loan' for a power station to be built by a British company.

The World Development Movement, a Third World charity, says Thailand, Nigeria, Jordan, Ecuador and Oman have also seen large increases in aid coincide with significant sales of British arms. Thailand, where aid has increased 625 per cent since 1980, is the sixth biggest buyer of British arms since 1988, spending £110m. Ecuador, where aid increased by 157 per cent in the same period, is the fifth

biggest arms buyer, and spent £130m.

Michael Meacher MP, a former Labour overseas development spokesman, claimed:□'The aid budget has just been ruthlessly hijacked to conclude arms sales. This is just another example of government dishonesty.'

If Mr Major is called before an all-party Foreign Affairs Committee investigating the financing of the Pergau dam, MPs will want to know why he pushed through the £234 m aid for Pergau, despite being told by Sir Tim Lankester, Permanent Secretary at the Overseas Administration, that it was a 'bad buy'.

The Foreign Office initially said last week that linking arms with aid was illegal under the 1966 Overseas Development Act.

Douglas Hurd, the Foreign Secretary, admitted the two had been linked in defence protocol drawn up by George Younger, then Defence Minister, visiting Malaysia for discussions in 1988. But it had been recognised as a mistake soon afterwards and references to arms deleted from the final version.

The Foreign Office later changed tack and suggested it was not necessarily illegal to link aid with arms after all. On a close reading, the act did not rule out such linkage deals. Ministers, it said, had done nothing wrong. As if the Pergau waters were not deep and murky enough, reports last week claiming to fill in more details of the alleged aid-for-arms deal also established a link with arms to Iraq.

Two secret army bases said to be planned in Malaysia as part of the £1bn deal supposedly involve British construction companies.

Figure 2.20 Government under fire over arms for aid (*Source:* Michael Durham, *The Observer*, 30 Jan. 1994)

Figure 2.21 Pergau dam, Malaysia: Britain's £234 million aid for the dam is linked with £1.3 billion defence deals

---

?

13 Use Figures 2.19–2.21 and Table 2.6. Discuss the moral justification for linking aid with the arms trade. Include your own view on this trade and give reasons for your opinion.

---

promote the interests of the poor, protect the environment or undertake community development. There are NGOs based both in the rich nations in the North and in the poor countries in the South which provide a variety of functions and support in the developing countries. Some of these are involved in grassroots work through funding, technical advice and education programmes. Most of the finances for the work done by NGOs comes both directly from governments and from fund-raising activities.

Growth of the NGOs
During the 1950s and 1960s people in both the developed and developing countries became dissatisfied with the development progress of the poorer nations. This encouraged the growth of the NGOs. The role of the NGOs became apparent as the established official development agencies, such as the

Table 2.7 Major NGOs and the structure of their spending (*Source: New Internationalist*, no. 228, Feb. 1992)

Agency	Income US$	Income from government (%)	Development/ education (%)	Fundraising (%)	Administration (%)	Domestic programme (%)	Overseas programme (%)
New Zealand							
Christian World Service	552 580	18.4	3.5	6.1	18.0	U	72.3
Save the Children	2 307 456	5.2	F	7.5	4.6	1.0	85.3
World Vision	9 388 086	0	2.0	11.7	10.0	0	76.6
Australia							
Aus. Catholic Relief	7 407 200	35.4	7.0	n/a	7.0	4.0	71.4
Foster Parents Plan	6 680 423	8.0	0	12.8	17.7	0	69.4
Freedom from Hunger	4 970 000	59.1	5.3	19.3	5.2	1.1	69.1
Canada							
Devt. and Peace	17 153 456	47.2	15.0	A	13.0	2.4	69.6
Oxfam Canada	17 578 258	61.8	4.5	9.7	3.0	2.5	76.6
Save the Children	17 584 455	45.1	5.8	15.4	9.5	1.5	73.0
United Kingdom							
Action Aid	10 584 455	17.1	2.5	12.4	6.3	0	78.3
CAFOD	36 287 720	37.5	4.4	3.1	1.9	0	90.6
Christian Aid	41 105 500	33.8	7.6	11.8	F	0.5	76.6
United States							
CARE	293 508 000	77.4	F	4.5	2.8	0	92.2
Christian Children	102 959 701	n/a	A	10.4	9.3	4.2	76.2
Church World Service	43 090 436	12.4	5.1	11.6	6	0	76.9

F = under fundraising   U = undisclosed   A = under administration

14 Research one recent development project by an NGO and one by an official agency.
a Analyse their strategies for development.
b Assess the success of each of these projects according to their original aims.

15 There are now a large number of international NGOs covering wide areas of development in the poor countries. Construct a questionnaire to examine public awareness of NGOs (see Appendix A2). You could include questions about:
a which NGOs are most well-known
b the type of aid they supply
c which NGOs are most deserving of support.

16 Using your questionnaire, carry out a survey and then write a brief report summarising your results.

Tea? Pay them a fair price!

On a Sri Lankan tea plantation Kusumalatha and her son cannot get fair wages. Satyodaya, a Christian Aid partner, helps people like them.

Christian Aid

Figure 2.22 Changing your point of view: NGOs' supply of information for humanitarian purposes

World Bank and the United Nations Organisations, seemed to be failing many poor nations. These international institutions concentrated most of their efforts on promoting 'economic growth', rather than responding to the basic needs of people. Consequently, the NGOs became a major instrument for development and the 1980s was known as 'the decade of NGOs'. The hope that the NGOs would provide alternative solutions to the problem of under-development in the poorer countries was based on the fact that NGOs have a particular ability to reduce poverty and to pursue sustainable development. They achieve this through their grass-roots involvement; by their ability to reach remote communities; by working more cost effectively than bureaucratic government and commercial institutions; and by remaining flexible and innovative. NGOs are popular with the receiving countries for their use of local resources, their promotion of self-help and self-reliance (Fig. 2.22).

NGOs differ not only in the type of projects they support, but also in the degree of their involvement in local development projects. In terms of specific activities, four different generations of NGOs can be identified.

First-generation NGOs
NGOs in this category are concerned mainly with relief and welfare. More often than not, they assume the role of the 'doer', while the community they serve is generally passive. The NGOs that adopt this approach believe that, with a little short-term assistance, poor communities would be able to get themselves back on their feet.

Second-generation NGOs

These focus on developing the capacities of the local people so that they can then work to meet their own needs. We can therefore see the second-generation NGOs as *initiating* self-reliant local action. Thus their role is one of 'mobiliser', rather than 'doer'. However, some critics of this type of NGO suggest that this practice is little more than a handout in a sophisticated guise. When such NGOs cease operations, the local community may not be able to maintain those projects which the NGOs began.

Third-generation NGOs

These are NGOs which look beyond specific or individual problems and seek to change the policies of institutions at local, national and global scales. In this generation, the NGOs are the 'catalyst of change' i.e. to bring about development in any community, they work through grassroots organisations, especially in the planning, design and implementation of projects. NGOs that operate in this way are said to be approaching the problem of poverty and under-development from a more 'people-centred' approach.

Fourth-generation NGOs

Fourth-generation NGOs both adopt the people-centred approach and also place a high emphasis on local initiatives. Such NGOs assist projects that are built around existing organisational units to create a much more self-reliant community. This strategy is based on the idea that decision-making must be returned to the people, who have both the capacity and the right to contribute positively to the process of development in their community.

The greatest challenge facing NGOs, is how they can increase their impact on the development of the poor nations in which they operate. To become more effective, NGOs find that they have to diversify their operations into such areas as advocacy and actively influencing government policies. This is clearly seen in the environmental lobby groups which pressure institutions into changing policies. For example, Shell's decision to tow the Brent Spar North Sea oil storage platform on-land for decommissioning (rather than dump the platform at sea as originally planned) was, to some extent in response to protests and public action encouraged by Greenpeace up until June 1995.

?

17 To what extent do you think the first generation NGOs could provide solutions to the growing problems of poverty in the developing countries?

18 What are the potential problems NGOs face today in raising funds in your country?

19 Essay: Discuss the view that the developing countries have become increasingly reliant on the developed countries since the end of colonialism.

Summary

- Many development problems facing the developing countries have their roots in the colonial past.
- The political and economic relationships between the rich and the poor nations reinforce dependency of the developing countries on the developed countries.
- The modern international capitalist system gave birth to such institutions as the World Bank and the IMF. These institutions try to influence development in the developing countries through loans and mega-projects.
- The World Bank notion that international trade and competition could result in growth, and so benefit everyone has not materialised.
- Capitalism tends to increase poverty and inequality in the developing countries.
- Aid, in all its forms, may do more harm than good in the long term. Some development experts have suggested that aid is another form of dependency.
- NGOs play an increasingly important role in providing aid to the developing countries at a more grassroots level.
- NGOs provide information about the developing countries and help foster a humanitarian attitude towards the predicaments of the poor nations.

3 Population dynamics and structure

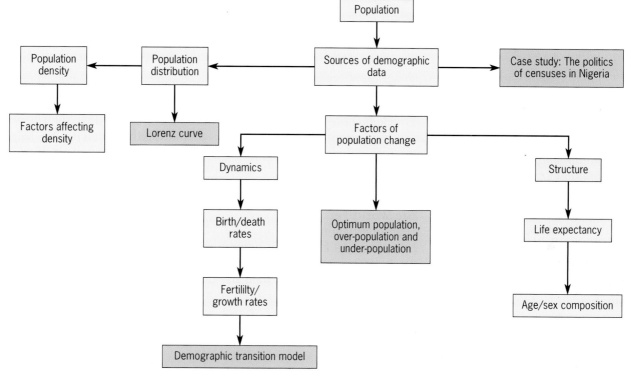

3.1 Introduction

This chapter examines various aspects of population in relation to development. We will firstly consider data collection and the sources of information about population. With such information, we can look at **population distribution**, or the arrangement of people over a geographical area, and population density, the number of people per unit of area. We will then analyse population structure, involving the numbers of people in different age and sex groups, together with the changes in population characteristics over time.

3.2 Sources of demographic data

Census information

Statistics about the population of any region or country are essential for planners if any development is to go ahead (Fig. 3.1). **Demography** is the scientific study of the various aspects of population, such as gender, age, birth and death rates, and information about the population is usually obtained through a census. This is a statistical survey which the United Nations define as 'the total process of collecting, compiling and publishing demographic, economic and social data pertaining, at a specified time or times, to all persons in a country or delineated territory'.

The United Nations recommends that a census is carried out every ten years, although it prefers censuses to take place every five years. In **developed countries**, the census requires heads of households to complete a form answering questions about all members of their household. The questions are related to age, sex, marital status, birthplace, ethnic background, education and

Figure 3.1 Inspecting the plans for the Nigerian Federal Capital, Abuja. The city planners, including experts from Milton Keynes, had to construct buildings and an infrastructure to cater for an increasing population.

Figure 3.2 Collecting data for the 1991 census, Burkina Faso. The enumerator is responsible for collecting data in a particular district and must make sure that all census questions are answered. When individuals are unable to read or write, the enumerator has to interview them.

Figure 3.3 World population: international participation in the World Fertility Survey programme, 1984 (*Source:* World Fertility Survey, UN). Countries are shown with area proportional to population.

economic activities. Other questions might be included relating to household structure, housing tenure, amenities and transport. Governments make the process of conducting a census easier by dividing the country or region into areas known as 'enumeration districts' (Fig. 3.2).

Vital registration

In developed countries, and in some **developing countries**, there is a legal requirement for people to register significant events such as births, deaths and marriages. People usually go to the local register office for this. In the UK, vital registration statistics are regularly used to update a previous census.

Special surveys

Special surveys are often used to supplement insufficient or poor-quality data provided by the census or vital registration. For example, in the UK, the General Housing Survey (GHS) is an annual sample survey carried out by the Office of Population Censuses and Surveys (OPCS). Different topics, such as leisure and/or smoking are covered every two to three years, or whenever the government may need specific information.

The World Fertility Survey

At an international scale, the World Fertility Survey (WFS) aims to assess the state of human fertility throughout the world. The first pilot study was carried out in 1973. Women were then asked about the history of their pregnancies, duration of marriage and their use of contraception etc.

The WFS came about as a result of the poor quality of demographic data available for the developing world and the need for better population data – both for scientific study and for policy applications. The Survey was funded by a number of international and national agencies, mainly the United Nations Fund for Population Activities (UNFPA) and the United States Agency for International Development (USAID). By 1984, 42 developing countries and nineteen developed countries had been covered by the survey (Fig. 3.3). The WFS provided a wealth of information which has helped to clarify some of the

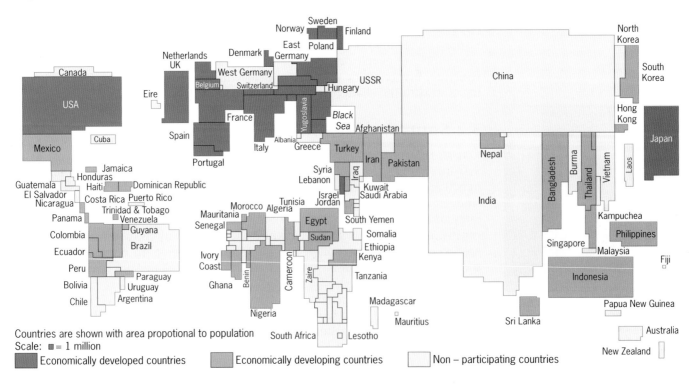

Countries are shown with area propotional to population
Scale: ■ = 1 million

■ Economically developed countries   ■ Economically developing countries   □ Non – participating countries

1 List as many likely uses of vital registration and census data as you can think of for planners at a local, regional and national scale.

2 Select an appropriate sampling technique and explain how you would carry out a survey to determine the average size of households in your local community.

3 Suggest some likely problems caused by using unreliable census data for planning purposes in the areas of:
a health
b education
c employment.

relationships between population change, economics and development. From such data, governments were able to formulate national population policies. For example, a great deal of detailed WFS information about fertility in Asia, South America, and the Middle East helped to determine levels, trends and factors influencing infant and child mortality in these locations.

3.3 Problems of data collection in developing countries

In some developing countries the census may be the only national survey which ever takes place. In fact, some countries, like Ethiopia and Afghanistan, have had very few census surveys. This is usually due to government instability, a weak infrastructure or disruption caused by war. Additionally, vital registration in most of the developing countries is inadequate and those people who do register may not be representative of the whole population. Often, they are better educated, wealthier and they understand the need and procedures for vital registration. Conversely, people who live in the more remote areas are often under-represented because they are less accessible. This inadequacy of data collection is a problem for demographers (people specialising in the study of population) who depend on using accurate and trustworthy information. Overall, though, we know that wide demographic variations exist between the relatively better-off urban dwellers and the poorer rural inhabitants. Even in developed countries, people may refuse to fill in their census forms. This occurred in the UK when individuals tried to avoid paying the new community charge, 'poll tax', introduced by the Conservative government in April 1990. As a result, the 1991 census returns were perhaps the least reliable since World War 2. However, in most developing countries there are many other factors which may distort the accuracy of census data (Table 3.1).

Table 3.1 Selected reasons for unreliable census data

• Households may be omitted due to incomplete mapping of enumeration areas.	• Language barriers e.g. in Cameroon there are 30 major language groups.
• Lack of trained staff to administer the census.	• In areas where there are low literacy levels, some people have difficulty filling in the forms.
• Nomads and the homeless may be difficult to record.	• Age misreporting: a person may not have a birth certificate and in some cases the enumerator may have to guess ages; people may describe themselves as being younger or older than they actually are, e.g. teenage girls and older women shift their ages into the fertile age band; where status is associated with age, people may give an older age.
• Transport difficulties in remote rural areas (often made worse by seasonal weather patterns e.g. monsoon).	
• In northern India and the Middle East, male enumerators are not allowed to interview women.	

The politics of census surveys in Nigeria

Nigeria has the largest total population in Africa, with an estimated 108 million people in 1994 (see Fig. 1.10). The first attempts to enumerate the population were in 1863, and since then there have been 10 censuses. These Nigerian census surveys illustrate how unreliable government statistics can be.

Official estimates
The 1991 census involved 500 000 staff covering 225 000 enumeration districts over three days. In 1989 the government's official population estimate for 1991 was 109.2 million (Fig. 3.4) while the 1991 census revealed a total of only 88.5 million.

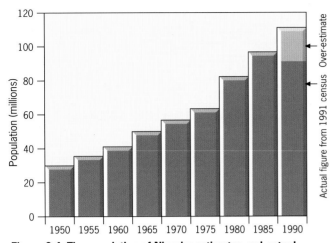

Figure 3.4 The population of Nigeria: estimates and actual

Inaccuracies

The population estimates were based on the census of 1963, which was considered the most accurate of all Nigerian censuses. However, the then western and eastern regions accused the northern region of inflating its figures so that it could keep political control of the country. The response from the northern region was to accuse the others of also over-inflating their population totals in order to receive an unfair share of the government's revenue. This tribal rivalry escalated into the Biafran war (1967–70) when eastern Nigeria (Biafra) claimed independence but was then defeated by the Nigerian government forces. More recently, the government has created a number of new states in an attempt to reduce regional tensions and encourage more integration of the population (Fig. 3.5).

Population control

In May 1989, the Nigerian government introduced a population control policy. The government recommends that couples should limit themselves to having a maximum of four children instead of the current average of six. The dependency ratio (the proportion of the non-working population to the working population) has risen steadily since the 1960s and this has created an extra burden on the economy as well as on the health and education services. Over half of the total population are under 15 years of age and such a high **child dependency ratio** (see Appendix A3) gives the government little choice other than to try controlling Nigeria's population growth rate.

4 The text suggests there is over-reporting of local populations in Nigeria. Suggest ways in which the Nigerian population census could be made more reliable.

5 Bearing in mind the population doubling time for Nigeria of 23.34 years (Fig. 3.5), what resource implications does this have for the country? (See also Figs 1.11–1.13)

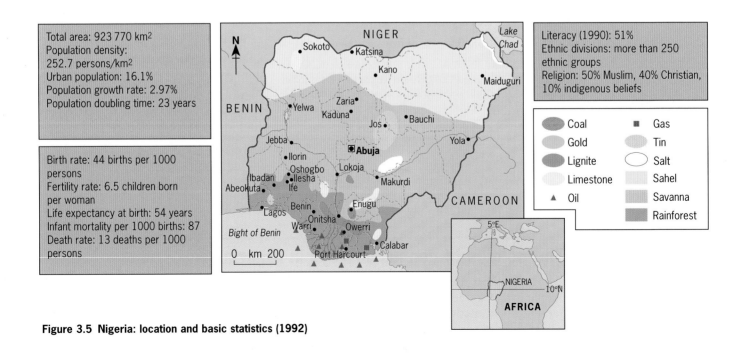

Total area: 923 770 km²
Population density:
252.7 persons/km²
Urban population: 16.1%
Population growth rate: 2.97%
Population doubling time: 23 years

Birth rate: 44 births per 1000 persons
Fertility rate: 6.5 children born per woman
Life expectancy at birth: 54 years
Infant mortality per 1000 births: 87
Death rate: 13 deaths per 1000 persons

Literacy (1990): 51%
Ethnic divisions: more than 250 ethnic groups
Religion: 50% Muslim, 40% Christian, 10% indigenous beliefs

Figure 3.5 Nigeria: location and basic statistics (1992)

6 Divide the graph in Figure 3.6 into three stages. Describe each stage and comment on it.

7a With reference to Table 3.2, use an appropriate mapping technique to show the 1994 population growth rates for five developing countries and five developed countries on a blank base map of the world.
b Suggest reasons for the differences shown.

3.4 World population growth rates

After domestic agriculture became established and settled communities developed, the world population grew to about 300 million by AD 1 (Fig. 3.6). The rate of growth from then on was very slow (about 0.1 per cent per annum).

Since 1750, the world has witnessed a rapid rise in the number of people, with average annual growth rates of 0.5 per cent between 1750 and 1900. During the first half of the 20th century, the world population grew at an average rate of 0.8 per cent and by the second half of the century this increased to 1.7 per cent. In mid-1994, the average annual growth rate was 1.6 per cent.

By 1994, many countries in Africa, Asia and Latin America were experiencing high population growth with annual rates of 2.0–4.5 per cent (Table 3.2). The industrialised nations, such as the United Kingdom or France were experiencing slower growth with annual growth rates of less than one per cent (Table 3.2). In contrast, some countries were even experiencing population decline (Table 3.3).

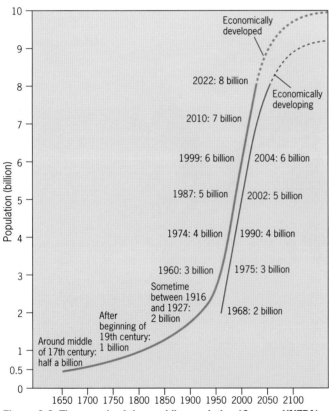

Figure 3.6 The growth of the world's population (*Source:* UNFPA)

Table 3.2 Population growth for selected countries, 1994-2050 (*Source:* UN Population Division, 1994)

Country	Mid-year population 1994 (thousands)	Annual growth rate (%)	Projected population by year 2050 (thousands)
Angola	10 674	3.7	41 182
Australia	17 853	1.4	26 060
Bangladesh	117 787	2.2	238 512
Belgium	10 080	0.3	10 068
Brazil	159 143	1.7	264 349
Canada	29 141	1.2	39 870
China	1 208 841	1.1	1 605 991
Egypt	61 636	2.2	117 398
Ethiopia	53 435	3.0	194 203
France	57 747	0.4	60 475
The Gambia	1081	3.8	2 762
India	918 570	1.9	1 639 863
Japan	124 815	0.3	110 015
Mexico	91 858	2.1	161 450
New Zealand	3 531	1.2	4 667
Nigeria	108 467	3.0	338 510
Peru	23 331	1.9	43 820
UK	58 091	0.3	61 635
USA	260 631	1.0	348 966

Table 3.3 Annual percentage growth of population for countries with static/declining population (*Source:* The World Bank, 1979; *World Development Report*, 1994)

Country	1960–70	1970–80	1980–92	1992–2000
Bulgaria	0.8	0.4	–0.3	–0.4
Hungary	0.3	0.4	–0.3	–0.4
Portugal	0.0	0.8	0.1	0.0

8 Look at Table 3.3.
a Discuss the factors which may lead to relatively static or declining population growth rates.
b What might be the • social, • economic and • demographic implications of such declining population growth rates?

Population doubling time

The high population growth rates which we see in many poor nations should be viewed in relation to the population doubling time associated with such rates. With a two per cent growth rate, the population doubling time would be about 35 years, while a growth rate of three per cent means it will only take 24 years for the population to double. Similarly, within a period of 17 years, a country with a population growth rate of four per cent per annum would double itself

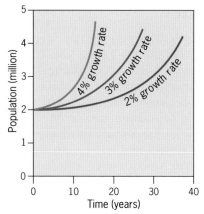

Figure 3.7 Samples of population doubling time

Figure 3.8 World population distribution and density (*Source:* Population Concern)

(Fig. 3.7). Such an understanding of population doubling time is important for assessing demands on both human and physical resources (see section 5.2).

3.5 Population distribution and density

Population distribution refers to the way in which people are spread out across the earth's surface. In contrast, population density describes the number of people living in a given area. Population density (*PD*) is calculated as follows:

$$PD = \frac{\text{Number of people in an area/country}}{\text{Size of area/country (km}^2)}$$

As such, population density indicates the concentration of people per unit area. It shows the number of people who will be living in each square kilometre if people were distributed evenly over the land.

Both the density and distribution of population vary widely on a global scale (Fig. 3.8). In fact, a majority of the world's population is in developing countries as Table 3.4 and Figure 3.9 illustrate.

Mollweide projection

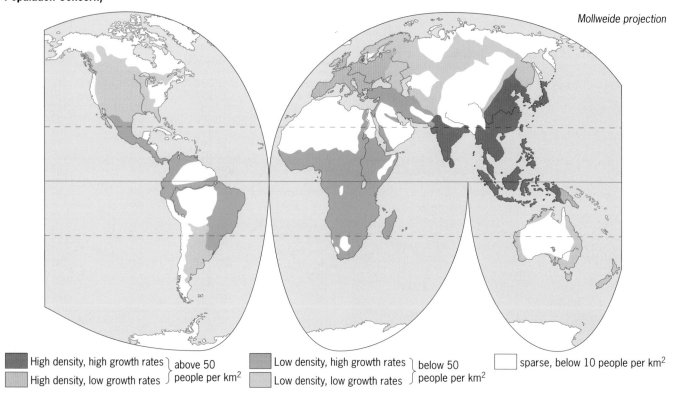

■ High density, high growth rates	above 50
▨ High density, low growth rates	people per km²
▨ Low density, high growth rates	below 50
▨ Low density, low growth rates	people per km²
□ sparse, below 10 people per km²	

?

9a On a blank world map, shade the world's ten largest nations using Table 3.4.

b Referring to Figure 1.1, draw the North–South dividing line on your map and comment on how many of the largest nations are in the South.

Table 3.4 World's ten largest nations, 1994 (*Source:* UN Population Division)

Rank	Country	Population (millions)	World population (%)
1	China	1209	21.5
2	India	919	16.3
3	United States	261	4.6
4	Indonesia	195	3.5
5	Brazil	159	2.8
6	Russian Federation	147	2.6
7	Pakistan	137	2.4
8	Japan	125	2.2
9	Bangladesh	118	2.1
10	Nigeria	108	1.9

Similarly, on an international scale, the population densities of different countries vary (Figs 3.10–3.11). In Western Europe, the UK is one of the most densely populated countries, with 604 people per square kilometre. This national average density figure often hides the fact that population density varies across the country (Fig. 3.12). On a regional scale, population densities also vary, as can be seen in the case of northern England (Fig. 3.13) and on a local scale as in urban areas such as Greater London (Fig. 3.14).

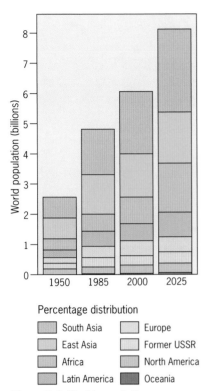

Percentage distribution

- South Asia
- East Asia
- Africa
- Latin America
- Europe
- Former USSR
- North America
- Oceania

Figure 3.9 World population distribution by major areas, 1950–2025 (*Source:* UN)

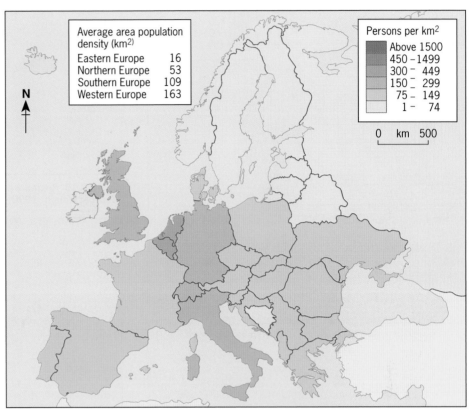

Figure 3.10 International population density: Europe, 1990

Average area population density (km²)
Eastern Europe 16
Northern Europe 53
Southern Europe 109
Western Europe 163

Persons per km²
Above 1500
450 – 1499
300 – 449
150 – 299
75 – 149
1 – 74

Figure 3.11 International population density: Northern Africa, 1990

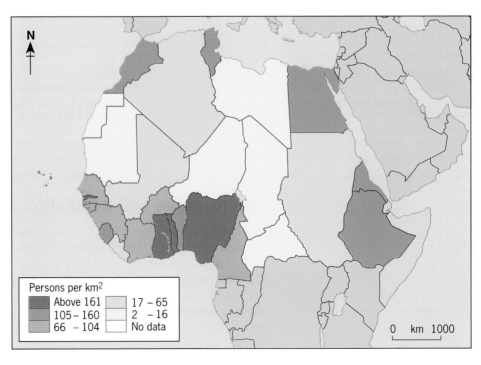

Persons per km²
Above 161
105 – 160
66 – 104
17 – 65
2 – 16
No data

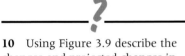

10 Using Figure 3.9 describe the changes and projected changes in the world's population distribution from 1950 to 2025.

11a Describe the variations in population density throughout
• Europe and • Northern Africa, as shown in Figures 3.10 and 3.11.
b Suggest why some countries have high population densities while others have lower densities.

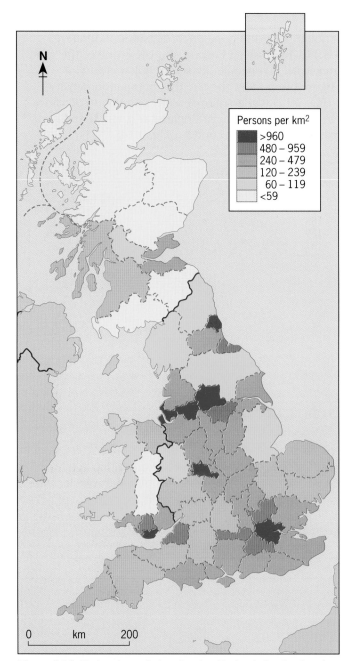

Figure 3.12 National population density: England, Scotland and Wales, 1990

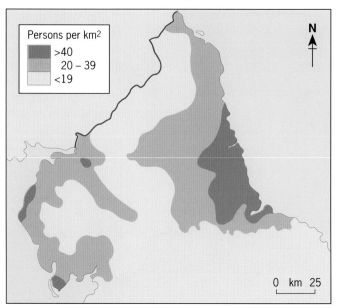

Figure 3.13 Regional population density: Northern England, 1990 (*Source:* Waugh, 1990)

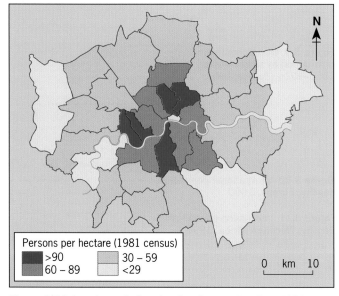

Figure 3.14 Local population density: Greater London, 1981 (*Source:* 1981 census)

Lorenz curve and population distribution

The Lorenz curve (Fig. 3.15) is a graph used to show inequalities in distributions. In fact there are many phenomena, such as population, industry and employment, which will show unequal distributions over a given area. On Figure 3.15, the straight diagonal line represents a perfectly even distribution of the population over a selection of continents. The curve shows the level at which population is concentrated within the various regions. The larger the area between the diagonal line and the curve, the greater the concentration of population (or industry, employment, etc.) relative to the total area.

Table 3.5 Distribution of the world's population by region, 1994 (*Source:* UN Department for Economic and Social Information)

Region	World population (%)	Cumulative population (%)	World's area (%)	Accumulative area (%)
Africa	12.6	12.6	22.3	20.3
Asia	60.5	73.1	20.3	40.4
Europe	12.9	86.0	20.1	62.7
South America	8.4	94.4	15.2	77.9
North America	5.2	99.6	15.8	93.7
Oceania	0.4	100	6.3	100

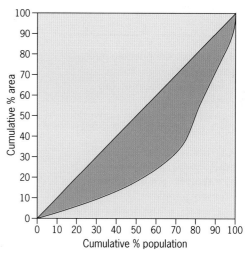

Figure 3.15 Lorenz curve for world population distribution, 1960

?

12a Using the data provided in Table 3.5, draw a Lorenz curve to illustrate the distribution of the world's population (see Appendix A4).
b Compare and comment on the differences between your own graph and Figure 3.15.

Figure 3.16 Lowland area: the west coastal plain of Taiwan. The main north-south highway crosses the length of the plain, and by 1993 the area had about 80 000 factories.

Figure 3.17 Irrigated vegetable plots in the Gobi Desert, Mongolia, where the average temperatures range from –25°C in January to 32°C in July

Physical factors influencing population density

There are many environmental and human factors which influence population densities. Some of the environmental factors are as follows:

Relief

Mountainous areas are less attractive to settlement than lowland plains. Soils are often thin on steeply sloping land, making it difficult to develop agriculture. Also, at high altitudes air has a low oxygen content and temperatures decrease very rapidly with increased altitude. High mountains, even on the equator, can be as cold as polar areas, with a mean monthly temperature persistently lower than 10°C. Such areas are therefore usually sparsely populated.

Lowland areas, being relatively flat, tend to attract settlement and often support large numbers of people (Fig. 3.16). Communication lines, such as canals, railways, roads and airports, as well as industry, are easily constructed here. This also attracts more people. In addition, lowland areas are usually intensively farmed.

Climate

Where average monthly temperatures rarely exceed 10°C, the range of crops people can grow is limited. Transport is also hampered by frost and snow. In fact, few people live where temperatures are so low, such as in Lapland where there is an average of only one person living per square kilometre. Similarly, people do not tend to live where it is excessively hot and dry. As crop cultivation is impossible in desert regions without expensive irrigation, high population densities are relatively rare in arid areas. For example, in central-west Nigeria, about 50 people live per square kilometre (see Fig. 1.11), while in the Gobi Desert there is an average of only 1.4 people per square kilometre (Fig. 3.17).

In contrast people are attracted to temperate climates, where temperatures are neither too cold nor too hot, and rainfall is distributed evenly throughout the year. Here, intensive crop cultivation is possible. This is clearly seen in the Mid-West USA, known particularly for its corn production. Another example is north-west Europe, which is also one of the most densely populated parts of the world. Similarly, we see high population densities maintained in hot and humid areas near the equator where cultivation takes place all year round, such as the 200–400 people per square kilometre in Bangladesh.

3

13a List all the possible *human* factors which might influence population distribution and densities.
b Assess their impact on world population distibution (Fig. 3.8).

14a Study Figure 3.8 and list those regions or countries which are • sparsely populated and • densely populated.
b For each of the areas you have listed in **14a**, give reasons for the variations in their population densities.

Figure 3.18 Brunei: tropical rainforest. Brunei is situated on the north-west coast of the island of Borneo and has an annual rainfall of 250cm along the coast.

Vegetation
Dense forests, which are difficult to clear, and deserts, where natural vegetation is sparse, are usually regions of very low population density (Fig. 3.18). The most obvious examples of this are the Saraha Desert and the Amazon rainforest.

Conversely, as previously mentioned, areas of grassland and easily removed broad leaved woodlands in the temperate regions tend to support dense populations. Examples include the Mid-West conurbations of the east coast of the USA. These areas usually have deep fertile soils which, again, are ideal for agriculture.

Optimum population, over-population and under-population

Optimum population
In economics theory, the **optimum population** of an area is the number of people who, when working with all the available resources and with existing levels of technology, will produce the highest possible per capita income. As such, the optimum population should be able to provide for the highest standard of living possible. We can therefore say that the standard of living is determined by the interaction between physical and human resources as expressed by the following formula:

$$\text{standard of living} = \frac{\text{natual resources} \times \text{technology}}{\text{population}}$$

This concept is a dynamic one, i.e. it changes with time as technology improves, as population totals and structure (age and sex ratios) change, and as people discover new raw materials to replace those which are exhausted or have changed in value.

Over-population
Over-population is a situation where there are too many people, given the existing resources and levels of technology, for them to maintain 'adequate' standards of living. It is also important to stress that over-population is not necessarily associated with high population densities. For example, in countries which are largely deserts, the **carrying capacity** will be small and a few people per square kilometre may represent 'over-population'.

The carrying capacity relates to available resources and the existing levels of technology. It indicates the number of people who can be adequately supported

15 In relation to the theoretical optimum, what will happen if the size of the population • increases, • decreases?

16 Use Table 3.6.
a Work out the population density of both the Netherlands and Bangladesh.
b Describe the standard of living for each country (you could refer to section 1.3).

17a For each country, use the formula to describe the relationship between population and the other factors.
b Suggest additional factors that may affect the link between population and resources.

18 Using specific examples of countries which are • developing and • developed, describe the symptoms of over-population. Figures 3.19 and 3.20 may help you.

by the productive capacity of the land (in terms of food output, water availability and the general resource base). If the carrying capacity is exceeded, given existing levels of technology, then a country or region may be described as over-populated. In this case, living standards are lowered and the resource base may be damaged from over-use. Theoretically then, if the numbers of people were reduced, or if new technology resulted in a more productive use of resources, then standards of living should improve.

The Netherlands and Bangladesh: a comparison

The Netherlands and Bangladesh are two countries which we might consider as over-populated. In fact it is clear that there are large, densely populated areas in both countries (Table 3.6). The Netherlands is not well endowed with natural resources but it has been able to use technology to produce high-quality agricultural products for export to generate income (Fig. 3.19). Bangladesh also has insufficient mineral and energy resources, but it has not been able to use technology to generate export income (Fig. 3.20) in the same way.

Under-population

Under-population is the opposite to over-population. It occurs when far more resources are present in an area than can be used by the people living there. In theory, Canada is still under-populated in that it *could* support a population of 50 million and still maintain its standard of living (Fig. 3.21). In 1994 the population of Canada was 29.1 million and the population density was three people per square kilometre. Australia is another country which we can classify as under-populated. Both Canada and Australia could export their surplus food, energy and mineral resources and still have high incomes, good living conditions, high levels of technology and high levels of immigration (Table 3.7). It is also likely that, if the population were to increase, standards of living would rise because of increased production and exploitation of resources.

Table 3.6 Selected indicators of development (*Source:* Human Development Report, 1993; UNDEP; World Development Report, 1994)

	Total population, mid-1995 (millions)	Land area (km²)	Life expectancy at birth, 1994 (years)	GNP per capita, 1992 (US$)	Human Development Index, 1990	Adult literacy 1992 (%)	Population per doctor, 1989	Urban population, 1992 (%)	Exports, 1990 (US$ million)	Imports, 1990 (US$ million)
Netherlands	15.5	3 730	77	20 480	0.970	99	450	89	131 839 Machinery, foodstuffs, chemicals,	126 195 Machinery, foodstuffs, chemicals, minerals, fuels
Bangladesh	119.2	114 000	56	220	0.189	35.3	6 890	14	1 305 Jute, fish	3 524 Machinery, foodstuffs, petroleum

Figure 3.19 Intensive, mechanised farming in the Netherlands

Figure 3.20 Basic farming methods in Bangladesh

?

19 Use the formula to describe the relationship between population and resources for Canada and Australia (Table 3.7).

20 Using library resources, find an example of a developing country that you consider to be under-populated. Write a feature for a news magazine assessing its characteristics.

Figure 3.21 Underpopulation: Canada has more resources than can be fully exploited by its population

Table 3.7 Selected indicators of development (*Source: Human Development Report*, 1993; UNDEP; *World Development Report*, 1994)

	Total population, mid-1995 (millions)	Land area (km²)	Life expectancy at birth, 1994 (years)	GNP per capita, 1992 (US$)	Human Development Index, 1990	Adult literacy, 1992 (%)	Population per doctor, 1989	Urban population, 1992 (%)	Exports, 1990 (US$ million)	Imports, 1990 (US$ million)
Australia	18.0	7 686 850	78	17 260	0.972	99	436	77	39 539 Agricultural produce, oil, gas, textiles, machinery	38 843 Machinery, chemicals, petrol, agricultural produce
Canada	29.6	9 916 140	77	20 710	0.982	99	455	85	126 995 Cars, machinery, chemicals, foodstuffs, tobacco metals	116 461 Machinery, clothing, paper, iron steel

3.6 Factors of population change

There are three major factors of population change: fertility, mortality and migration. These variables account for population change over time and space. While fertility and mortality are discussed below, see Chapter 4 for migration.

Fertility
There are a number of methods for measuring fertility.

Crude birth rate
The crude birth rate (CBR) is the most common measure of fertility. It gives an overall picture of the number of births per 1 000 population in a year, i.e:

$$\text{CBR} = \frac{\text{total number of births}}{\text{total population}} \times 1\ 000$$

However, CBR does not take into account the age and sex distribution of the population.

Age-specific fertility rate
The age-specific fertility rate (ASFR) is a measure of the number of children born to each age group, in relation to the number of women in that age group.

Table 3.8 USA age-specific fertility rates, 1988 (*Source:* US Dept of Health and Human Sciences)

Age	Births	Population	Rate
10–14	10 588	8 144 000	1.3
15–19	478 353	8 924 000	53.6
20–24	1 067 472	9 574 000	111.5
25–29	1 239 256	10 928 000	113.4
30–34	803 547	10 903 000	73.7
35–39	269 518	9 660 000	27.9
40–44	39 349	8 198 000	4.8
45–49	1 427	7 135 000	0.2

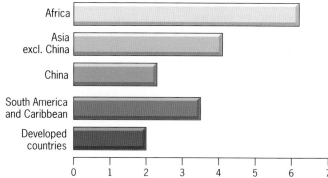

Figure 3.22 The average number of children born to women in different world regions

21 The average family size in developing countries tends to be much larger than in developed countries. Use Figure 3.22 to respond to this comment, suggesting reasons for your observations.

Seven age groups are conventionally used across the span 15–49 years. ASFRs are normally expressed per 1 000 women in each age group (Table 3.8).

Total fertility rate

The total fertility rate (TFR) is one of the most useful measures of fertility. It is the average number of children born to a woman during her lifetime. This varies noticeably across the world. For example, in Sierra Leone, there was a 1994 TFR of 6.5, while the UK had a TFR of only 1.8. The TFR is obtained from the total of all the age-specific fertility rates and assumes that these remain constant throughout a woman's child-bearing years. Like any other statistical estimates, the TFR value does not necessarily mean that women will, in future, continue to have that number of children.

Replacement level fertility

The replacement level fertility (RLF) is the level at which each generation of women has only enough daughters to replace themselves in the population. The 'replacement' levels vary for different populations, depending on the level of mortality and the sex composition of the population. For example, while in theory we could say that a woman with two daughters has replaced herself twice, in practice these births may only just reach the actual 'replacement level' if child mortality is high. Consequently, a total fertility rate of 2.12 children is usually considered as the replacement level. This is because mortality may prevent a proportion of the female children from reaching their productive years and also, on average, slightly more boys are born than girls.

Mortality

Mortality is the ratio of deaths to the population of a given area. Mortality is often measured using such indices as crude death rates, infant mortality rates or life expectancy.

Crude death rate

The crude death rate (CDR) gives an overall picture of mortality and is expressed as the number of deaths per 1 000 population in one year, i.e:

$$CDR = \frac{\text{total number of deaths}}{\text{total population}} \times 1\ 000$$

According to the 1994 population data, Sierra Leone had a CDR of 25 per 1 000 while the CDR for the United Kingdom was 11 per 1 000. This means that for every 1 000 people in the United Kingdom, 11 deaths were recorded in 1994.

The CDR can be very misleading, though, because the index is generally influenced by the age structure of the population. For example, although France

Table 3.9 Infant mortality rates and life expectancy for selected countries, 1994 (*Source:* UN Population Division)

Country	Infant mortality (per 1000)	Life expectancy at birth (years)
Malawi	143	46
Burundi	102	50
Sierra Leone	166	39
Afghanistan	163	43
Switzerland	6	78
United Kingdom	7	76
Germany	6	76
Sweden	5	78
Mexico	36	71
Colombia	37	69
Peru	64	66
Bangladesh	108	56
India	82	60
Australia	7	78

Table 3.10 Life expectancy at birth (years) in world regions (*Source:* UN)

	1950–5	1980–5	2020–5
Africa	37.8	49.4	64.5
S. America	51.1	64.2	72.3
N. America	69.1	74.4	77.5
E. Asia	42.7	68.4	75.9
S. Asia	39.9	54.9	70.1
Europe	65.3	73.1	77.2
Oceania	60.8	67.9	74.9
Former USSR	64.1	70.9	76.7
World	46.0	59.5	70.5

22a Using Spearman's rank correlation (see Appendix A1), analyse the relationship between infant mortality rates and life expectancy for the countries listed in Table 3.9.
b Comment on your result.

23 Using Table 3.10, choose a suitable graphical technique to show changes in life expectancy for all the world regions listed.

and Togo both had CDR values of 13 per 1 000 in 1994, a person can expect to live on average some 22 years longer in France than in Togo. The age structures of the two populations in this case are significantly different. While 15 per cent of France's population is aged 65 years and over, only 3 per cent of the population in Togo are within this age group.

Age-specific death rate
Unlike the CDR, the age-specific death rate (ASDR) is a mortality measure for just one age group in the population. The ASDR is calculated using the formula:

$$ASDR = \frac{\text{number of deaths in a specified age group}}{\text{population of the age group}} \times 1\,000$$

It is also expressed as a number per 1 000 per year. The age-specific death rate of the population aged 0–5 years is generally referred to as 'child mortality'.

Age- and sex-specific death rate
Usually, age-specific death rates are calculated separately for each sex because of the differences in mortality between the sexes – women tend to live longer than men (Fig. 3.23). An age- and sex-specific death rate (ASSDR) is therefore the number of deaths during a year among persons of a given age and sex per 1 000 people of that age and sex category, i.e:

$$ASSDR = \frac{\text{number of deaths in a specified age and sex category}}{\text{population of age and sex category}} \times 1\,000$$

Figure 3.23 What a difference! (*Source:* Quillin, 1992)

Infant mortality rate
The infant mortality rate (IMR) is a measure of the number of deaths of infants before their first birthday, per 1 000 live births in a year. Since children are much more susceptible to sickness and disease than adults, the number of infant deaths recorded in a country is usually a reliable indication of the state of health of the country. This is especially so, because children respond easily to the state of their mother's health and the state of pre- and ante-natal services. Countries such as Malawi, Burundi, Sierra Leone and Afghanistan have very high infant mortality rates (Table 3.9).

Life expectancy
Life expectancy measures the average number of years a person can expect to live. High mortality in the early age groups often lowers the average life expectancy. Similarly, as general mortality declines, life expectancy will increase (Table 3.9). Just like the age-specific death rate, life expectancy can be calculated for different sexes.

24 Using the annual population growth rates for a range of countries listed in Table 3.2, estimate the time it will take for the population of each country to double (see section 3.4).

Maternal mortality rate

Maternal mortality rate (MMR) is a measure of the number of women who die as a result of complications in pregnancy and childbirth. It is expressed per 1000 live births in a specified year. MMR is higher in many poor countries, especially in Africa where women are 200 times more likely to suffer a pregnancy-related death than Western European women. There are a variety of reasons, but the higher MMR for developing countries generally results from poorer access to health facilities; higher fertility rates (giving women less time to recover from previous pregnancies); and a poorer diet (lowering a woman's resistance to illness).

Calculation of population growth rates

The difference between the crude birth rate and the crude death rate is the rate at which a population is either increasing or decreasing (see Tables 3.2, 3.3). This is referred to as **natural population change** but it takes no account of the effects of migration. When the net effects of migration are considered, this is known as **actual population change.**

With a CBR value of 45 per 1 000 (4.5 per cent) and a CDR value of 15 per 1 000 (1.5 per cent) recorded for Nigeria in 1994, the annual population growth rate is calculated as follows:

$$4.5\% - 1.5\% = \text{annual growth rate of } 3.0\%$$

Demographic transition model

Following a study of changes in birth and death rates in several developed countries in North America and Western Europe, researchers have developed a model which suggests that all countries pass through similar population cycles, or **demographic transition stages** (Fig. 3.24). The model suggests that changes in birth and death rates are linked to the development process.

25a From Figure 3.24, describe how the population total changes through each stage of the demographic transition model.
b Use Tables 3.2 and 3.3 to decide whether you could add a fifth stage to the model. If so, describe its characteristics.

26a With reference to Figure 3.25, make a list of the factors which brought about changes in the birth and death rates in the United Kingdom between 1700 and 1940.
b Describe how both the birth and death rates reacted to each of the factors you have listed.

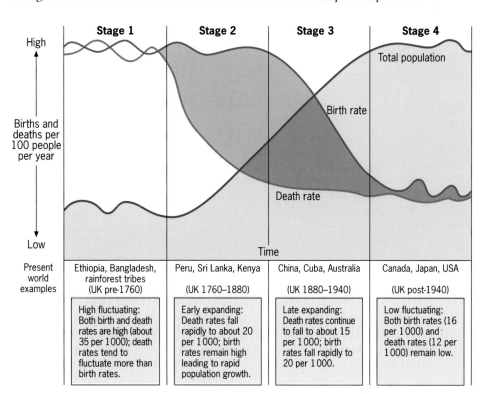

Figure 3.24 The demographic transition model

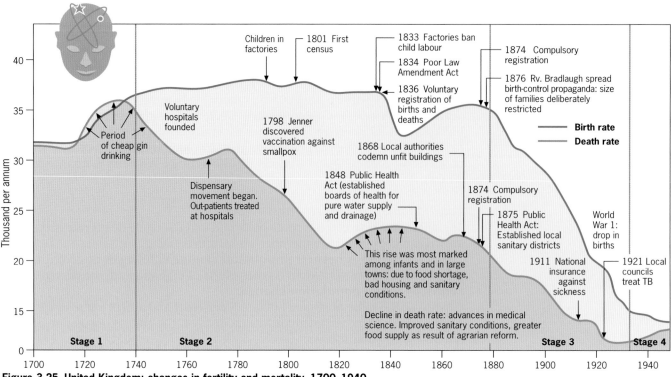

Figure 3.25 United Kingdom: changes in fertility and mortality, 1700–1940

27a Study Figures 3.26 and 3.27 and decide which stage of the demographic transition model each country in north Africa has reached in relation to birth and death rates.
b Suggest what you think will happen to the total population of each country over the next few years. Give your reasons.

Although the dynamics of population change in developed countries has been generalised here, the model helps us understand the reasons for population growth in the developing countries.

Many factors contribute to variations in both birth and death rates. All countries therefore have differing demographic transitions, depending on the social and economic circumstances which influence their birth and death rates. For example, changes in fertility and mortality may be affected by a variety of factors such as legislation, medical advances and even fashion (Fig. 3.25).

Although the developed countries have passed through the four stages of the demographic transition, most developing countries experience persistently high birth rates. Stages 2 and 3 of the demographic transition model is more typical, therefore, of most developing countries in the late 20th century.

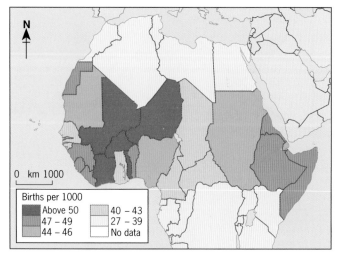

Figure 3.26 Northern Africa: birth rates, 1992

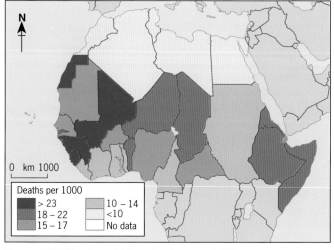

Figure 3.27 Northern Africa: death rates, 1992

3.7 Factors affecting fertility

There are various factors which particularly affect fertility in the developing countries. Some of these are outlined below:

Demographic factors

Families often try to compensate for high infant and child mortality by having a large number of children (Fig. 3.28). This is in the hope that some of the children will survive. In fact, social scientists have calculated that, in sub-Saharan Africa, where the average IMR is over 100 deaths, a woman must have an average of 10 children to be 95 per cent certain of a surviving adult son.

Where a population has a high child dependency ratio (see section 3.3 and Appendix A3), the result of a declining IMR will be more children surviving into adulthood. This can have long-term implications for future population growth rates. For example, more female children will survive to reach child-bearing age. Thus the birth rate remains high – even if fertility rates have since declined. This is a case of past fertility and mortality rates affecting future population growth and is known as **population momentum.**

Figure 3.28 Fai Mankoh (left) has 6 wives and 36 children. Some traditional African societies seek to increase the numbers of surviving children through family structures: polygamy is practised in Nigeria, Ghana, Mali and Cameroon.

Economic factors

In many developing countries, children are regarded as an economic asset. This means that they are viewed as producers rather than consumers and so parents (or other adults) will encourage them to contribute to the family income (compare with section 5.6).

Whereas children in developing countries are used as income generators, in the developed countries they are often viewed as a financial burden. For example, in the United States it is estimated that the cost of supporting a child to the age of 18 is in excess of US\$100 000. The economic motivation for having many children in developed countries is therefore reversed.

Social and cultural factors

There is a strong correlation between increasing female literacy and decreasing fertility rates (see section 6.5). In fact, low literacy rates and high dropout rates from school, especially among girls, mean that many young women enter into marriage and so have children early (see Table 6.9). Similarly, women's reduced access to formal employment and other income-earning opportunities means that they are forced to devote most of their time and energy to child-bearing and **informal** home and agricultural work (see Table 6.4). In contrast, developed countries show that with 'emancipation', women are more likely to have fewer children, and at a later age, than in developing countries.

There is no doubt that family size will reduce if the socio-economic conditions of many poorer nations improve. However, opinions differ as to how to reduce fertility rates in the developing countries (Fig. 3.29).

We also need to view high fertility rates in the cultural context. This is because in many developing countries, cultural factors play a significant role in the number and frequency of child birth and, hence, in the size of families. For example, in some African countries religious traditions emphasising ancestry and descent require babies to be named after dead relatives. People therefore view a lack of children as evil and childless couples as cursed. Demographic and cultural factors come together when, as part of their 'bride price', women in some African cultures, e.g. Nigeria, are obliged to produce as many children for their husbands as possible. When these women become widowed, any claim on their deceased husband's property is denied. As a result, the only security women have is their children, which suggests why many women would like/need to have as many children as possible.

?

28 Read Figure 3.29.
a Identify the two opinions on how best to reduce fertility rates in developing countries.
b Which view do you agree with? Give your reasons.
c Devise a plan to promote the successful adoption of your view for reducing fertility rates in a developing country.

Birth of a new world order

THE truth about population has become dangerously obscured. A proper concern for women's rights, and for the alleviation of chronic poverty, have ossified into ritual condemnations of anyone making a priority of population. Old shibboleths have persisted decades after their demolition by the empirical evidence of demographers.

None have persisted more obdurately than the idea that 'development is the best contraceptive'. From this perspective, doing anything about reducing human numbers becomes dependent on first reducing poverty – on the grounds that this was how things had happened in the world's richer nations when they went through their demographic transition. Only as per capita income rises will people be persuaded to have fewer children.

Unwelcome though this may be for the development lobby, this is basically cobblers. In country after country, average fertility rates have been falling dramatically over the last 20 years – with or without the necessary increases in per capita income.

Bangladesh is one of the most interesting examples of this so-called 'reproductive revolution'. It is one of the world's poorest nations, with high infant mortality and a largely agrarian society, in which most families still depend on children for labour and security in old age. But between 1970 and 1991, fertility rates declined from 7 to 5.5 children per woman (a 20 per cent reduction). And the key to that was the increase in the number of married women using contraception: up from 3 per cent to 40 per cent.

In short, contraception is the best contraceptive, not 'development'. Some researchers have gone as far as to say that differences in contraceptive prevalence (the percentage of women using contraception) explain about 90 per cent of the variation in fertility rates, and that for every 15 per cent increase in contraceptive prevalence, each woman will bear on average one child less.

What's more, though women's education is indeed one of the key factors in increasing contraceptive prevalence, it is not a precondition of it. In Egypt itself, where illiteracy still exceeds 50 per cent in many rural areas, contraceptive use has doubled in 10 years (making it the first Muslim country with more than 50 per cent of couples using contraception) and fertility rates are down from an average seven children per woman in the early 1960s to four today. That drop has been achieved largely through an unprecedented media blitz, including the screening of up to 600 hours of material relating to population and family planning every year.

To argue that the availability of contraception is the key determinant in reducing average fertility does not mean that one abhors any the less strongly either the poverty or the illiteracy of women taking advantage of that contraceptive availability. But it does rather change one's perception of what we can realistically do to address these problems.

For one thing, availability on its own is not enough. Fertility surveys around the world have shown that what really counts is quality of care, real freedom of choice (between different contraceptives) and the degree to which family services are integrated into overall reproductive healthcare strategy.

That's what makes the Cairo conference programme for action such an astonishing document. It's at least as much about women's reproductive rights and healthcare services as it is about family planning per se. It's a triumph for women's organisations which have gone on pointing out the obvious in the teeth of male-dominated health departments concerned only about the increasing number of 'contraceptive acceptors'; that coercion is not only heinous but counterproductive; that 'empowering' of women to take control of their own fertility will fail and keep on failing.

At long last the penny seems to have dropped. Family planning is an important health measure in its own right. Where women have six or more children, the lifetime risk of dying from maternal causes is five times higher than where they have two or less. The welcome convergence between the family planning establishment and mainstream women's organisations has been highly significant in the drafting and promoting of the Cairo programme for action.

Figure 3.29 Cairo Population Summit, September 1994 (*Source:* Jonathon Porritt, *The Guardian*, 2 September 1994)

Modernisation and the changing fertility trend
As people adopt Western culture in many developing countries, some traditional customs become less important. As a result, there is less emphasis on high fertility, particularly with a declining child mortality and increasing familiarity with family planning programmes. Recent demographic household surveys show that birth rates have fallen by 15–25 per cent in Botswana, Zimbabwe and Kenya. Similarly, social scientists report a fertility decline of over 10 per cent in southern Nigeria.

3.8 Age-sex structure of population

The age-sex structure of a population is best illustrated as a population pyramid, which is another form of bar graph (Fig. 3.30, see Appendix A5). The population is normally divided into five-year age groups e.g. 0–4; 5–9; 10–14 on the vertical axis. The horizontal axis represents the percentage of the total male or female population in each age group and is divided in two, according to gender. As well as illustrating the effect of past changes, population pyramids can also indicate both short- and long-term future changes in population.

We can use population pyramids to show the results of migration, the age and sex of migrants and the effects of wars and major epidemics. Certain population pyramid shapes are also characteristic of each stage of the demographic transition model.

?

29a Draw four hypothetical population pyramids to reflect the characteristics of the four stages of the demographic transition model (Fig. 3.24).
b Comment on the development of the population structure shown by your graphs.

Figure 3.30 Population by age and sex, 1950, 1990 and 2025 (*Source: US Bureau of the Census, Center of International Research, UNDIESA, 1991*)

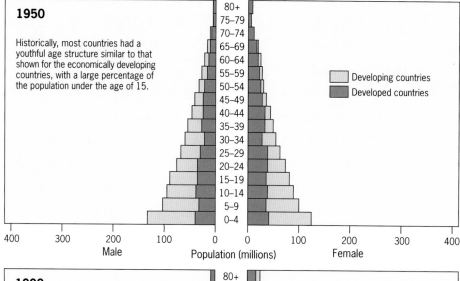

1950

Historically, most countries had a youthful age structure similar to that shown for the economically developing countries, with a large percentage of the population under the age of 15.

Developing countries
Developed countries

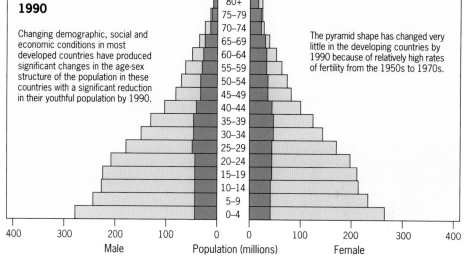

1990

Changing demographic, social and economic conditions in most developed countries have produced significant changes in the age-sex structure of the population in these countries with a significant reduction in their youthful population by 1990.

The pyramid shape has changed very little in the developing countries by 1990 because of relatively high rates of fertility from the 1950s to 1970s.

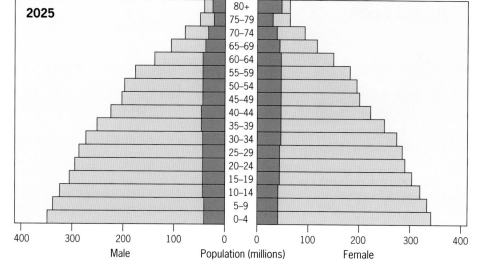

2025

?

30 Use Table 3.11. On a blank world map, draw pie graphs for each region showing the percentage in each age sector in 1990 and 2025:
• child dependants (0–14);
• economically active (15–64);
• aged dependants (over 65).
Compare the differences in the proportion of elderly people between developed and developing regions.

31a Discuss the social, economic and demographic factors responsible for the varying proportion of elderly people in different regions of the world.
b What implications does the growing proportion of elderly people have for service provisions such as health care and transport?

32 Essay: With reference to specific countries, describe and explain the social and economic implications of • top-heavy and • broad-based population structures.

Elderly people and population structure
An essential feature of the world population structure is the growing proportion of elderly people. We consider the elderly population to be 65 years old and above and this is usually the retirement age for many countries, including the

Table 3.12 The world's oldest nations, 1992 (*Source:* US Bureau of the Census, Center for International Research, International Database on ageing)

Country	Percentage population >65
Sweden	17.9
Norway	16.3
United Kingdom	15.7
Belgium	15.4
Denmark	15.4
Austria	15.3
Italy	15.2
France	15.0
Germany	15.0
Switzerland	14.9
Greece	14.8
Spain	14.1
Finland	13.9
Luxembourg	13.8
Bulgaria	13.8
Hungary	13.7
Portugal	13.6
Netherlands	13.2
Japan	12.8
United States	12.6

Table 3.11 Percentage of elderly people by regions, 1990–2025 (*Source:* US Bureau of the Census, Center for International Research, International Database on ageing)

Region	Year	65 years and over	75 years and over	80 years and over
Europe*	1990	13.7	6.1	3.2
	2010	17.5	8.4	4.9
	2025	22.4	10.8	6.4
North America	1990	12.6	5.3	2.8
	2010	14.0	6.5	4.0
	2025	20.1	8.5	4.6
Oceania	1990	9.3	3.6	1.8
	2010	11.0	4.8	2.8
	2025	15.0	6.6	3.6
Asia*	1990	4.8	1.5	0.6
	2010	6.8	2.5	1.2
	2025	10.0	3.6	1.8
South America/Caribbean	1990	4.6	1.6	0.8
	2010	6.4	2.4	1.2
	2025	9.4	3.6	1.8
Near East/North Africa	1990	3.8	1.2	0.5
	2010	4.6	1.6	0.8
	2025	6.4	2.2	1.1
Sub-Saharan Africa	1990	2.7	0.7	0.3
	2010	2.9	0.8	0.3
	2025	3.4	1.0	0.4

*Data excludes the former Soviet Union

Figure 3.31 Increasingly growing old: by the year 2025 it is estimated that more than 1 in 10 Europeans are likely to be 75 years old or older

UK (Fig. 3.31). Of all the world regions, Europe has the highest proportion of population aged 65 and over (Table 3.11) although Japan, too, is dealing with the problems of an ageing population (see section 4.7).

The 'oldest old'

The term 'oldest old' refers to the population 80 years and over. Persons in this category constituted 16 per cent of the world's elderly population in 1992, i.e. 22 per cent in the developed countries and 12 per cent in the developing countries. In many European countries, the population aged 80 and over represented about 25 per cent of the elderly population (Table 3.12).

Summary

- Reliable population statistics are essential for effective government policies and planning.
- Unreliable data in the developing countries can act as an obstacle to development.
- The concepts of optimum, over- and under-population relate to the size of population, the available resources and the existing levels of technology.
- The world's population is unevenly distributed. Some areas are over-populated, while others are under-populated.
- Fertility, mortality and migration are the three components of population change.
- All countries pass through demographic transition stages which are linked to the development process.
- The population structure typical of developing countries consists of a high percentage of people under 15 years, resulting in a high child dependency ratio.
- Many developed countries are characterised by an ageing population.

4 *Population movements and urbanisation*

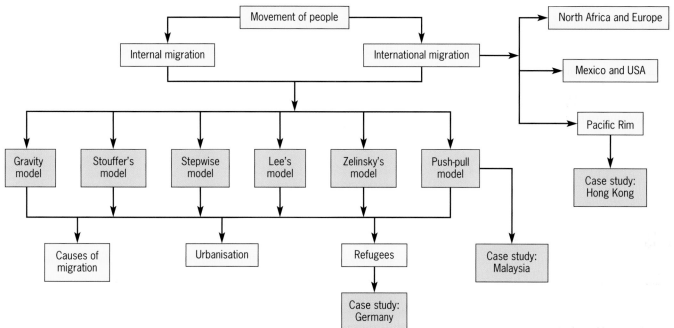

4.1 Introduction

In both the **developed** and **developing countries** patterns of human migration are a result of changing social, economic, political and environmental circumstances. In this chapter we will discuss some of these causes of migration. Over recent years, attention has increasingly centred on the issue of internal population movement, particularly in the developing countries. International migration is another area of growing concern which has implications for both developing and developed countries – not least in its effects on the allocation and utilisation of resources.

4.2 Historic population movements

Early migration
Historical evidence suggests that early human groups spread outwards from north-east Africa. The earliest human remains found in Europe are approximately half a million years old. This indicates that people had already migrated from East Africa to Europe (often now referred to as the **old world**) by that time. These migrations took place during periods of glacial advance in the last ice age when water taken up in ice sheets lowered the sea's surface to create land bridges. These made it easier to migrate (Fig. 4.1). It took humans an estimated 3 million years to spread over much of the earth's surface.

Ethnic (racial) diversity
As people inhabited different parts of the world, they grouped together and developed their own distinctive identities. The term 'race' refers to descent from one of these distinctive groups. Long periods of interbreeding and inter-regional migrations have since resulted in a great mixing of races and racial diversity.

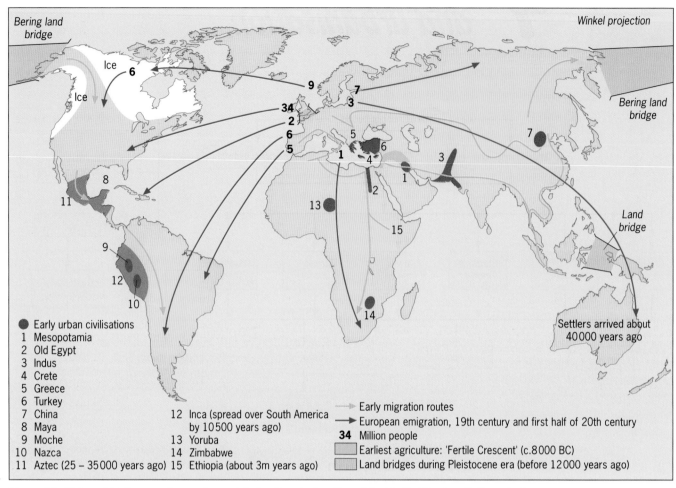

Bering land bridge

Winkel projection

Ice
Ice

Bering land bridge

Land bridge

Settlers arrived about 40 000 years ago

● Early urban civilisations
1   Mesopotamia
2   Old Egypt
3   Indus
4   Crete
5   Greece
6   Turkey
7   China
8   Maya
9   Moche
10 Nazca
11 Aztec (25 – 35 000 years ago)

12 Inca (spread over South America by 10 500 years ago)
13 Yoruba
14 Zimbabwe
15 Ethiopia (about 3m years ago)

→ Early migration routes
➡ European emigration, 19th century and first half of 20th century
34 Million people
▨ Earliest agriculture: 'Fertile Crescent' (c.8 000 BC)
▨ Land bridges during Pleistocene era (before 12 000 years ago)

Figure 4.1 Major migrations: early peoples and during the nineteenth and first half of the twentieth centuries

Table 4.1 Population total increase in Western Europe, 1750–1980 (*Source:* JN Biraben (1979) *Essay sur l'evolution du Nombre des hommes*, 1979; UN World Population trends 1981, UN Population Bulletin 14, 1982)

Year	Population (millions)	Increase since previous year; average per year, per 1 000 population
1750	111	—
1800	146	5.5
1850	209	7.2
1900	295	6.9
1950	392	5.7
1960	425	8.1
1970	462	8.4
1975	474	5.1
1980	484	4.2
projected		
2000	512	2.8
2100	504	—

For example, the Caucasoids met Mongoloids (American Indians) in North and South America and through intermarriage produced the Mestizos. The world became a 'multi-racial' (pluralistic) place at a very early stage primarily because of early migrations and intermarriages.

We can see differences between the ethnic groups in both their physical and cultural characteristics, e.g. language, dress and even diet. It is therefore possible for us to identify the major races:

a Negroid: includes the indigenous peoples of Africa south of the Sahara, their descendants and the people from Melanesia (Pacific Islands).
b Mongoloid: includes most of the peoples of Asia, the Inuit (eskimo) and the North American Indians.
c Caucasoid: refers to peoples originating from Europe and North Africa.

Migration during the industrial revolution
Apart from the early migrations, the world's major mass movement of people occurred during the industrial revolution in Europe. This was a time when Europe experienced a population 'explosion' (Table 4.1). In fact, one of the major characteristics of the industrial revolution in Europe was high population growth due to rapidly declining death rates while birth rates remained persistently high (see section 3.6 and Fig. 3.24). This led to population pressure which, alongside social changes, encouraged many people to migrate, especially to North America (known as the **new world**) (Fig. 4.1). An estimated 40 million Europeans emigrated to North America and other relatively uninhabited regions, such as Australia and South Africa, between 1820 and 1900.

1 Use Figure 4.1 to write an historical account of the early movement of people across the world.

2a Read Figure 4.2.
a How did Europe cope with its labour problems after World War 2?
b In what ways were the **immigrants** to Britain different from those migrating to other European countries?
c In your group, discuss what you consider to be the results of such migration.

3 In 1963 President Pompidou stated that 'immigration is a means of creating a certain easing in the labour market, and of resisting social pressure'. Comment on this statement saying whether or not you agree with it.

Figure 4.2 Attracting workers to the industrial centres of Europe (*Source: Jonathan Power, 1972, The New Proletarians*, Community & Race Relations Unit of the British Council of Churches)

Post-World War 2 and the migratory balance

The direction of population movements from Europe was reversed after World War 2. This was a time when the devastated European economies needed rebuilding and Europe was suffering from serious labour shortages because of men lost in fighting. The European governments encouraged migrants, usually from the European colonies, to work in industries such as transport, care and construction (Fig. 4.2).

During 1956, 30 000 West Indians arrived in the UK: most came by boat to Southampton and then train to London.

THE SECOND WORLD WAR led to unforeseen new demands. By 1944 Germany had seven million foreign workers. Every fourth German tank, lorry, and field gun was made by a foreigner. Much of this, of course, was forced labour.

But at the end of the war, in 1945, the consensus of expert opinion was that most European countries would not be able to provide enough employment for their own citizens. The big worry was Western Germany which had received eight million refugees from the East. But in fact the reverse happened. The expanding economies of the West European countries soon took up the slack and before long attention was swivelling outwards to foreign sources of labour. In Britain it began in 1940 with a cargo of West Indian immigrants. They were closely followed by Indians and Pakistanis. The numbers of immigrants increased year by year until, in the late fifties and early sixties, Britain's economy went into the permanent doldrums. Ironically, at this time, racism and xenophobia pushed anxious governments into building high walls of protection to limit the immigrants who no longer wanted to come. All in all, in this time of immigration Britain absorbed 800 000 workers and their families – small fry compared with what was going on in some other European countries…

The British have the feeling that the great influx of Commonwealth immigrants in the last two decades is a special British phenomenon – a legacy of Empire. But this is only true inasmuch as the British tend to have black workers rather than white ones. But all European countries have experienced what the British have experienced – a great influx since the war of large numbers of foreign workers. In Germany they are nearly all white – Greeks, Turks, Yugoslavs, Spaniards, and Italians. In France the principal groups are Portuguese, Spanish and North African. In Belgium they are mainly Italians, Turks, and Greeks. In Holland, more similar to Britain, there are large numbers of Indonesians and people from the Dutch West Indies, Although Turks, Greeks and Italians are numerous too.

They are the new proletarians – doing the menial jobs, poorly paid with little job security (unless they are Italians or Greeks, fellow members of the EEC), separated from their families, living in housing that is often appalling.

Willy Brandt succinctly summed up their contribution when he said: 'In every way, foreign workers help us to earn our daily bread… although foreign workers are in Germany because at home they live in indigent circumstances, Germany needs them urgently. They're dependent on us. But we are even more dependent on them for otherwise they would not be here.'

4.3 Definition of migration

The United Nations defines migration as the movement of a person or persons from one place to another, involving a permanent (one year or more) change of address. There are different types of migration classified according to whether the movement is within a country (internal migration) or from one country to another (international migration).

Internal migration

This involves movement between regions within the same country and over relatively short distances. There are various types of movement in this category depending on their direction (Table 4.2 and Fig. 4.3).

International migration

International migration involves relatively long distance movements between countries. **Emigration** is the term used to describe the departure of a person from one country to live permanently in another. Conversely, immigration is the entrance of a person into a country with the aim of living there permanently (see Figs 4.1 and 4.24)

4a Using the media or your library, research recent examples of both migration types.
b Identify some of the difficulties each type of migrant had to face as they moved. Consider how the people in the host area responded to the migrants.

Table 4.2 Types of internal migration

Type of migration	Direction of movement	Reason and example
Rural-to-urban	People moving from countryside to urban areas	People searching for work led to: • growth of cities in Europe during industrial revolution, • rapid urbanisation in developing countries in late twentieth century.
Urban-to-rural	People moving from the city or town to the countryside	Many people see cities as unattractive and in developed countries people try to move away from the urban areas. This process is referred to as **counter-urbanisation**, e.g. England's South-East where families move out of London into the semi-rural home counties.
Inter-urban	People moving from one town or city to another	Changing work opportunities force people to relocate.
Intra-urban	People moving within the same urban area or city	Increased transport results in high levels of residential mobility e.g. post World War 2, people moved to the edge of cities (suburbanisation).
Rural-to-rural	People moving from one area of the countryside to another	Common in agricultural communities where there is a need to change farming locations, e.g. sheep shearers migrating between ranches in the USA and Australia; nomadic pastoralists, northern Africa.
Transmigration	Forced, or government-organised, mass movement of people	Brazil, 1970s: the government displaced people from the poorest parts of Brazil to settle in areas of cleared rainforest. Indonesia, from the 1980s several million people were moved to the country's less populated outer islands, from Jakarta and other overcrowded cities (resulting in conflict and environmental degradation).

Figure 4.3 Squatters near Curitiba, southern Brazil. Large plantations have taken up much land and left many people homeless and landless, forcing them to move close to the cities in search of work. In 1980 18.45 million people migrated within the South-East region of Brazil. In contrast, 35.14 million people migrated to the relatively inaccessible Central-West region. Brasilia has grown rapidly mainly as a result of rural-urban migration.

4.4 Migration theories and models

There are two main categories of migration models. First are those which try to predict and explain migration using some mathematical or probability concept. An example of such an approach is the gravity model. Second, there are largely descriptive models which focus on various social factors that may influence patterns of migration. Whether expressed in mathematical or descriptive form, migration models generally provide some specific explanation for population movements.

Mathematical migration models

Gravity model

The gravity model is based on E G Ravenstein's laws of migration (1885). He developed these to explain the migration process in late nineteenth century Britain.

An essential feature of the gravity model is its suggestion that migrants tend to move over short distances, with the number of migrants decreasing as the distance over which migration takes place increases. This idea is known as the **distance decay effect** which states that the volume of migration is inversely proportional to the distance travelled, and directly proportional to the relative sizes of the origin and destination places (Fig. 4.4). This is mathematically expressed as follows:

$$M_{ij} = \frac{P_i P_j}{D_{ij}^2}$$

where
M_{ij} = the volume of migration from place i to place j
P_i = the population size of place i
P_j = the population size of place j
D_{ij}^2 = the distance between places i and j

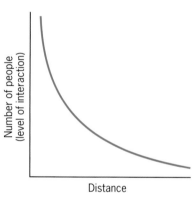

Figure 4.4 The distance decay effect

(y-axis: Number of people (level of interaction); x-axis: Distance)

5a For the five largest cities in the country where you live, find out: • the population size of each, • the distance between each city and the capital.
b Calculate the *predicted* interaction between each city and the capital using the formula provided.
c List the factors which could lead to more or less interaction between cities than you have predicted using the gravity model.

Stouffer's intervening opportunity model

Stouffer's migration model suggests that the level of movement of people between two places is dependent upon the type and number of **intervening opportunities** between them. Intervening opportunities are the nature and number of possible alternative migration destinations that may exist between place A (migration origin) and place B (migration destination). An essential feature of this model is that the nature of places, rather than their distance, is more important in determining where people move to. People will move from place A to place B based on the real or perceived opportunity at place B (e.g. work). According to Stouffer's model, therefore, the number of persons moving

Stouffer's intervening
opportunity model

over a given distance is directly proportional to the number of opportunities at that distance, and inversely proportional to the number of intervening opportunities.

Using Strodbeck's (1949) version of this method, the basic idea of Stouffer's Intervening Opportunity model can be mathematically expressed as follows:

$$y = k \; \frac{\nabla x}{x}$$

where y = the expected number of migrants from a place to a particular concentric zone or distance band around that place

∇x = the number of opportunities within this band

x = the number of opportunities intervening between origin and midway into the distance band

k = a constant of proportionality

Behavioural migration models

Stepwise migration model

The stepwise migration model is a behavioural one developed from E G Ravenstein's laws (1885) that population movements occur in stages and with a 'wave-like' motion. According to this idea, major settlements, such as capital cities, tend to attract migrants from the smaller cities, which in turn attract migrants from smaller towns and villages. Migration therefore occurs in 'steps' and in the form of a 'ripple' that stretches across an entire region (Fig. 4.5).

a Hierarchical stepwise movement

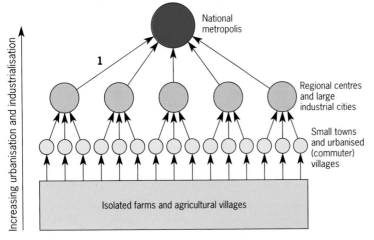

b Varied stepwise movement

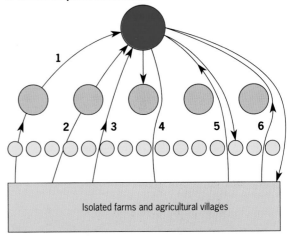

Types of stepped migratory movement originating from rural areas:

1 Progressive movement from rural area to small town, to regional centre to national metropolis
2 Progressive movement from rural area to regional centre and then national metropolis
3 Direct movement from rural area to national metropolis

4 Intention to move from rural area to national metropolis but eventually residing in regional centre
5 Intention to move from rural area to national metropolis but eventually residing in small town
6 Intention to move from rural area to national metropolis but eventually returning to rural area without residing elsewhere

?

6 Referring to Figure 4.5, draw your own version of the stepwise model identifying the stages of Chinese migration.

Figure 4.5 Stepwise migration model (*After: Ravenstein*)

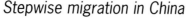

Table 4.3 Pacific Rim countries: overseas Chinese (*Source: Financial Times*, 22 June 1989)

Country	Ethnic Chinese population in millions
Thailand	7.0
Hong Kong	5.5
Malaysia	4.88
Indonesia	4.12
Singapore	1.99
USA	0.894
Canada	0.4
Philippines	0.6
Australia	0.17
UK (for comparison)	0.126

Stepwise migration in China

Several events in China have led to increasing numbers of Chinese emigrating to countries of the Pacific Rim. A famine in the early 1960s, resulting from a change in political direction, caused many Chinese to escape to nearby countries such as Thailand and Malaysia. The adoption of the 'Open Door' policy, in 1978, also resulted in a steady stream of Chinese migrants moving to the urban centres around the Pacific. In the early 1990s, there were about 30 million Chinese living in Pacific Rim countries (Table 4.3).

We can see the influence of such Chinese migration by looking at Malaysia. Here, one-third of the population are indigenous Chinese and most of these, as in many other Pacific Rim countries, are successful business people who maintain their cultural and economic links with China. They are often reluctant to break with Chinese traditions and religions, and usually regard Chinese as their first language. In fact, many have now left Malaysia, 'stepping on' to greater cultural tolerance and better business opportunities in Singapore.

There are also 400 000 Chinese in Canada, with two-thirds of these living in Vancouver and Toronto. Most Chinese here come from Hong Kong, though, showing the 'stepwise' progression, as a typical feature of international migration.

Lee's migration model

Lee's model tries to explain the factors of migration in terms of positive and negative characteristics of both the origin and destination places. Migrants must expect to receive some added advantage in moving from one place to another. Also, potential movements from an origin, such as a rural area, to a final destination, such as a capital city, are often influenced by the existence of possible alternative destinations. These present themselves as intervening opportunities for migrants whose movements to the final destination may be slowed down or even stopped by these intervening places (Fig. 4.6).

Intervening obstacles may prevent migration from taking place, or may reduce the numbers moving. Distance may be such an obstacle (see gravity model), while social or economic factors may also act as obstacles.

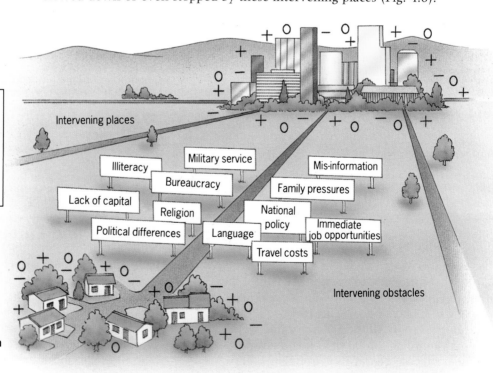

– Negative factors
+ Positive factors
0 Neutral factors

Figure 4.6 Lee's general migration model

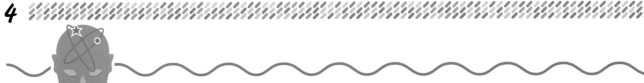

Zelinsky's model of mobility transition

Zelinsky's model of mobility transition is a parallel theory to the **demographic transition model** (see section 3.6). Zelinsky's model attempts to describe definite regularities in migration types through space and time. In doing so, it seeks to explain the pattern of migration from what Zelinsky considered to be the pre-modern traditional society through the different stages of modernisation to the advanced industrial society. The essential feature of the model is based on Rostow's stages of economic growth (see section 6.6).

Zelinsky's model suggests that as modernisation proceeds, different forms of migration patterns emerge. Once a particular pattern of migration is started, it rises steadily until it reaches its peak and then declines. Thus different types of population movement succeed one another as the dominant wave (Fig. 4.7).

?

7a How might long-distance travel be affected by modern developments in transport, such as Concorde?
b Might these developments in transport mean that another stage could be added to Zelinsky's model? If so, describe the main features of this stage.

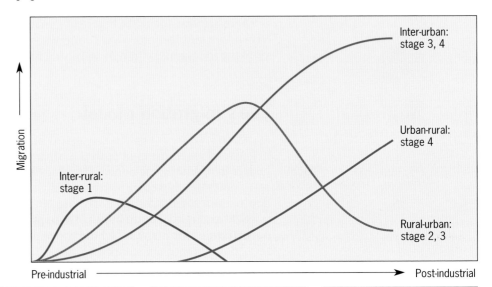

Figure 4.7 Zelinsky's mobility transition model

Stage 1: occurs mostly in a subsistence economy. People move about very little and usually only make daily journeys to work in the fields, or less frequent journeys from village to village to sell farm produce.

Stage 2: migration to other countries and cities becomes important. People begin to move home in search of better opportunities. Farm mechanisation reduces the demand for rural workers while industrialisation provides work in urban areas.

Stage 3: overseas emigration tends to fall. Movement from the countryside to the cities remains important. Migration from one city to another and within particular cities also occurs.

Stage 4: migration from the countryside to the cities declines and urban-rural migration (counter-urbanisation) begins. People tend to move home frequently but within or between cities e.g. 1/5 of the population of the USA change residence annually. Ease of travel encourages daily long-distance journeys for e.g. work or education. Long-distance travel for holidays is another feature of this stage.

Migration between North Africa and Europe

It has been estimated that about six million people from North African countries now live within the European Union (Fig. 4.8). It is also now evident that increasing numbers of people are arriving in Europe from countries south of the Sahara. While we could consider distance an 'obstacle' to migration, this movement suggests that the environmental and political push factors (see push-pull model, section 4.5) in the semi-arid origin countries, e.g. Chad and

Ethiopia, are much stronger than the distance obstacle. Italy and France are the most popular destinations with migrants from North Africa. We can explain this by proximity, but also by historic ties. Algeria, Morocco, Tunisia, Libya, Mali, Chad and Burkina Faso are all former colonies of France and many people in these countries still speak French as their main language, despite subsequent independence.

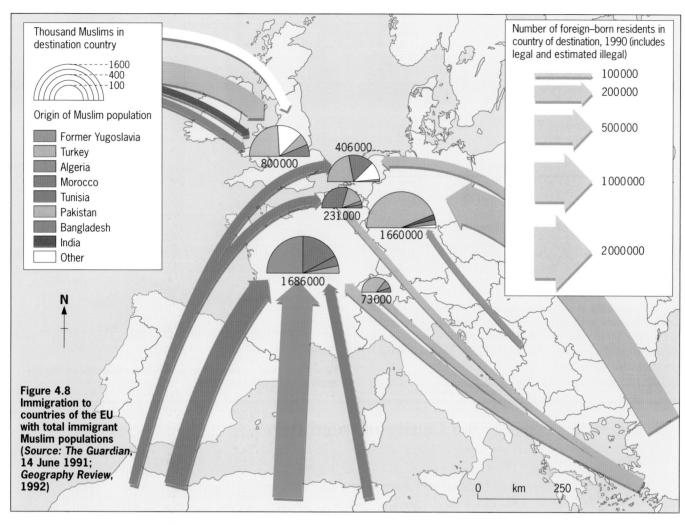

**Figure 4.8
Immigration to
countries of the EU
with total immigrant
Muslim populations
(*Source: The Guardian,*
14 June 1991;
Geography Review,
1992)**

The impact in Italy and France

Both Italy and France have been under great pressure
to tighten their immigration policies. This is principally
because of the rapid increase in the numbers of
migrants during the 1980s, especially from North
African countries such as Senegal, Ghana and the Cape
Verde islands.

Italy

Italy introduced visa requirements from July 1990 for
'visitors' from the Mahgreb (or North African
countries). Italy's 2000 km coastline makes it
particularly vulnerable to landings of illegal immigrants
and the authorities fear that such migrants will find it
easy to travel into other countries of the European
Union since internal border controls were abolished
(1994).

France

France has prohibited 'new' immigration since 1974.
None the less, the composition of immigrant groups
seen in 1975 is a pattern which has continued
throughout the 1980s and early 1990s (Fig. 4.9). In
fact, there is a clear relationship with the location of

the origin of each group. Distance travelled obviously
determines the type of migrant most likely to move.

People joining family members already resident in
France are still allowed entry, and this leads to an in-
flow of 120 000 immigrants a year. In 1990, 440 000
Algerians, 50 000 Tunisians and 16 000 Moroccans
entered Marseilles on tourist visas which entitle them
to stay for up to three months. Many immigrants in
France are Muslims (Fig. 4.8), but unlike the French,
they often have large families and take cheaply-paid
work. Because most migrants enter France now as
refugees, the processing of their applications can take
months. During that time, refugees have rights to both
reside and work in France.

8 Study Figure 4.8.
a Describe the geographical pattern of the origin and
destination of Muslim migrants in West Europe.
b Using this information, find evidence for some of the
likely issues that such immigration could cause.

Migration between North Africa and Europe

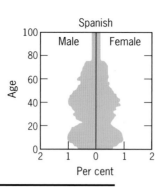

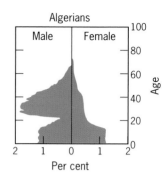

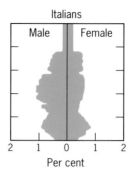

9a Describe the composition of each of the immigrant groups in France as shown in Figure 4.9.
b Comment on the numbers of • dependants, • those who are economically active, and • the implications for France.
c With reference to an atlas, suggest reasons why the composition of migrants from south of the Sahara is different from the other groups of immigrants in France.

10 How far is the scale of migration *from* countries in North Africa consistent with Zelinsky's model? Have these countries reached the same stage of development as European countries at the turn of the century (when large-scale international migration also occurred)?

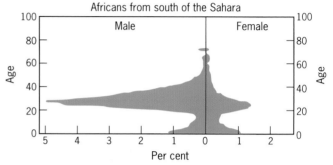

Figure 4.9 France: population pyramids for selected immigrant groups, 1975 (*Source:* JMB)

4.5 Causes of migration

The traditional models of migration suggest that population movements largely reflect inequality in the distribution of resources and opportunities. These differences force people either towards or away from an area.

Push-pull model

Imbalance in both economic activities and opportunities creates the potential 'push' and 'pull' forces which drive and sustain population movements (Table 4.4). According to the migration models, the operation of these two forces (push and pull) generally determines the level, type, and nature of migration.

On the one hand, the 'push' factors are features of the home area which create pressures and so cause people to move away. For example, unemployment, natural disasters and political/religious crises. On the other hand, the 'pull' factors operate at places outside the migrant's home area to attract individuals to a new location. In fact, the major reason why people move from one place to another is economic. The main pull factor is therefore the promise of work, and the person in search of work is thus known as an **economic migrant** (Fig. 4.10, see Fig. 4.2).

11a Read Figure 4.10 and identify some of the major problems which result from large-scale internal migration.

12a Study Figure 4.11 and make a list of all the different reasons indicated for migration.
b Using Table 4.4 and all the reasons you identified in **a**, sort all the 'push' and 'pull' factors into the following:
• physical factors
• economic factors
• social factors
• political factors.

Table 4.4 Factors affecting migration (*Source:* Selmes (ed), 1985)

Push		Pull	
Natural disaster	Bereavement	Political asylum	Marriage
Heavy taxes	Inaccessibility	Higher education	Promotion
Harsh climate	Poverty	Resource exploitation	Scenic quality
High rents	Discrimination	Fertile soils	High living standards
Growth of family	Unemployment	Lack of natural hazards	Good welfare services
Persecution	Lack of housing	Propaganda	Freedom of speech
Planning decisions	Civil unrest	Relatives and friends	Good wages

China's 'gold coast' pulls millions in search of work

Every few minutes a public address system outside Shanghai railway station broadcasts warnings to a forecourt packed with people. They are told that it is illegal for employers to recruit workers at the station and it urges those who have arrived in the city in the hope of finding work to go home.

Despite the regulations, a man in a suit and camel-hair coat negotiates with potential employees. There are shouts of 'Wenzhou!' or 'Ningbo!', as private bus operators tout for custom to fill seats to other boom towns along the coast. Elderly men and women in tattered clothes beg for pennies.

One young beggar, her 10 months old baby swaddled to her chest, asked for a contribution to her train fare home. She and her husband had spent all their savings to get here, she said, but now had nothing to eat.

The scene is repeated in stations throughout southern and eastern China.

About 140 million people in the countryside do not have enough work, according to official estimates. Frenzied construction and industrialisation near the coast acts as a magnet. In Guangzhou, the capital of Guangdong province next to Hong Kong, 100000 people arrive each day.

The railways cannot cope. Last month up to 50 people died in a stampede at the station in Hengyang, in the central province of Hunan. More than half were young women under the age of 20. Local officials said 160000 people were leaving the town each day.

But there is work for many. Much of coastal China is a building site, staffed by migrants who are a source of cheap labour for local and foreign investors. After a spate of murderous factory fires late last year, the official media has railed against conditions. The labour ministry said it would set up a telephone hotline for abused workers.

In Shanghai, most of those still job hunting at the station are from the neighbouring, but poor province, of Anhui. One young man is with a group of about 30 from one village. 'What can we do?' he asked. 'There's no work there.' Two men came from the village last year. They live in a dormitory on a construction site in Pudong, the new town over the river from old Shanghai, where office blocks and factories have shot up.

City officials said 2.5 million of Shanghai's population of 13 million are migrants. The local media blame them for an increase in crime. It is claimed that 80 per cent of bicycle thieves are migrants. Murder, rape and armed robbery increased by 80 per cent in 1993.

Taxi-drivers, who are protected by metal grilles and reinforced plastic, said they will not pick up migrants. 'It's not safe. Shanghai is lawless these days,' one said.

Despite recent efforts to slow down the Chinese economy, industrial output in January was still up more than 30 per cent on last year. Shanghai's economy grew by 15 per cent last year and hopes to achieve 12 per cent this year, three per cent above the national target.

But the boom is unevenly spread. So each year, one of the world's great annual migrations gathers momentum, as poor farmers take off to claim their share of the benefits.

Figure 4.10 The uneven spread of wealth results in one of the world's great annual migrations (Source: Simon Long, The Guardian, 2 March 1994

At the walls of Citadel Europe

Most of today's emigrants wish to change their identities and, in so doing, reject what they leave behind in their homeland. They are not fleeing to any particular country, but from the Soviet Union. Today's wave of emigration from the USSR is also very different from the migration of peoples in demo-cratic states. A form of 'security' still reigns here; while people will have been exposed to all manner of persecutions, they have also been subject to the will of the state. These people long to free themselves from this imposition; to flee constraints and pressures of totalitarianism.

They also want, quite simply, to see those things which for so many long years remained forbidden fruit. Yet ask someone today why they want to emigrate and one will probably hear this: 'I'm just sick and tired of this dirt, the fear of hunger, the endless time spent standing in queues.'

The Guardian, 14 June 1991

Calls to shut out immigrants

Poles, Ukrainians and other second-world-war refugees were initially recruited followed, increasingly, by Commonwealth immigrants from the Caribbean. London Transport, the National Health Service and other employers actively recruited in the West Indies for workers.

The Guardian, 19 Nov. 1991

Fear of Fortress Europe

Economic deprivation and political repression have driven large numbers of people to leave developing and southern European countries and move to the richer north. The break-up of the former Eastern bloc has opened the door to the West for hundreds of thousands of immigrants. Meanwhile, the abolition of internal borders within the EC after 1992, accompanied by new restrictions to keep out non-EC migrants, is acting to encourage refugees to enter the EC while they can.

The Guardian, 14 June 1991

Across the river and into the States

'There isn't any work in Mexico,' says Hernandez. 'That's why the frontier is the way it is.' He is not exaggerating. Unemployment in Mexico runs at 40 per cent. Another 20 per cent of adults are estimated to be underemployed. Mexico's population stands at about 85 million, of which 40 million are under 18 years of age. In El Paso, 69 per cent of the inhabitants are of Mexican origin.

The Guardian, 19 Nov. 1991

Figure 4.11 Some causes of migration

Internal migration in Peninsular Malaysia

In the **newly industrialising country** of Malaysia (Fig. 4.12) we can see high rates of internal migration which exist mostly because of spatial inequalities of wealth. In fact, most of Malaysia's internal migrations involve short distance movements both within and across states (Fig. 4.13).

Total area: 329 750 sq km

Land area: 328 550 sq km

Climate: tropical; annual southwest (April to October) and northeast (October to February) monsoons

Natural resources: tin, crude oil, timber, copper, iron ore, natural gas, bauxite

GDP growth rate 8.6% (1991)

Unemployment rate: 5.8% (1991)

Industries: rubber and oil palm processing and manufacturing, light manufacturing industry, electronics, tin mining and smelting, logging and processing timber; petroleum production; agriculture processing.

Population:
1992: 18 742 000
2025 (projected): 34 889 000

Urban population: 34.6%

Population growth: 2.53%

Birth rate: 30 births per 1000 persons

Death rate: 4.7 deaths per 1000 persons

Ethnic divisions: Malay and other indigenous 59%, Chinese 32%, Indian 9%

Figure 4.12 Peninsular Malaysia

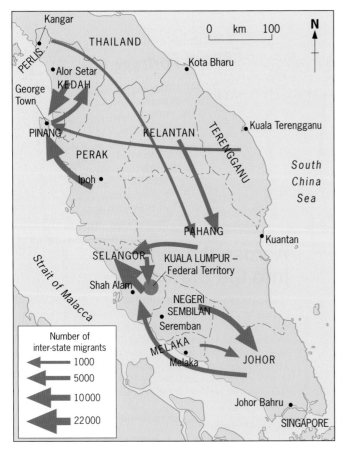

Figure 4.13 Peninsular Malaysia: migration flows, 1990
(*Source:* Jegede, O'Hare, 1994)

13   Using Table 4.5 and Figure 4.13, compare the levels of migration into and out of the 12 states of Peninsular Malaysia. Identify:
a   regions of high in-migration.
b   regions of high out-migration.

Growth areas

The most important development areas in Peninsular Malaysia which have attracted migrants in recent years include first, the economic core of the country, i.e. the Federal Territory (Kuala Lumpur) and the state of Selangor. Second, many migrants have been attracted to significant outer zones of development at Pinang and, more recently, in the southern state of Johor. In addition, a number of rural states such as Pahang and Kedah have witnessed significant in-migration at different times because of the Government sponsored rural development projects.

We can explain internal migration in Malaysia, as in many other developing countries, in terms of the location of economic activities and social amenities such as industry, schools, and health facilities. Industry and other economic activities tend to be concentrated in urban areas, so these therefore become attractive to potential migrants.

Experts have now recognised that the governments of developing countries could play a significant role in controlling the mass movement of people from rural to

Table 4.5 Inter- and intra-state migration (origin-destination matrix), 1990
(*Source:* Internal Migration in Peninsular Malaysia, Dept of Statistics, Malaysia 1991)

To destination state:	Johor	Kedah	Kelantan	Melaka	Negeri Sembilan	Pahang	Pinang	Perak	Perlis	Selangor	Terengganu	Federal Territory	Total*
From origin state:													
Johor	75 121	1 450	1 008	3 719	2 855	1 879	*	744	246	6 790	1 664	2 428	97 904
Kedah	1 948	42 645	1 334	*	*	817	7 096	3 613	1660	1 646	594	1 077	62 430
Kelantan	1 807	402	47 878	*	712	4 417	471	273	64	2 387	4 219	1 792	64 422
Melaka	3 245	468	*	19 205	1 989	253	397	328	119	2 941	*	1 451	30 396
Negeri Sembilan	7 887	518	*	3 316	13 428	488	760	676	*	3 238	326	1 325	31 962
Pahang	6 230	1 231	2 842	1 019	2 316	35 009	*	2 073	*	6 372	1 712	941	59 745
Pinang	2 500	9 681	285	307	308	900	26 241	4 324	253	1 500	63	1 692	48 054
Perak	8 647	4 511	397	709	394	3 135	10 447	63 223	*	8 891	319	5 369	106 042
Perlis	291	1 123	*	*	*	2 400	858	63	5340	493	*	125	10 693
Selangor	3 935	3 904	1 596	1 065	2 679	4 048	2 602	4 242	*	31 234	2 063	5 498	62 866
Terengganu	2 522	*	1 757	*	*	2 259	2 878	508	*	1 565	15 447	371	27 307
Federal Territory	8 583	2 175	2 956	1 748	306	3 851	3 177	5 679	*	21 950	1 244	*	51 669
Total†	122 716	68 108	60 053	31 088	24 987	59 456	54 927	85 746	7 682	89 007	27 651	22 069	653 490

*No data †Number of people moving into each state from all other states, and including movement within the state

Table 4.6 Inter- and intra-state migration (origin-destination matrix), 1981
(*Source:* Internal Migration in Peninsular Malaysia, Dept of Statistics, Malaysia 1981)

To destination state:	Johor	Kedah	Kelantan	Melaka	Negeri Sembilan	Pahang	Pinang	Perak	Perlis	Selangor	Terengganu	Federal Territory	Total*
From origin state:													
Johor	63 859	2 477	1 455	4 454	3 219	3 920	827	5 000	476	4 345	867	5 302	96 201
Kedah	1 546	54 051	1 114	411	683	3 464	9 448	4 483	774	3 127	733	2 989	82 823
Kelantan	1 083	1 398	36 786	61	222	3 111	272	1 349	*	1 457	3 255	1 225	50 219
Melaka	4 228	417	307	15 649	3 948	1 077	124	885	43	2 325	46	1 827	30 876
Negeri Sembilan	2 485	290	702	2 821	20 820	1 899	222	1 474	86	3 607	259	3 627	38 292
Pahang	2 408	1 106	3 413	460	2 122	36 485	711	3 675	*	3 713	2 559	3 976	60 628
Pinang	350	3 796	714	469	266	771	28 841	3 389	*	3 005	99	2 251	43 852
Perak	2 237	2 964	905	346	1 442	5 270	7 506	62 164	268	8 265	754	9 295	101 416
Perlis	46	1 662	*	*	153	235	390	141	2 888	86	*	472	5 987
Selangor	3 745	1 485	1 511	1 076	2 811	5 120	998	6 394	166	30 510	1 715	9 405	64 936
Terengganu	1 427	684	1 669	*	175	2 615	74	192	*	423	28 766	496	36 098
Federal Territory	3 309	1 230	2 041	2 778	1 810	2 172	2 009	5 869	481	14 224	1 079	*	37 002
Total†	86 723	71 560	50 617	28525	37671	66139	51 422	95 015	5 182	74 578	40 033	40 033	64 8330

*No data †Number of people moving into each state from all other states, and including movement within the state

urban areas. Governments can do this by discouraging the urban concentration of economic and social activities and by promoting rural-oriented development projects.

Analysis of migration flows in Malaysia

In 1990, the total population of Peninsular Malaysia, was 14.2 million. Just less than three quarters of a million persons or 5.1 per cent of the population migrated that same year. Intra-state migrants, i.e. those moving within a state, formed the majority at 51.6 per cent of total migrants; but an estimated 40 per cent were inter-state migrants, i.e. they moved between the states. About 8.4 per cent of the total migrants left the Malaysian peninsular altogether; a minority of these went to other parts of Malaysia, including the islands of Sarawak and Sabah, with the rest going to other countries. These patterns of movement are very similar to migration flows in 1981 when 6.0 per cent of the total Malaysian population were classed as migrants. Similar proportions of people were then moving within and between states, or emigrating from the peninsular region.

Internal migration in peninsular Malaysia

Figure 4.14 Peninsular Malaysia: base map

Table 4.7 Total migrants as a proportion of total population of destination state

	Population, 1981	No. of migrants, 1981	Percentage	Population, 1990	No. of migrants, 1990	Percentage
Johor	1 640 488	96 201	5.9	2 074 297	97 904	4.7
Kedah	1 117 510	82 823	7.4	1 304 800	62 432	4.8
Kelantan	895 354	50 219	5.6	1 181 680	64 422	5.5
Melaka	465 346	30 876	6.6	504 502	30 396	6.0
Negeri Semblan	574 327	38 292	6.7	691 150	31 962	4.6
Pahang	800 034	60 628	7.6	1 036 724	59 745	5.8
Pinang	955 618	43 852	4.6	1 065 075	48 054	4.5
Perak	1 807 423	101 416	5.6	1 880 016	106 042	5.6
Perlis	148 448	5 987	4.0	184 070	10 693	5.8
Selangor	1 517 504	64 936	4.3	2 289 236	62 866	2.7
Terengganu	541 608	36 098	6.7	770 931	27 307	3.5
Federal Territory	978 326	37 002	3.8	1 145 075	51 669	4.5

14 Study Tables 4.5 and 4.6.
a Use Figure 4.14 to draw a blank base map of Malysia.
b Choose another suitable technique to that shown in Figure 4.13 and illustrate the amounts of intra-state migration, i.e. the numbers moving *within* each state, for both 1981 and 1990.
c Comment on any differences between the two sets of migratory patterns identified in **b**.

15a Using the figures in Table 4.6, identify the main destinations of the majority of people leaving each state in 1981.
b Draw flow lines to illustrate the direction and size of these movements on a base map of Malaysia. (Your map should be similar to that in Figure 4.13.)
c Comment on the location of each main destination state for those migrants involved in inter-state migration in 1981 and 1990.

16a Using the material on migration models, suggest which models can be applied to the inter-state migration patterns in Malaysia. Give reasons.
b Identify the main receiving states and the main losing states for both 1981 and 1990. Give possible explanations for any changes which may have occurred in the period between 1981 and 1990.

17 Study Table 4.7.
a Choose an appropriate graphical technique to illustrate the percentage of the state population who were migrants for 1981 and 1990.
b Which states have experienced the greatest change with regard to the sizes of their migrant populations?

Short-distance migration

Short-distance migration has tended to dominate population movement in Malaysia (Tables 4.5 and 4.6). We can see this particularly well in the movement of people between Selangor and the Federal Territory. In recent years there have been considerable population shifts between these two states with people moving out of the neighbouring Federal Territory into Selangor. In 1983, Selangor, a state which normally reports moderate total migration rates of between 4.0 and 5.4 per cent, showed a migration rate of 8.9 per cent. In that year, Selangor experienced a housing boom which attracted many migrants, many of whom were drawn from the neighbouring Federal Territory. In fact, people often live in Selangor and commute daily to work in the Federal Territory.

Rural-to-rural migration

The rapid industrialisation process throughout Asia has produced a large number of big cities. For Peninsular Malaysia, though, the predominant direction of movement appears to be rural-to-rural migration. For instance in 1990, almost 60 per cent of the Peninsula's *intra-state* migrants were categorised as rural-to-rural with only 14 per cent classified as rural-to-urban. Similarly, although only 35 per cent of the region's *inter-state* migrants were described as rural-to-rural, this direction of movement was still the main characteristic, and double the rural-to-urban flow at 16.5 per cent. The dominant pattern of rural-to-rural migration, especially for intra-state migrants, is particularly noticeable in the agricultural states of Kedah, Kelantan, Pahang, Perlis and Terengganu.

Rural-to-urban migration

In Malaysia, rural-to-urban migration seldom assumes the importance we might expect of a newly industrialising country where the average annual urban growth rate between 1980 and 1991 was 4.8 per cent. Rural-to-urban drift reaches almost 20 per cent of total intra-state migrant flow in the fast industrialising state of Johor, yet only 14.5 per cent of migrants moving into the state from elsewhere apparently move to its urban areas. For inter-state migrants, the urban focus of drift is much greater in the highly urbanised Federal Territory where one half of all migrants moved either from a rural to an urban, or from an urban to another urban destination. The amount of urban-to-rural drift is surprisingly high for both intra- and inter-state migrants at 21.5 per cent and 30 per cent respectively.

A number of factors may have contributed to the rural-to-rural or urban-to-rural bias in migration flow.

One has been the influence of government-sponsored rural development projects. Many of these are significant for generating employment, and have taken place on an extensive scale in several states in the Peninsular. The construction of the Pergau Dam (1994) in southern Pahang State is the most recent example of such a project (see section 2.6).

?

18a Suggest possible reasons for the change in the scale of migration into the Federal Territory between the years 1980 and 1991.
b Given the migration patterns you have identified, which stage of Zelinsky's mobility transition model do you think Malaysia fits into (see Figure 4.7)?

19a Add to your list from **12a** any other reasons for migration that you can think of.
b For each reason, decide whether it is an example of 'selective' or 'non-selective' migration.
c Discuss some of problems resulting from each example for the • receiver and • loser states.

Selective migration

Depending on the reason for migration, some types are more '**selective**' than others. For example, if famine is the cause of migration, everybody will want to move in search of food. In this case, migration may be described as 'non-selective'. On the other hand, if the cause of migration is to find work then it is usually the young adults (often without families) who will move (see Fig. 4.9). This type of migration is clearly more selective in that it involves only certain people.

Religious migration

Religion is a powerful factor causing people to move across the world (Fig. 4.15). Traditional, usually temporary, pilgrimages include Hindus, Jains, Sikhs and Buddhists journeying to Varanasi in north-east India, while many thousands of Roman Catholics tend to head either to Rome (residence of the Pope) or to Lourdes (where in 1858 a girl saw visions of the Virgin Mary).

Figure 4.15 Pilgrimage to Mecca, Saudi Arabia: it is the ambition of most Muslims to travel to the birthplace of Mohammed at least once in their lives

Per cent

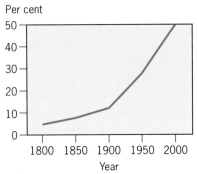

Figure 4.16 World urbanisation (*Source:* Selmes, 1995)

4.6 Rural-to-urban migration and urbanisation

Rural-to-urban migration has been an important feature of population movement, especially in the developing countries from about the 1970s (see Fig. 4.3). This urban-oriented movement of people has given rise to the swiftly growing number of cities – a process known as **urbanisation.** On a global scale, nearly half of the world's population live in urban areas and this trend is expected to continue (Fig. 4.16).

The global pattern of urbanisation
Generally, there are higher levels of urban population in the developed than in the developing countries (Fig. 4.17). In fact, 75 per cent of the population in developed countries live in big cities and towns compared with 25 per cent in developing countries. However, there is a wide variation in the level of urbanisation between countries both in the developed and developing areas.

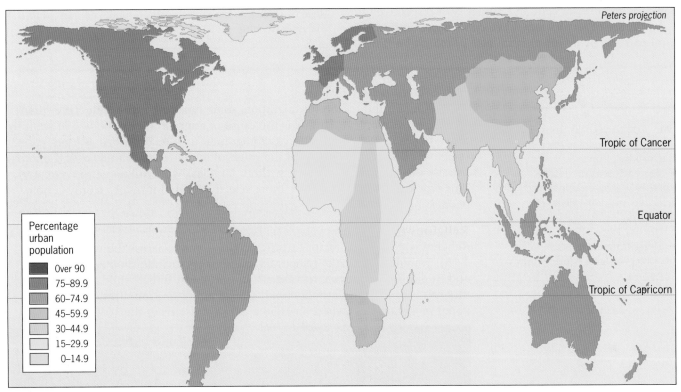

Figure 4.17 World pattern of urbanisation

?

20a Using a suitable graphical technique, illustrate the variations in the levels of urbanisation in the regions shown in Fig. 4.17.
b Comment on the pattern shown.

The growth of cities in developing countries
According to the United Nations' standard definition of urbanisation, settlements of over 20 000 people are generally classified as urban. Similarly, we consider settlements of more than 100 000 people to be cities, while we refer to settlements of more than 10 million people as megacities.

When we look at the global urban population we can see that the rate at which cities are growing in the developing areas is phenomenal. In terms of absolute totals, 25 per cent of the people resident in cities in the developing countries far exceeds the total urban population of the developed countries. It is estimated that by the year 2000 the urban population in the developing countries will rise to 1000 million (1 billion).

The rates of urbanisation are particularly high in South America and Sub-Saharan Africa (Table 4.8). In 1960, only 14.9 per cent of African people lived in cities. This rose to 24.2 per cent in 1980 and by the year 2000, it is estimated the proportion of the urban population in Africa will be as high as 37.9 per cent.

Figure 4.19 Lack of living space in Cairo, Egypt: 1 000 people migrate into the city every day and many are forced to live on roof tops. Others, some 3 million, find space in the city's cemetery, 'City of the Dead'.

21 Study Figures 4.18 and 4.19.
a Explain how rural-to-urban migration causes poverty in cities.
b Discuss the effects of rural-to-urban migration on resources in
• rural areas, • urban areas, • in a country as a whole.

Table 4.8 Levels of urbanisation as a percentage of total population (*Source: World Development Report, 1994*)

| | Urban population as percentage of total population | | Average annual growth rate of urban population (%) |
	1970	1992	1980–92
Egypt	42	44	2.5
Ghana	29	35	4.3
Kenya	10	25	7.7
Pakistan	25	33	4.5
India	20	26	3.1
China	18	27	4.3
Thailand	13	23	4.5
USA	74	76	1.2
Mexico	59	74	2.9
Jamaica	42	54	2.1
Peru	57	71	2.9
Argentina	78	87	1.7
UK	89	89	0.3
France	71	73	0.4
Poland	52	63	1.3
Italy	64	70	0.6
Australia	85	85	1.5

Consequences of increasing urbanisation in developing countries

One population issue for many countries is that cities grow at the expense of surrounding rural areas (see section 9.3). The consequences of this are felt at both the local and national levels (Fig. 4.18). In developing countries, the most obvious result of large numbers of migrants moving to urban areas is overcrowding (Fig. 4.19). We may describe such places as over-populated when the resources available (including land) cannot meet demand. As a result, at a national level, the rapid growth of urban areas demands investment through urban-oriented development programmes. Conversely, rural and peripheral areas tend to lack such investment.

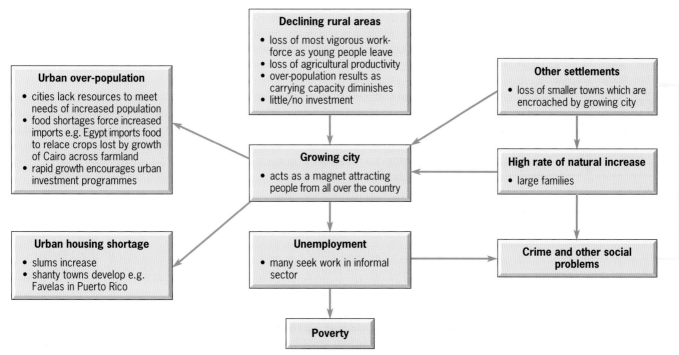

Figure 4.18 The effects of rural-to-urban migration in developing countries

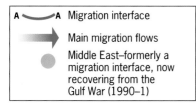

A ⌣ A Migration interface

→ Main migration flows

● Middle East–formerly a migration interface, now recovering from the Gulf War (1990–1)

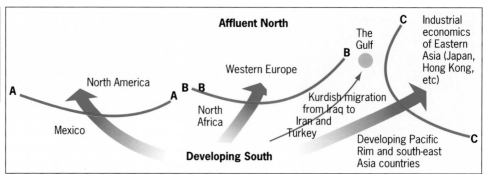

Figure 4.20 North-South migration pressure-points (*Source: Geofile*, Jan. 1992)

Figure 4.21 'Wetback' tries to enter the USA from Mexico illegally by crossing the Rio Grande River. It is estimated that for every person caught, at least one other succeeds.

22a Using an atlas, identify the Pacific Rim countries and their gross domestic products (GDP).
b Classify the Pacific Rim countries into those which have experienced: • net immigration, • net emigration over the last two decades.
c Describe the relationship between the net migration and GDP for each country.

4.7 International migration

The pressure from people wanting to migrate from developing countries to developed countries in search of economic security, has increased since the **economic gap** between the rich North and the poor South has widened. Migration occurs across the traditional **North–South divide** (see section 1.1), and there are three 'pressure points' where migration flows are strongest (Fig. 4.20). The first of these, migration between North Africa and Europe, we have already considered in the case study in section 4.4.

Mexico and the United States
The United States government is keen to attract the immigration of highly qualified professionals. In fact, in November 1990, the government passed a new immigration law specifically to make it easier for professional people to enter the USA. At the same time, though, the government is concerned about the continuing immigration from Mexico.

During the 1980s a total of 8 million migrants entered the USA. This was the largest number for a single decade since the beginning of the 1900s. Of these 8 million, 3.5 million were Mexicans who took up US residence between 1980 and 1989. In 1990, more than one million people were caught trying to enter the USA and were sent back to Mexico (Fig. 4.21). Although most migrants are Mexicans, a considerable number also reach the Mexican border from countries in South and Central America. It has always been relatively easy to enter Mexico from the south and many people, especially from Central America, have taken advantage of this with the intention of 'stepping' on to the USA.

Pacific Rim countries
In this part of the world, large-scale migration between, and to, Pacific Rim countries has occurred only since World War 2. Historically, this is because neither the Chinese nor the Japanese have wanted to emigrate, while migrants originating in Europe went to other areas such as Australia, Canada, the USA and South America. However, numerous factors have, over the last few decades, encouraged greater numbers of migrants throughout the region:

• Increasing population pressure; e.g. with a population size (124m) double that of the UK, pressure increases because the mountainous areas of Japan mean much of the land is unsuitable for human settlement.

• Difficult political situations; e.g. China's Cultural Revolution of the 1960s resulted in widespread famine. Those peasants who could, then emigrated to either Malaysia or Singapore (see section 6.7).

• Different levels of development; e.g. civil wars have prohibited development in some countries, such as Vietnam and Cambodia, while successful industrialisation exists in such countries as Hong Kong and Singapore. War refugees and economic migrants are therefore common between such countries.

The migration problem in Hong Kong

From the late 1980s the number of Chinese emigrating from Hong Kong increased considerably (Table 4.9). This was partly in response to the expiry of Britain's 99-year lease of the island from China, with Hong Kong's subsequent return to Chinese rule in 1997. Additionally, other residents were 'frightened' into leaving China because of the Tiananmen Square massacre in Beijing on 4 June 1989. Facing serious challenges to its authority, the Chinese communist government massacred over 2000 students demonstrating for democracy and against party corruption. Subsequent emigration occurs as a 'brain drain' sees the departure of professionals and intellectuals seeking more secure working environments in other western countries (Table 4.10). To combat this, China has actually urged Hong Kong to persuade its professional and well educated would-be migrants *not* to leave. The Chinese authorities fear that the economy of Hong Kong will be damaged if this type of selective migration (see section 4.8) continues. In fact, by the end of 1989 about 30 per cent of companies in Hong Kong had themselves organised jobs abroad for their emigrating and professional staff. The intention is to attract the employees *back* to Hong Kong after they have received their foreign passports.

Table 4.9 Hong Kong: emigration (*Source:* Hong Kong government, quoted in *Financial Times*, 6 March 1991)

Year	Number of emigrants
1980	22 400
1981	18 300
1982	20 300
1983	19 800
1984	22 400
1985	22 300
1986	19 000
1987	30 000
1988	45 800
1989	42 000
1990	62 000

Table 4.10 Destination of emigrants from Hong Kong (thousands) (*Source: Financial Times*, 22 June 1989)

Country	1986	1987	1988	1989 (est)
Canada	5.6	16.3	24.6	16.4
USA	7.7	7.4	11.8	12.6
Australia	4.4	5.2	7.8	10.9
Others	1.2	1.1	1.6	1.9
Total	**19.0**	**30.0**	**45.8**	**42.0**

Immigration to Hong Kong

Since the 1970s, large numbers of Vietnamese 'boat people' have been arriving in Hong Kong (Fig. 4.22). These migrants are hoping to improve their economic well-being, as well as to avoid a Communist regime which they see as threatening and hostile. However, once in Hong Kong they are forced to live in overcrowded camps. The problem of where to settle the boat people has never really been solved by the international community. Many are encouraged to return to Vietnam but most wish to settle in Canada, which accepted 75 000 during the first wave of emigration.

Other countries, apart from Canada, have also accepted many boat people. However, by 1995 it had become harder for the Vietnamese to prove genuine political refugee status and so avoid being forced to return to Vietnam.

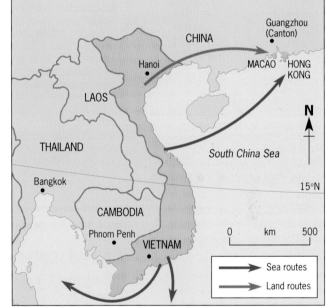

Figure 4.22 Hong Kong: Vietnamese migration routes

23 You are the personnel manager for a Hong Kong based company. Write some publicity material aimed at your well-qualified and well-trained employees to persuade them to stay with you in Hong Kong.

24 Use Tables 4.9 and 4.10.
a Draw a graph with a logarithmic scale on the vertical axis to show the increasing scale of emigration from Hong Kong.
b Draw divided bars to represent the destinations of emigrants from Hong Kong for each year.
c In light of the selective nature and scale of migration, discuss the likely social and economic problems Hong Kong might face in the future.

Table 4.11 Foreigners living in Japan, 1988 (*Source: Financial Times Survey*, 10 July 1989)

Country of origin	Number
North and South Korea	677 140
China	129 269
USA	32 766
Philippines	32 185
UK	8 523
Thailand	5 277
Vietnam	4 763
Brazil	4 159
Malaysia	3 542
Canada	3 510
West Germany	3 222
France	2 744
India	2 730
Australia	2 585
Indonesia	2 379
Bangladesh	2 130
Pakistan	2 063
'no nationality'	1 658
Singapore	1 084
Cambodia	1 021
Total	**941 005**

25 Read Figure 4.23 and answer the following:
a How has Japan attempted to solve the problems of an ageing population?
b Why might the Japanese authorities have to change their attitude towards immigration in the future?

26a Using Table 4.11 draw proportional symbols on a base map of the world to show the countries of origin of foreign workers in Japan.
b Describe the pattern of migration shown by your map and decide which migration models it relates to (section 4.4 and 4.5).

Japanese migration

Japan has had a long history of opposition to immigration, due partly to its strong sense of cultural identity. However, by the end of 1988 there were almost one million foreigners living in Japan (Table 4.11). Legal immigration in Japan is restricted to skilled workers and so most of the immigrants from Europe, North America and Australia are professional people employed by international companies. In contrast, there are at least 200 000 illegal immigrants in Japan and many of these are from the northern Chinese province of Fujian.

The Japanese are undecided on their future immigration policies. The acute shortage of unskilled labour in Japan partly explains why there is so much Japanese production overseas (it has been estimated that by the year 2000 one fifth of Japanese manufacturing output will be produced by Japanese companies located abroad). Japan's labour shortage, coupled with its ageing population, presents the authorities with serious problems (Fig. 4.23).

LIFE expectancy in Japan is the highest in the world. By the year 2025, 25% of the Japanese will be aged over 65. The high welfare costs associated with old age began to concern the Japanese government in 1986, when the 'Silver Columbia' project was adopted. This aimed to settle aged Japanese in purpose-built villages abroad, where medical and other expenses were expected to be cheaper. So far the programme has not met with much success – the elderly Japanese were apparently not interested in villages near Melbourne in Australia – but the attempts continue. In 1989 it was planned to set up a colony of retired academics and other professionals on the coast of Spain between Barcelona and Lloret de Mar, near the village of Canet de Mar (*Financial Times*, 24 July 1989). In 1991 a new scheme, 'Extended Leisure Stays Abroad', was begun on the Atlantic coast of Senegal, 80 kilometres north of Dakar. A retirement city is to be built on an area of 400 sq km; it will have its own airport and twenty-six golf courses. The Japanese government is still encouraging voluntary expatriate settlement in Australia (a village is to be built in Wollongong), Uruguay and Hawaii, an earlier venture in the Philippines came to an unfortunate end when it was overrun in a military coup (*Financial Times*, 24 February 1991). If these schemes do not succeed, Japan may in the end have to relax its immigration regulations so that young immigrants from South East Asia can enter the country to look after its elderly people.

Figure 4.23 A different migration problem in Japan (*Source: Geofile*, no. 184, 1992)

4.8 Refugees and international response

The original UN definition of 'refugee' was based on the concept of individual persecution and was not originally designed to deal with the large-scale flows of people which are more common in the early 1990s (Fig. 4.24). The UN's definition of a refugee is someone who, 'owing to well-founded fear of being persecuted for reason of race, religion, nationality, membership of a particular social group or political opinion, is outside the country of her or his nationality and who is unable … to return to it'. A true refugee is believed to want to return to his or her country of origin once the source of oppression, and so the reason for migration, has been removed.

Migrant or refugee?
In the early 1990s there were an estimated 20 million people on the move throughout the world. This is a larger number than at any other time since World War 2 and was greatly influenced by some of the dramatic political events of the late 1980s. With *perestroika* and the collapse of communism in the Soviet Union, over half a million Jews emigrated to Israel between 1986 and 1995. Until the unification of Germany in 1990, vast numbers of economic migrants left East Germany for the Federal Republic (see case study following). The Gulf War (1991), led to temporary migrations with Iraqi Kurds crossing the borders to Turkey and Iran (see Fig. 4.20). In addition, immigrant workers from

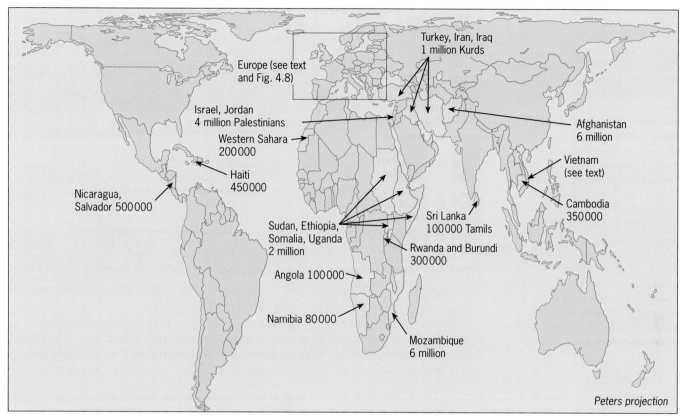

Figure 4.24 Major migrations: estimated number of refugees and displaced persons fleeing to neighbouring countries, 1990–1 (*Source: Geofile*, Jan. 1992)

developing countries, resident in Kuwait at the time of the Iraqi invasion, were forced to return home. By March 1991 35 000 Sudanese, 100 000 Bangladeshis, 100 000 Sri Lankans and 200 000 Indians had left the Gulf. Their countries of origin thus lost much-needed earnings (remittances from the Gulf had amounted to one third of Bangladesh's foreign exchange earnings).

As a proportion, there are more people who migrate from one developing country to another rather than from one developing country to a developed country. Consequently, the developing countries bear the brunt of population movements caused by push factors such as civil war and environmental degradation. The people who are affected by such problems are, respectively, often referred to as **war refugees** or **ecological refugees** who may, or may not, consider themselves to be persecuted.

Overall, people in the 1990s are arriving in groups rather than individually and this causes confusion over the definitions 'migrant' and 'refugee'. The term refugee is therefore becoming increasingly synonymous with the term migrant.

Asylum

As shown by the example of Italy (see section 4.4), many of the developed countries are tightening up their immigration laws. Since it is now harder for a migrant looking for better economic opportunities to gain permanent residential status in a developed country, many are now using the 'refugee route' to gain permission to stay (Fig. 4.25). Perhaps it is more appropriate to use the term **asylum seeker** to describe those economic migrants who call themselves refugees.

The European Union

To gain entry to the EU, increasing proportions of migrants are seeking asylum (Fig. 4.26). However, a person is only allowed to appeal for asylum once within

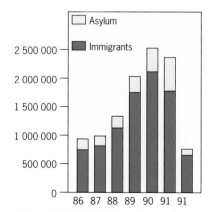

Figure 4.25 Official asylum seekers versus immigrants

27a If one of the main intentions of developed countries is to encourage potential migrants from developing countries to stay at home, assess the value of the following solutions:
• increase the amount of aid to developing areas
• encourage investment in developing areas
• reinstate border controls and legal barriers to immigrants entering developed countries
• allow some immigration to compensate for the declining workforce (resulting from lower fertility rates in developed countries, see sections 3.4, 3.6–3.8).
b Give your own view and response to the scale of immigration to developed countries from the developing countries.

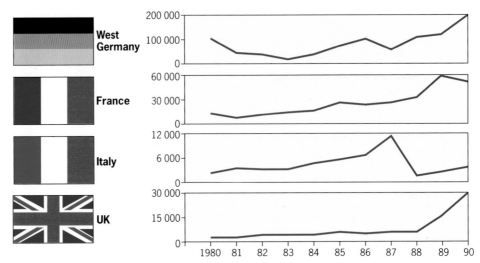

West Germany

France

Italy

UK

Figure 4.26 Numbers of people seeking asylum, 1980–90 (*Source: The Guardian*, 19 Nov.1991)

the country of her/his choice and if this application is turned down, s/he has no choice other than to return to their country of origin.

Although individual European countries still have their own immigration laws, the EU intends to align all the separate immigration procedures. The aims of such a single policy are to slow down the rate of immigration, to allow for legal immigration and to assist the social integration of future immigrants.

Refugees in Germany

With the dramatic political events of 1989, and the collapse of communism (Fig. 4.27), there was a huge upsurge in the numbers of people moving from eastern Europe, including the former Soviet Union, into western Europe. As frontiers across Europe were lifted, the first large-scale movement of people was of former East Germans migrating into the old West Germany, followed by migrants from other countries (Fig. 4.28, see Fig. 4.8).

Results of refugees

The long-term consequences of migration into former West Germany, as well as immigrants arriving since unification, have concerned the German authorities. Some economists view the migrant 'guestworkers' as a boost to the economy. The migrants will provide much needed labour to replace Germany's own, ageing workers (see section 3.8). Conversely, other oberservers highlight the problems of rising unemployment – for both nationals and migrant workers (Table 4.12). During times of recession and social hardship, people often look for a scapegoat (Fig. 4.29).

Figure 4.27 The fall of the Berlin Wall, 9 November 1989. In 1988, 50 000 people had emigrated from East to West Germany; in 1989 there were 300 000 emigrants.

28 'Racism is the result of ignorance and fear. It should be dealt with swiftly and firmly.' Discuss, giving your own views on this statement.

Table 4.12 Germany: 'guestworkers' and unemployment

Year	'Guestworkers' (% of total population)	Unemployment (% of total population)
1970	4.3	0.5
1974	6.7	1.5
1978	6.5	2.5
1982	7.6	6.9
1986	7.4	8.1
1990	8.2	5.1

On 9 November 1989, the East German government allowed its citizens to travel freely to the West for the first time since the completion of the Berlin wall in 1961. In the 10 months before the collapse of the Berlin wall, 20000 East Germans had left for the West; in the week that followed 3 million East Germans travelled across the old border (many to visit relatives and return).

23000 East Germans entered West Germany through Czechoslovakia (since partitioned into the Czech Republic and Slovakia) over a two-day period.

With Hungary dismantling its Communist Party in October 1989, East Germans then 'on holiday' in Hungary were able to dash for the Hungarian border with Austria and so cross into Western Europe. By the end of 1989 an estimated 20000 East Germans had 'escaped' through this route.

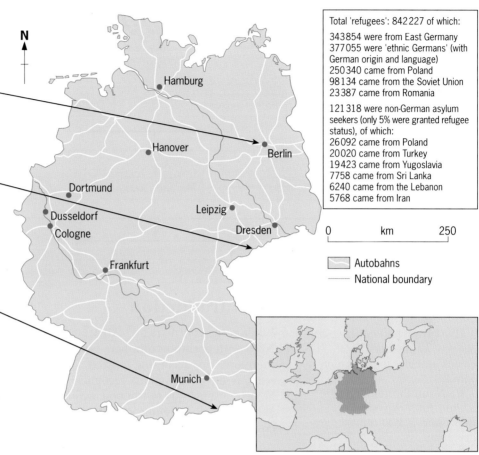

Total 'refugees': 842227 of which:

343854 were from East Germany
377055 were 'ethnic Germans' (with German origin and language)
250340 came from Poland
98134 came from the Soviet Union
23387 came from Romania

121318 were non-German asylum seekers (only 5% were granted refugee status), of which:
26092 came from Poland
20020 came from Turkey
19423 came from Yugoslavia
7758 came from Sri Lanka
6240 came from the Lebanon
5768 came from Iran

0   km   250

☐ Autobahns
— National boundary

Figure 4.28 Migration into Germany

Figure 4.29 Social tension and racial violence sweep Germany: Turkish immigrants, originally temporary 'guestworkers' but staying in Germany permanently, become 'scapegoats' with residents blaming them for unemployment, scarce housing resources and poor social services.

29 Essay: Describe some of the reasons for the large scale international migration of the 1990s. Discuss the advantages and disadvantages of international migration both for the source and destination countries.

Summary

- Population movement is an essential feature of human society.

- Migration has occurred in 'waves' throughout history giving rise to multi-racial societies.

- Migration can be categorised into two major types: internal and international. Each type has implications for available resources and development.

- Rapid urbanisation in the developing countries mostly results from the mass exodus of people from rural to urban areas.

- Environmental disasters, political unrest and the spread of disease have led to large scale migration from one developing country to another.

- Increasing poverty in many developing countries has resulted in the growing numbers of people migrating to the developed countries as economic migrants.

- Many developed countries are tightening their immigration policies in response to the increasing refugees, economic migrants and asylum seekers from the developing countries.

- The breakdown of communism in Eastern Europe increased the immigration problem in Western Europe and other developed areas.

- Racial tension has increased in many areas as more people are on the move. This accounts for the rise of nationalism in many West European countries.

5 Population policies and food supply

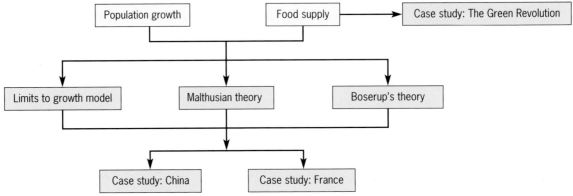

```
Population growth        Food supply  ──────▶  Case study: The Green Revolution

        │                    │
        ▼                    ▼                         ▼
Limits to growth model   Malthusian theory      Boserup's theory

                              │
                ▼                       ▼
        Case study: China       Case study: France
```

?

1a Design a questionnaire (see appendix A2) to investigate people's attitudes to population control.
b Carry out the questionnaire and find out how your interviewees would combat over-population.
c Do responses vary with age, gender, social, and ethnic groups?
d Summarise your findings, stating whether, and how, opinions are divided over population control.

5.1 Introduction

While some countries are experiencing rapid population growth, others are faced with declining numbers (see Tables 3.2 and 3.3). Population policies therefore vary according to each country's **demographic** situation. On a global scale, while governments recognise that population is rising fast, there seems to be no consensus as to the best way to control this growth. Opinions are divided along cultural, religious and ideological lines as to the need for population control.

Growing populations, which characterise many **developing countries** (see sections 3.4–3.8), then have serious implications on the availability and use of resources (Fig. 5.1). Debt, dependency on cash crops and lack of investment all place the production of essential commodities, such as food, under great stress. In this chapter, we will examine reasons for the unequal distribution of food supply and then discuss specific policies which are geared towards controlling population growth and decline.

• The average American consumes 300 times as much energy as the average Bangladeshi. The 16 million babies born each year in the rich North will have four times as great an impact on the world's resources as the 109 million born in the poor South.

• UNICEF estimates that preventing 7 million babies dying each year will lead to the prevention of between 12 and 20 million births by the end of the century. There will undoubtedly be a time-lag while parents gain confidence in the improved survival chances. However, no country has ever managed to achieve a low birth rate while infant deaths remain high.

• The United Nations states that 'food supplies might be adequate if they were evenly distributed in relation to needs'.

Figure 5.1 Population and resource issues (*After: New Internationalist,* Oct. 1987)

• Population growth rates are slowing down everywhere in the world. According to the United Nations Fund for Population Activities (UNFPA), the world's population will stabilise at around ten billion by approximately the year 2050 (double what it was in the early 1990s). In some countries numbers are already declining.

• People who do not have access to contraception still plan their families. In Greece, where contraception was not legalised until 1980, women bore an average of only 2.3 children in 1978. In theory these women could have had many more children.

• In the poorer countries, scarcity among the poor is partly due to an uneven distribution of land ownership and lack of person power in rural areas, for example, in South America, 47 per cent of the land is owned by just 2 per cent of the people.

5.2 Population growth and food shortages

There are two main theories relating to population growth and food supply.

Malthusian theory

Thomas Malthus was an English clergyman and economist who lived from 1766 to 1834. In his text *An essay on the principle of population*, 1798, Malthus expressed a pessimistic view over the dangers of **over-population** (see section 3.5) and claimed that food supply was the main limit to population growth.

Principles of Malthus

Malthus believed that the human population increases geometrically (i.e. 2, 4, 8, 16, 32, etc.) whereas food supplies can grow only arithmetically (i.e. 2, 4, 6, 8, 10, 12, etc.) being limited by available new land. Malthus added that the 'laws of nature' dictate that a population can never increase beyond the food supplies necessary to support it (Fig. 5.2).

Checks

According to Malthus, population increase is limited by certain 'checks'. These prevent numbers of people increasing beyond the **optimum population**, which the available resources cannot support (see section 3.5). Malthus identified two types of check which limit further population growth. Preventive, or 'negative', checks are methods which people can choose to reduce human fertility e.g. abstinence or delaying marriage. Conversely, 'positive' checks are anything which increases mortality e.g. low living standards and unhealthy living conditions resulting in disease, war and famine.

At the time Malthus was proposing his ideas, inadequate food and clothing were common features of daily life in the then rapidly growing urban areas of England. Towns were heavily polluted by new factories during these early stages of the industrial revolution and malnutrition and disease were frequent.

Malthus saw the checks as nature's way of controlling excessive growth in the population, and they fall into three categories:

1 Misery: This includes the effects of disease, famine or war, i.e. 'all the causes which shorten the duration of human life'.

2 Vice: Malthus warned against the dangers of practising any kind of 'family planning', believing that it could only lead to promiscuity.

3 Moral restraint: Delayed marriage and abstinence from sexual relations were considered highly advisable by Malthus in order to avoid the consequences of over-population.

Malthusian theory and food supply

As long as fertile land is available, Malthus believed that there would be more than enough food to feed a growing population. However, as population in-creases so do the demands for food. There is therefore greater pressure to farm more intensively and cultivate poorer, more **marginal land**. According to Malthus, though, food production can only increase to a certain level determined by the productive capacity of the land and existing levels of technology. Beyond the ceiling where land is used to its fullest extent, over cultivation and, ultimately, soil erosion occurs, contributing to a general decline in food production. This is known as the **law of diminishing returns** where, even with higher levels of technology, only a small increase in yield will event-ually occur. These marginal returns ultimately serve as a check to population growth. Malthus did acknowledge that increases in food output would be

Figure 5.2 Representation of Malthus' view on population growth and food supply

2a Draw a continuous flow diagram putting the following labels in sequence according to Malthusian theory:
• Increased demand for food
• Economic distress
• Early marriage
• Population growth
• Suffering and delayed marriage
• Food prices drop
• Increase in wealth
• Food prices rise
• Less demand for food
• Population decrease
• Increased demand for food
b Explain why your diagram illustrates the pessimistic view of Malthusian theory.

Malthusian theory

possible with new methods in food production, but he still maintained that limited food supply would eventually take place and so limit population.

The carrying capacity of the land

The **carrying capacity** refers to the number of plants, animals or humans which can be adequately supported (carried) by the land (see section 3.5). The maximum carrying capacity of the environment is referred to as the saturation level, while for populations it is the **population ceiling**. Malthus was the first to suggest the idea of a population ceiling and assess different scenarios when a population approaches carrying capacity (Figs 5.3–5.4).

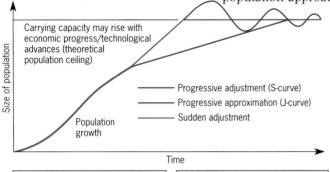

S-curve: population growth adjusts gradually to the carrying capacity; population growth rates slow down and the population total stabilises around the maximum number of people who can be supported by the existing carrying capacity.

J-curve: population growth may overshoot the carrying capacity causing fluctuations in growth rates; such fluctuations gradually diminish until the population total stabilises around the level of the carrying capacity.

Figure 5.3 Population growth adjustments to carrying capacity

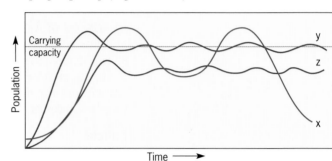

Figure 5.4 Population change and resource limits

?

3 Study Figure 5.3
a Describe how the population rates change as the carrying capacity is reached.
b Which of these possible scenarios is the most realistic? Explain why (see section 3.6).

4 Study the relationship between population growth and carrying capacity in Figure 5.4. Suggest what events or government policies could produce:
a the curve x.
b the curve y.
c the curve z. Describe how the population rates change as the carrying capacity is reached.

5a Decide whether each statement in Figure 5.1 supports or contradicts Malthusian theory.
b Essay: Rapid population growth is the only explanation for poverty. Discuss.

Figure 5.5 Opposing views on the reasons and outcomes of population growth

POPULATION GROWTH IS CAUSED BY A LACK OF MORAL RESTRAINT AND, UNLESS CHECKED, WILL LEAD TO POVERTY, HUNGER AND DISEASE!

POPULATION GROWTH IS CAUSED BY INEQUALITIES AND THE UNFAIR DISTRIBUTION OF RESOURCES. UNLESS THIS MALADMINISTRATION IS CHECKED, THERE WILL BE REVOLUTION!

Limitations of Malthusian theory

Anti-Malthusians criticise the theory as being too simplistic. A shortage of food is just one possible explanation for starvation, disease and war (Fig. 5.5). In fact, Marxists argue that the theory's reasoning (geometric population growth which outruns an arithmetic increase in food supply) ignores the reality that it is actually only the poor who go hungry. Marx claimed that poverty results from the poor distribution of resources, not physical limits on production. Except on a global scale, the world's community is not 'closed' and so does not enjoy a fair and even distribution of food supplies. Even so, Malthus could not possibly have foreseen the spectacular changes in farming technology which mean we can produce enough food from an area the size of a football pitch to supply 1 000 people for a year, i.e. there is enough land to feed the whole world.

Thus evidence of the last two centuries contradicts the Malthusian notion of food supply increasing only arithmetically. Rather than starvation, food surpluses exist and agricultural production increases. In 1992 European surpluses reached 26 million tonnes and there are indications that this trend will continue, contrary to Malthusian theory.

Boserup's theory

In 1965, Esther Boserup, a Danish economist, asserted that an increase in population would stimulate technologists to increase food production (the optimistic view). Boserup suggested that any rise in population will increase the demand for food and so act as an incentive to change agrarian technology and produce more food (Fig. 5.6). We can sum up Boserup's theory by the sentence 'necessity is the mother of invention'.

Boserup's ideas were based on her research into various land use systems, ranging from extensive **shifting cultivation** in the tropical rainforests to more intensive multiple cropping, as in South-East Asia. Her theory suggests that, as population increases, agriculture moves into higher stages of intensity through innovation and the introduction of new farming methods. The conclusion arising from Boserup's theory is that population growth naturally leads to development.

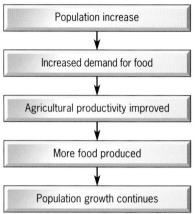

Figure 5.6 Boserup's view on the relationship between population growth and food supply

Limitations of Boserup's theory

Like Malthus, Boserup's idea is based on the assumption of a 'closed' community. In reality, except at a global scale, communities are not 'closed' because constant in- and out-migration are common features. It has therefore been very difficult to test Boserup's ideas. This is because migration usually occurs in areas of over-population to relieve the population pressure which, according to Boserup's theory, then leads to technological innovation.

In addition, Boserup herself admits that over-population can lead to unsuitable farming practices which may degrade the land. Consequently, some geographers have partly blamed population pressure for **desertification** in the Sahel. From this it is clear that certain types of fragile environment cannot support excessive numbers of people. In such cases, population pressure does not always lead to technological innovation and development.

6 Using Figure 5.6, draw a graph similar to Figure 5.2 to illustrate Boserup's theory. (Note that the carrying capacity will increase in stages, as the intensity of cultivation increases.)

Economists versus environmentalists

The conflict between the views of Malthus and Boserup continues today. We can see this controversy in the debate between optimistic economists and pessimistic environmentalists (Table 5.1).

7 Write a summary of Malthus' and Boserup's ideas and compare their views on the relationship between population growth and food supply.

8 Why do you think some commentators refer to the Malthusian viewpoint as 'pessimistic'?

9a With reference to Table 5.1 and evidence from other chapters, find specific examples to justify the viewpoints of the economists and environmentalists on population and resources.

b Organise a class debate to determine which of the viewpoints is more convincing.

Table 5.1 Economists versus environmentalists

Proponent	View of people and resources	View of population growth	Example of belief
Economist's view Professor Julian Simon, University of Maryland, USA	People are the 'ultimate resource' – not the problem; every newly-born human is a fresh source of ingenuity who can provide many more solutions to problems than they can ever cause.	Population growth is responsible for technical improvements in social infrastructure, e.g. transport and communication, which sustain further high population growth.	Energy provision is one of the global problems of the late 20th century: Simon sees future generations as the discoverers of new forms of much-needed energy.
Environmentalist's view Paul Ehrlich; neo-Malthusians	People are condemned to live in poverty and hunger because of food shortages, lack of development and limited resources; natural environments can only support a limited population.	People always reproduce faster than food supplies will increase.	Deforestation, global warming, desertification, depletion of the ozone layer, wars and AIDS are all signs of an impending Malthusian crisis.

5.3 Application of Malthus and Boserup

There is evidence to suggest that the ideas of both Boserup and Malthus may be appropriate at different scales. On a global level, the growing suffering and famine in some developing countries today may reinforce Malthusian ideas. On the other hand, at a national scale, some governments have been motivated by increasing population to develop their resources and so meet growing demands.

Population and resource crisis in Mauritius

Figure 5.7 Mauritius

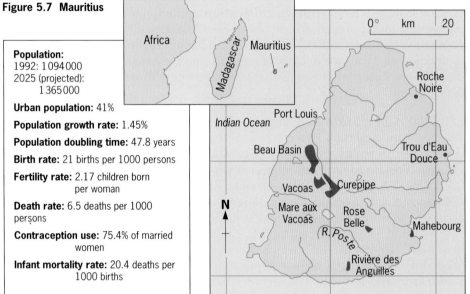

Population:
1992: 1 094 000
2025 (projected):
    1 365 000

Urban population: 41%

Population growth rate: 1.45%

Population doubling time: 47.8 years

Birth rate: 21 births per 1000 persons

Fertility rate: 2.17 children born
    per woman

Death rate: 6.5 deaths per 1000
persons

Contraception use: 75.4% of married
    women

Infant mortality rate: 20.4 deaths per
    1000 births

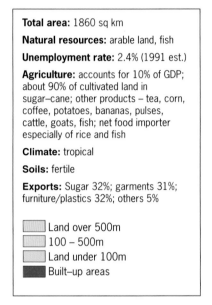

Total area: 1860 sq km

Natural resources: arable land, fish

Unemployment rate: 2.4% (1991 est.)

Agriculture: accounts for 10% of GDP; about 90% of cultivated land in sugar–cane; other products – tea, corn, coffee, potatoes, bananas, pulses, cattle, goats, fish; net food importer especially of rice and fish

Climate: tropical

Soils: fertile

Exports: Sugar 32%; garments 31%; furniture/plastics 32%; others 5%

- Land over 500m
- 100 – 500m
- Land under 100m
- Built–up areas

One example where there is a rapidly growing population is the island of Mauritius (Fig. 5.7). Here however, the government has co-ordinated efforts to improve standards of living in spite of this population pressure.

Human expansion

In the 1950s Mauritius was facing a 'Malthusian crisis' when the relationship between its population and resources became unbalanced (Fig. 5.8). A sharp decline in the death rate followed by a rise in birth rate

meant increased pressure on the economy, which was almost totally reliant on sugar production.

Falling birth rates

In response to the population increase, by 1953 the Mauritan government had developed an organised family planning programme. This aimed to:

- improve the social position of the people
- improve the status of women
- restrict early marriage
- provide better health care
- encourage emigration
- set up an integrated family planning service.

Gradually, a hierarchical network of government health and family planning clinics developed and by 1985 only 14 per cent of the urban population and 11 per cent of the rural population were more than 30 minutes' travelling time from a clinic.

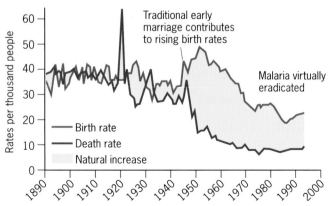

Figure 5.8 Mauritius: demographic transition, 1890–1992
(*Source: Geography Review,* **May 1995**)

10 You are researching Mauritius as a possible location for a transnational company. Write a brief description of the history and population geography of the island as background information for your research.

Other factors which contributed towards reducing birth rates included: a change in attitude towards family size, postponement of marriage (mainly as a result of harsh economic conditions in the 1960s) and a shift in the status of women as female education improved. As women looked for work opportunities outside the home, their roles changed. Only 22.3 per cent of women were in paid employment in 1975, whereas by 1990 this had risen to 35.75 per cent.

Improved living standards

Although population numbers have always been high in Mauritius (Fig. 5.9), the country has still been able to turn its economy around (Fig. 5.10). This is contrary to Malthus' pessimistic view.

The main routes to increased living standards include diversification of agriculture and investment in industry (see Fig. 5.7). As the workforce became relatively better educated than in other developing countries, economic transformations were considerable. In 1993, the GDP per capita was nearly US$3000, a 159 per cent increase since 1986.

Figure 5.10 Port Louis, Mauritius:
with economic growth and social change, the capital now has the appearance of an international centre

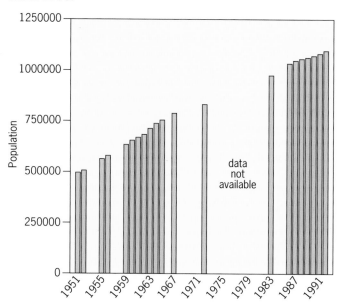

Figure 5.9 Mauritius: population growth (*Source: Geography Review*, May 1995)

International trade

As an ex-colony of the UK, Mauritius built links with Europe and maintains a stable and democratic government. This encourages a pro-Western stance which, during the Cold War, helped the country's trade relations with the USA.

Many **transnational corporations** (**TNCs**) have since been attracted to Mauritius. This is due in part to the large numbers of well-educated residents. More obviously, though, the TNCs are drawn to the country by its status as an Export Processing Zone (EPZ). This provides numerous financial incentives such as reduced corporation tax, free repatriation of capital, guarantees against nationalisation of companies (compare with Fig. 2.12) and investment in transport. In addition, Mauritius has a good supply of cheap labour ready to work in the transnationals.

The EPZ status, together with the more recent creation of a Free Port at Port Louis, have helped to improve the resources side of the population-resources imbalance. This works as the TNCs import raw materials into Mauritius for manufacture and then export as finished goods. One aspect of this is that Mauritius is now a textile exporter of world rank although it grows no cotton. Most raw materials are imported and the main resource provided domestically is the labour force.

11 Comment on the trend of natural population increase since the family planning programme was introduced (Figs 5.8 and 5.9).

12 Work in small groups.
a Using the Mauritius scheme, design a programme to reduce birth rates in another developing country which has a high population increase.
b Describe what prior research you would do, and how you would implement your programme.
c Get another group to evaluate your work and make modifications to improve the programme.

13a Compare the experiences of Mauritius with the theories of Malthus and Boserup.
b To which theory is Mauritius closer?

14 A poor country's fragile economy cannot keep up with population growth, so people will just get poorer and poorer. Use evidence from Mauritius to comment on this view of development, stating whether or not you agree with it.

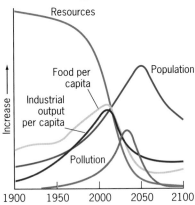

Figure 5.11 Limits to growth: resources and population (*After:* Meadows et al., 1972)

15 Study Figure 5.11.
a When does the model forecast world population will reach its limit?
b When does the model suggest both food and industrial output will peak and then decline?
c Comment on the relationship between these peak times.

16 The limits to growth model is sometimes referred to as 'Malthus with a computer'. Identify the similarities between the ideas of Malthus and the model's mathematically derived 'limits'.

17a Identify a finite resource in your country and find out the rate at which it is being exploited.
b What adjustments may be needed in order to conserve this resource?

The Club of Rome: limits to growth model

In 1968 representatives from ten countries met to form what is now known as the Club of Rome. The aim of the group was to research into world population issues. With an international research team from the Massachusetts Institute of Technology (MIT), the Club of Rome studied the effects and limits of continued world growth.

The Club concluded, in its 1972 report *The Limits to Growth*, that the world cannot support present rates of economic and population growth. The report warned against the consequences of general economic growth policies which rapidly use up the world's finite resources:

> If the present growth trends in world population, industrialisation, pollution, food production, and resource depletion continue unchanged, the limits to growth on this planet will be reached sometime within the next one hundred years. The most probable result will be a rather sudden and uncontrollable decline in both population and industrial capacity.
>
> MIT, *Limits to Growth*, (1972)

Identifying limits to growth
The MIT team used a large-scale computer model to simulate the behaviour of the world and forecast areas of, or limits to, growth. The team used five variables in the model: population growth, food per capita, industrial output, resources and pollution (Fig. 5.11).

Criticisms of the limits to growth model
Some development experts have criticised the limits to growth model for not considering possible advances in technology and the ability of market forces to adjust to supply and demand. Also, the model has been criticised for ignoring the human ability to develop new and **sustainable** methods of production.

In spite of these criticisms, some scholars agree with the basic idea of the model. They claim that, even with the best technology and resource management, there are still limits to the numbers of people who can be supported by the resources available in a geographic region. In summary, the model successfully focuses public attention on population growth, human future and the global environment. It shows that only by tackling all the major problems at once can humanity achieve ecological and economic stability.

5.4 The geography of food

Inequalities in world food distribution
In 1995 we globally produce enough food to give the whole world's population an adequate and balanced diet (see Fig. 5.1). We need, therefore, to question why so many people often go without food (Fig. 5.12). It is also important that we understand the reasons for these inequalities in world food distribution.

Farming systems and food output
The main source of food for all people is agriculture. Throughout the world it employs more than one billion people and they work in a great variety of

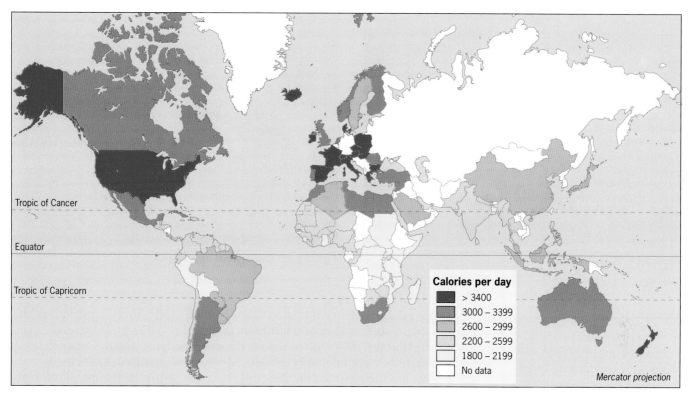

Figure 5.12 Average daily calorie intake by country, 1991 (*Source: FAO*). Malnutrition frequently leads to disease and often death; high rates of infant mortality are characteristic of countries with high levels of under-nutrition. An estimated 14 million children in Asia and Africa die every year from diseases caused by malnutrition.

?

18 Use Figure 5.12.
a Which countries have
• the lowest levels and
• the highest levels of calorie intake?
b Comment on the global pattern of food supply (see Fig. 1.1).

19 Use Figure 5.1 and give your personal response to the spatial inequalities in world food distribution.

20a Using Figure 5.12, trace the outlines of countries with a low low calorie intake.
b Use your tracing to overlay a map of different farming systems.
c Describe the relationship between levels of calorie intake and farming types.

Figure 5.13 Agriculture as a system

farming systems. A farming system relies on a series of inputs which produce a series of outputs (Fig. 5.13). Each system is affected by a number of different social, economic, political and environmental factors.

Subsistence agriculture

In most developing countries, much agricultural production relies on labour intensive methods. Traditionally, these consisted of ecologically sustainable practices such as shifting cultivation and **bush fallow** (Fig. 5.14).

However, such farming customs have not been able to provide enough income for the rapidly growing populations of developing countries. In response to this, large-scale rural-to-urban migration occurs (see section 4.5) and there is a decline in the level of **subsistence agriculture** as farmers switch to more commercial methods.

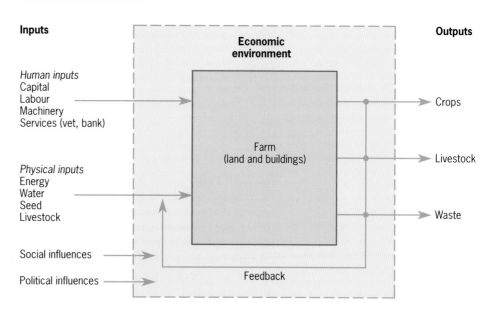

Figure 5.14 Subsistence agriculture

Figure 5.15 Commercial agriculture

21 Study Figures 5.14 and 5.15.
a Compare the differences between the two farming systems.
b Suggest how each system may affect people in terms of: • use of resources, • employment, • food supplies.

Commercial agriculture
Commercial agriculture is characterised by high capital investment in machinery and inputs such as chemical fertilisers (Fig. 5.15). While these increase agricultural output, they tend to reduce the need for farm labour. Commercial farming systems were originally introduced into developing countries by colonialists producing goods for their home market. With the decline of colonialism, the production of export crops in these old colonial areas, e.g. Brazil (see section 9.5), has increased. In some cases, such crops provide countries with their main source of revenue. Over three quarters of the exports from tropical countries are in the form of primary produce and there are many examples of countries which rely heavily on the production of just one crop (Table 5.2). This means that certain developing countries depend heavily on particular agricultural products, such as tobacco, cotton and coffee, placing both the national economy and farmers at the mercy of fluctuating world markets (see Chapter 8).

Table 5.2 Examples of countries reliant on a limited range of agricultural produce in their exports, 1990 (*Source:* Food and Agriculture Organisation *Trade and Commerce Yearbook*, 1990, Rome)

Country	Type of produce	Named produce as % of agricultural exports	All agricultural produce as % of merchandise exported
Réunion	Sugar	93.3	79.2
Cuba	Sugar	92.3	88.2
Uganda	Coffee	92.2	86.4
Ghana	Cocoa	85.8	41.2
Jamaica	Coffee	81.2	19.9
Swaziland	Sugar	78.3	38.1
Martinique	Bananas	66.4	60.8
Sri Lanka	Tea	66.2	39.0
Bangladesh	Jute	64.8	12.7
Ecuador	Bananas	60.0	28.7

Internal political crisis and food availability
Internal political crisis and inter-tribal conflicts often disrupt daily life and sometimes produce thousands of refugees (see Figs 4.24–4.25). During the latter part of the twentieth century, many countries in Africa have experienced such political upheavals. For example, Rwanda, Somalia, Chad and Ethiopia are countries which have recently witnessed large-scale population movements as people have been forced to flee from danger zones or from areas with little or no food supplies.

Figure 5.16 Care International delivering corn to Angola, December 1991: between 1980 and 1990 the USA supplied over 60 million tonnes of food aid

Food aid

One way the international community has responded to the increasing need for food in conflict areas is through the provision of food aid (Fig. 5.16).

Despite such aid efforts, many people still suffer from hunger and starvation (see Fig. 5.1). Both short-term and long-term food aid programmes have been vital during immediate crisis, but such aid cannot remove the more long-lasting food problems. Countries receiving aid may also find themselves tied financially to the donor country (see section 2.5).

5.5 Increasing food production

Only about ten per cent of the world's land surface is regularly farmed. Much of the rest is unsuitable for cultivation. In light of this global shortage of farming land and the increasing world population, people have tried firstly, to bring more land into cultivation and secondly, to increase production from current farming land.

The Green Revolution

Technology is one of the key factors for increasing food production on available agricultural land. Since the end of World War 2, technological advances were made through a 'package' of ideas known as the Green Revolution. This saw the development of new high yielding varieties (HYVs) or modern varieties (MVs) of staple crops such as wheat, maize and rice.

In 1943 investors from the USA established a research project with the Mexican government to improve local wheat and maize varieties. Yields of both wheat and maize increased threefold and researchers took the new seeds to the Indian sub-continent.

By 1960, the International Rice Research Institute had established a similar project at Los Banos, in the Philippines, to research the world's rice varieties. The first genetically engineered strain of rice was IR8, or 'miracle rice', which increased yields sixfold at its first harvest (Fig. 5.17). Technologists saw this miracle rice as a cure for the world's food problems.

Figure 5.17 Transplanting high-yielding rice varieties, Java, Indonesia

The Green Revolution

Both the new strains of wheat and rice produced dwarf plants capable of withstanding strong winds and heavy rain. They tolerated dry conditions, while their higher yields allowed farmers to reduce the land area devoted to cereals and so grow other crops.

Problems with HYVs

Rice is the traditional staple crop in most parts of Asia and this is where the new HYV strains of rice were originally introduced. The response of Asians to the HYVs was mixed. Some people complained that the taste was different and so reverted back to their traditional strains. For example, Thailand, the largest rice exporter in the world, was reluctant to adopt the new varieties for fear of losing customers who preferred the 'old' flavours. This explains why only 13 per cent of rice paddies in Thailand is planted with MVs.

Overall, HYVs are expensive. They require a higher level of fertiliser and irrigation (Fig. 5.18), so farmers have to buy a range of chemical fertilisers, pesticides and herbicides. Problems arise, then, with the typical peasant farmer who has little money for such inputs, and often poor access to irrigation. In addition, during the 1970s, farmers discovered that the new types of rice had little immunity to disease (unlike traditional varieties). The farmers therefore had to use more pesticides, often damaging the environment.

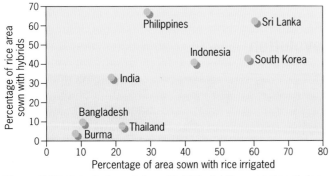

Figure 5.18 Selected countries with high-yielding varieties of rice and irrigation (*Source*: Grigg, DB, 1984, *An introduction to agricultural geography*, London: Hutchinson)

Biotechnology

Just as we have seen how technology and plant breeding programmes increase cereal production, so biotechnology affects both livestock and plant production. The Green Revolution has progressed since the early 1990s into genetic engineering where the use of artificial insemination, embroyo transfer and tissue culture increases agricultural production.

Major criticisms of the Green Revolution

Critics claim that the so-called Green Revolution is a long-term process going back as far as 1000 AD. Even then, improved varieties of rice were introduced from Vietnam to China to increase production. In contrast, the speed of Green Revolution changes in agricultural technology is startling, having begun only in the late 1940s. At the IRRI in the Philippines, for instance, technologists conducted over 50 000 cross-breeding programmes and released 29 MVs between 1966 and 1985. However, such euphoria over the 'miracle' crops is balanced by the problems involved (Fig. 5.19).

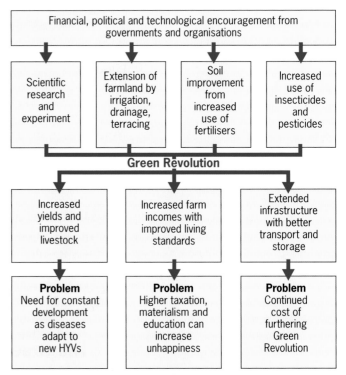

Figure 5.19 An appraisal of the Green Revolution

22 Study Figure 5.18.
a Comment on the geographical distribution of rice HYVs.
b Compare the location of HYVs with Figure 5.12.
c Use your observations to determine whether the Green Revolution can help those areas of the world where there are food shortages.

23 Use Figure 5.19 to evaluate the Green Revolution according to its:
a social benefits and disbenefits
b environmental benefits and disbenefits.

24 Essay: Referring to more than one developing country, assess the relative successes and failures of the Green Revolution, with regard to tackling world food inequalities.

5.6 Population policies

The first ever world population conference was held in Bucharest in 1974. Since then, a number of international institutions and **non-governmental organisations** (**NGOs**, see section 2.7) have focused on population control. These include the United Nations Fund for Population Activities (UNFPA) and the International Planned Parenthood Federation (IPPF).

Each of the institutions has different ideas and policies for population control and the appropriate strategy to adopt, whether anti- or pro-natalist. These fall into three ideological camps: • the neo-Malthusians; • those who consider the general lack of development to be the real problem, *not* high population growth; • those who believe that high rates of population growth in developing countries will naturally slow down with development.

The programme of Action on Development states that countries, as a matter of policy, should 'seek… reductions in maternal mortality through measures to reduce high-risk births, including birth to adolescents, eliminate all unwanted births and all unsafe abortion, [and] expand cost-effective obstetrical and gynaecological care'.

Figure 5.20 Recommending contraception (*Source: UN Draft Final Document of the International Conference on Population and Development, Cairo, 1994*)

Limiting fertility

Providing efficient and hygienic family planning is a major objective of governments and organisations (Fig. 5.20). As the number of births increases, we can see that the health risks to both babies and mothers also increases (Table 5.3). Each year, about 500 000 women die of complications due to pregnancy, child bearing or unsafe abortions. Over 90 per cent of such deaths occur in developing countries where poor health, frequent child bearing, and poor access to medical care are prevalent. The techniques used vary from coercive sterilisation to health care and education (Table 5.4).

Table 5.4 Methods to reduce population growth

Method of birth control	Examples of use
Contraception	Sub-Saharan Africa (>10%); Iran (22%); Philippines (25%); Haiti (10%); North America (69%)
Family planning programmes and child spacing (controlling of the number of, and intervals between, children)	Reduction of average fertility rate from 6.5 to 3.5 children per woman (years taken): USA (58); Indonesia (27), Colombia (15), Thailand (8)
Abortion	see text
Education	Poorly educated women in Brazil have an average of 6.5 children, those with secondary education 2.5.

?

25 Using Spearman's rank correlation method, calculate the strength of the correlation between maternal mortality rates and fertility rates as listed in Table 5.3.

26 In which ways can improvements in the economic status of women influence the number of children they have?

27a Compare Table 5.3 with Figure 5.12.
b Comment on the links between food availability with maternal mortality and fertility.

Table 5.3 Mothers' lives at risk by world regions (*Source*: Tinker et al, 1993, *Population Reports*)

	Estimated maternal mortality ratio (maternal deaths per 100 000 live births) 1988	Total Fertility Rate	Lifetime risk of maternal death
Africa	630	6.1	1 in 22
North	360	6.0	1 in 28
East	680	6.8	1 in 19
West	760	6.4	1 in 19
South	270	5.2	1 in 29
Asia	380	3.9	1 in 57
East	120	2.1	1 in 722
South	570	4.4	1 in 34
West	280	4.9	1 in 61
Europe	23	1.7	1 in 2 132
North America	12	2.6	1 in 2 671
South America	220	3.3	1 in 165
Oceania	600	2.6	1 in 54
World	390	3.7	1 in 58
Developed countries	26	1.9	1 in 1 687
Developing countries	420	3.9	1 in 51

Abortion

Abortion includes any means used to terminate a pregnancy. Throughout the world, women choose to abort more than 50 million pregnancies each year, while about 100 000 to 200 000 women die in the process (20–40 per cent of all maternal deaths).

The moral and ethical issues surrounding abortion are highly emotive, and the practice generates a lot of controversy. In the Russian Federation, abortion is one of the major forms of birth control and each woman has an average of four or five abortions in her life. Similarly, in the USA abortion is considered a constitutional right of women but there is also a growing anti-abortion campaign (Fig. 5.21).

Figure 5.21 Pro-life protesters in the USA, 1993

An unplanned pregnancy can be a disaster for a woman. It may affect her physical and mental health. It may cause her to lose her employment, thus ending her financial independence. It may also cause an intolerable strain on the economic circumstances of her existing family. The option of abortion is essential.

Harry Cohen, Labour MP for Leyton

The House Magazine, 12 June 1995

Abortion is violent and primitive. And it thrives on ignorance. People just don't know that the baby is a formed human being, with arms and legs and heart and eyes not a lump of jelly or tissue. The baby gets pulled out bit by bit, or sucked out in shreds by a machine.

LIFE

Abortion is wrong. God wants human beings to continue, this is a sacred order.

Turkey's Chief Cleric, Mehmet Ali Yilmaz

The Guardian, 11 August 1992

Do I acknowledge the pain of abortion? Yes. Do I think the state should control woman's choices? No. Do I think that birth control is a better choice? Yes. Abortion is indeed a cruel alternative to birth control.

Erica Jong, American novelist and feminist

The Observer, 29 Nov. 1995

Figure 5.22 Attitudes to abortion

28 'While ideological positions are divided, the possible effects of abortion on the growing world's population are widely recognised.' Read Figure 5.22 and state your own response to this statement.

29a Research newspaper articles on abortion.
b List arguments for and against abortion.
c Write a speech justifying your own view towards abortion.

Population and development in China

China is the third largest country in the world in terms of area (Fig. 5.23). In terms of population, though, China is the biggest nation with 1.2 billion people (1994), who make up 21.5 per cent of the world's total population.

Population changes

In 1949, General Mao Tse-tung took over the country's leadership, proclaiming the People's Republic of China a one-party, centrally planned, state. At that time, there were about 550 million Chinese. However, within ten years, the population had grown to 655 million (Fig. 5.24).

The 'Great Leap Forward' was initiated in 1958 to extend the socialist system of production. Mao hoped to give control to the peasants through industrialisation in rural areas and higher targets for agriculture. These plans, though, ended in disorganised production and

Population
1992: 1 165 771 000
2025 (projected): 1 590 783 000

Population density: 314.6 persons per km²

Population growth rate: 1.3%

Population doubling time: 53.4 years

Birth rate: 19.68 births per 1000 persons

Fertility rate: 2.18 children per woman

Death rate: 6.7 deaths per 1000 persons

Literacy: 73% (male 84%, female 62%) age 15 and over can read and write

Contraception use: 71.2% of married women

Infant mortality rate: 34 deaths per 1000 births

Total area: 9 596 960 km²

Natural resources: coal, iron ore, crude oil, mercury, tin, tungsten, antimony, manganese, molybdenum, vanadium, magnetite, aluminium, lead, zinc, uranium, world's largest hydropower potential

Figure 5.23 China

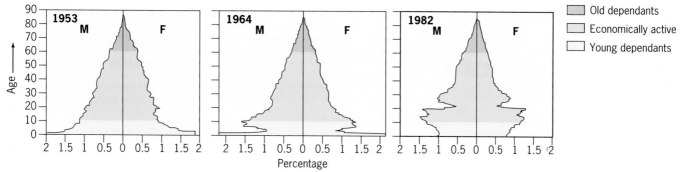

Figure 5.24 China: percentage age composition (*Source: Statistical year book of China*, 1985)

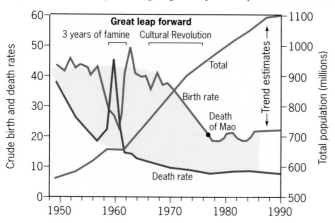

Figure 5.25 China's demographic transition
(*Source: Geography*, 1989)

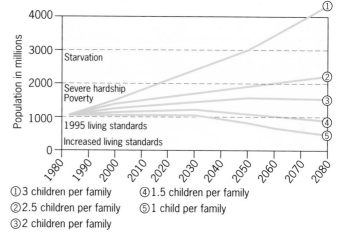

① 3 children per family   ④ 1.5 children per family
② 2.5 children per family   ⑤ 1 child per family
③ 2 children per family

Figure 5.26 China: population projections

famine, with the population declining by about 14 million between 1959 and 1962 (Fig. 5.25). Malnutrition and general distress meant that the average 25 million babies who would normally have been born were either not conceived or did not survive. Infant mortality was thus high, reaching about 284 per 1000. Now, in the mid 1990s, the IMR for China is about 30 per 1000, whereas it is 7 per 1000 in the UK.

Population pressure

Between 1955 and 1995, the population of China more than doubled. When increasing most rapidly, China's population grew by almost 24 million per annum, this is equivalent to the population of England and Wales being generated every two years.

The sheer size of the Chinese population puts increased demands on services such as food, housing, education and employment. In fact during the late 1970s, the government feared that further population increases would result in mass starvation by the end of the century (Fig. 5.26). By 1979, therefore, the government introduced a family planning programme. This is a national policy of one child to urban couples, while couples in the countryside are 'allowed' two children and 'may not have three'. The policy has met with some success (Fig. 5.28). There were 10 million fewer births in 1979 than in 1970 and during this time

the birth rate was halved (see Fig. 3.24). However, the government still found it necessary to extend the single child policy to rural areas by 1981.

The Chinese have defined their optimum population as being around 700–750 million. This would mean a reduction of about one-third of the current population.

?

30a Use Figures 5.24 and 5.25.
a Describe China's population trend.
b Suggest the impact of the Great Leap Forward and famine on the following generations.

31 Study Figure 5.26. Which of the government's five population projections does China's population trend fit (Figs 5.24 and 5.25)?

32a Make a comparison of China's population • projections and • policies with Malthus' and Boserup's theories.
b To which views are China's policies closest?
c What would be the response of • environmentalists, • economists, to China's strategy?

33 Some Chinese name their child 'the only one' in recognition of the fact that they are unlikely to have any more children. Read Figures 5.27 and 5.29 and identify Chinese attitudes towards government population control.

Population and development in China

China's criminal mothers

CHINA first got serious about population control in 1979. The policy of limiting every couple to one child, announced by Deng Xiaoping in 1979, was in place by 1981.

The policy, still in force today, requires women of childbearing age with one child to use IUDs, couples with two children to be sterilised and imposes abortion upon women who get pregnant without authorisation. By the mid-eighties, such birth control operations were averaging more than 30 million a year. Many, if not most, were performed on women against their will.

In 1981, when the Chinese government formally adopted a one-child policy, Chi An, a nurse in the Manchurian city of Shenyang, was recruited to help manage the programme in her factory. Despite her past experiences – she had been forced to end her second pregnancy – she obediently became part of the machine. She was responsible for sterilising women and inserting IUDs; she performed early abortions and assisted in late-term ones.

'The government said there would be a famine without the one-child policy,' she says now. 'We thought we were preventing a catastrophe.'

China draws a cold distinction: killing a newborn is murder; killing an infant even as its head crowns is a 'remedial measure' and a contribution to the public good. There were times when Chi An supervised the 'termination' of a pregnancy when the woman was in labour. But her conscience was silenced by fear of punishment if she failed to carry out her duty.

Chi An, now director of her factory's family planning clinic, had to sign a 'baby contract' with the Shenyang family planning office. If she kept the number of births in her factory below the target, she would receive a cash bonus and a commendation. If she allowed even one baby to be born over the quota, she would be fined and criticised.

January began with the pleasant task of announcing the names of the lucky women whose applications to bear a child had been approved by the factory family planning committee. The rest of Chi An's time was taken up performing pelvic examinations and pressuring into having an abortion those found to be pregnant. Those who refused 'remedial measures' were locked up in a warehouse until they relented. Factory officials would first threaten them, then Chi An would gently tell them they should go quietly to the hospital, for their own good. She always met her target. But then, in 1984, the factory's quota was slashed from 322 infants to 65. When Chi An complained, her superior told her 'the use of force is a necessary measure. Vice Premier Deng Xiaoping has instructed us: 'To reduce the population, use whatever means you must, but do it'.'

Figure 5.27 The other side of family planning (*Source*: Steven Mosher, *The Guardian*, 28 March 1994)

China admits one-child policy a failure

CHINA's national leaders have been forced to admit that the population is growing at a rate beyond the Government's control. Delegates to an emergency meeting in Peking to deal with the crisis heard that, by the year 2000, there will be 120 million more Chinese than planned.

The growth will deepen the economic crisis in a country where one-fifth of the world's population lives on only five per cent of its arable land and where the Agriculture Ministry recently warned that 20 million people were short of food.

It estimated that within 11 years there would be 1.32 billion Chinese, rather than the 1.2 billion forecast.

The one-child family policy, introduced in 1980 to avoid a fight for food in the mid-21st century, was designed to limit the population to 1.2 billion by the year 2000 and to lower it to 700 million within 75 years.

Figure 5.29 Family planning fails (*Source*: Jonathan Mirsky, *The Observer*, 15 Jan. 1989)

Rural women benefit from birth control

ZHENGZHOU (Xinhua) — Rural women are the biggest beneficiaries of implementation of the birth control policy, which has been pushed nationwide since the 1970s.

Most housewives interviewed share the view they have more energy and time for other pursuits and make their own families rich.

The families all observed the birth control policy. Most couples only have one child, or two children at most. Their per capita income is above 2500 yuan ($301) a year, 1000 yuan ($120) more than the average per capita income for all farmers in the province.

Tian Ju, a 36-year-old woman farmer from Sizhuang Village, Nanshuang Township of Mengxian County, has two daughters. Tian, together with her husband, has been running a workshop for producing felt and shoe-pads since 1992. The couple also contracted with the village for four mu (0.266 hectares) of farmland.

Products from the workshop are selling well in the market. From this alone, Tian earns more than 15000 yuan ($1807) a year. Local villagers all admire the family.

'If this were the past, I would have to try to have a boy,' said the housewife. The survey shows rural women now have a decisive voice on birth. Their opinions are respected by their husbands and relatives, thanks to the improved economic status of rural women and adoption of the birth control policy nationwide.

A total of 3 million rural female farmers in the province have attended training courses of various kinds to become workers in rural enterprises.

Figure 5.28 Good results from family planning (*Source: China Daily*, 1 June 1995)

Eventually, as only one child replaces two parents, China's population will start declining. Such projections are, though, being undermined as couples living in the boom, coastal areas become wealthier (see Fig. 4.10, section 9.6). Because of their economic improvements, they no longer fear the official penalties of increased housing, schooling and medical costs for larger families. Other social factors also limit the effectiveness of the single child policy (Fig. 5.29).

34 Read Figure 5.29.
a What are the moral implications of enforcing the population control policy in China?
b Use all the evidence to assess the short-term and long-term advantages and disadvantages of China's population policy.
c Comment on whether China's one-child policy is a success or failure. Give reasons for your responses.

France: boosting the population

Population policies in France (Fig. 5.30) have aimed at increasing fertility. After World War 1, France's population structure was weakened by the loss of so many young males during fighting (Fig. 5.31). The French were frightened then that their population would shrink in future and so weaken France's position as a major world power. In response to this, the government developed a national policy to repopulate itself. This involved, by 1920, making all forms of contraception illegal. Although no longer illegal, the population policy will continue through the twentieth century and is expected to cost the government in excess of UK£11 billion. The long-term target is for France to increase its population to about 100 million by the twenty-first century (Table 5.5).

35 Study Figure 5.31 and explain the fluctuations in France's population structure.

36a Using the figures in Table 5.5, calculate the percentage change in France's total population for each of the periods shown.
b Plot the percentage changes on a graph and describe the trends.

Total area:
547030 sq km

Population
1992: 56876000

2010 (projected): 58766000

2025 (projected): 58613000

Population growth rate: 0.41%

Birth rate: 13.4% births per 1000 persons

Fertility rate: 1.8 children born per woman

Infant mortality rate: 7.3 deaths per 1000 births

Figure 5.30 France

Table 5.5 France: population growth, 1881–1994 (*Source: The Statesman's Yearbook, 1991; World Development Report, 1994; UN Population Division*)

Year	Population in millions
1881	37.6
1891	38.3
1901	38
1911	39.6
1921	39.2
1931	41.8
1946	40.5
1954	42.7
1962	46.5
1968	49.7
1975	52.6
1982	54.3
1992	57.4
1994	57.7

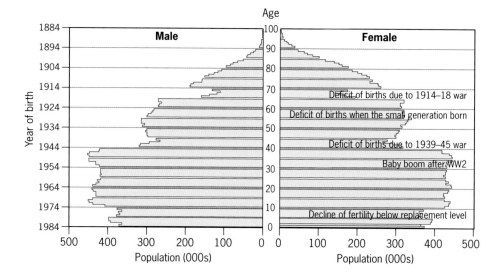

Figure 5.31 France: age-sex population structure (*Source: Quartorzieme rapport sur la situation demographique de la France, Population, 1985*)

5

France: boosting the population

Incentives

In 1995 the average number of children per couple is 1.8, but the aim is to see this increase. Because two-child families only maintain the replacement level for the population, the French policy gives incentives to encourage families to have three or more children (Table 5.6).

Assessment of France's population policy

In spite of the incentives to couples, France's total fertility in the last few decades has been on the decline (Table 5.7).

Table 5.6 French government incentives as part of the population policy scheme

- payment of up to UK£1 064 to couples having a third child
- generous maternity grant for women expecting a child
- guaranteed minimum family income for child-bearing couples of about UK£447 a month
- other family allowances to increase the purchasing power of three-child families
- increase in maternity leave from 4 to 6 months on full pay
- 100% mortgage and preferential treatment in the allocation of three bedroom council flats
- full tax benefits to parents until the youngest child reaches the age of 18
- 30% fare reduction on all public transport for three-child families
- pension schemes for mothers or housewives
- child-orientated development policies e.g. provision of crèche, day nurseries, child recreational facilities with access for non-working mothers
- nursing mothers are encouraged to work part time or take a weekly day off work

37 Suggest some social, economic and political reasons why some countries may wish to promote high population growth.
b What are the possible problems that governments' excessive promotion of large families may create for the nation in the future?

38a Assess the success of the French population policy in light of the information provided in this section.
b With reference to migration into France (see section 4.3), suggest how population policies might have been influenced by high levels of immigration.

39 With regard to population increase and the declining population in Europe (see section 3.4), how can policies encouraging couples to have large families be justified?

40a Compare China's attempt to control population growth with France's promotion of large families and consider which is more likely to succeed.
b What implications does this success or failure have for the two countries?

Table 5.7 Total fertility rates

Year	European average	France
1960	2.61	2.73
1965	2.74	2.84
1970	2.40	2.47
1975	1.98	1.93
1980	1.82	1.95
1985	1.59	1.81
1987	1.56	1.80
1988	1.57	1.81
1989	1.54	1.79
1990	1.54	1.78
1991	1.51	1.77
1992	1.48	1.73

Summary

- The international community recognises the need for population control.
- Malthus linked population growth with food shortages, poverty and disease.
- Boserup contradicted Malthus stating that population growth stimulates innovation and increased food production.
- Responses to population growth divide into economic and environmentalist views.
- Food availability is unequal across the world.
- Where there is famine, food aid is supplied for both humanitarian and political reasons.
- Technology and modern farming techniques help to increase food output. This benefits mainly the developed world, while some developing countries still suffer from food shortages.
- The success of the Green Revolution, based on high yielding varieties of cereals, has been uneven throughout the developing world.
- Population control is a controversial issue with mixed strategies and ideologies.
- A rise in the social status of women in developing countries has led to increasing access to contraception and family planning.
- In developed countries there is a growing anti-abortion movement.
- Some population policies are aimed at controlling fertility, while others encourage couples to have more children.

6 Human resources and industrialisation

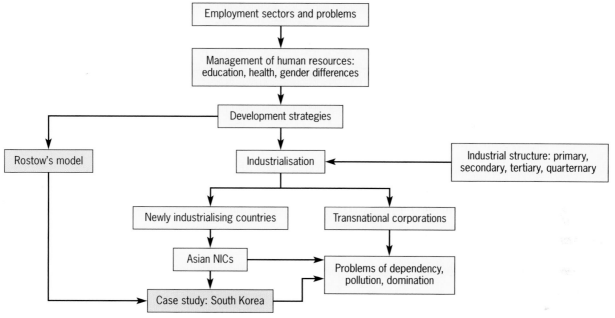

6.1 Introduction

The more a country develops its human, as well as its physical and technological resources, the more opportunity it has for transforming itself from economic dependency to self-reliance. In many cases, both **developed** and **developing countries** also view industrialisation as the key to economic change. This path is outlined in Rostow's model of economic development (see section 6.6). We can see that countries which are relatively successful in terms of industrial growth have also made practical use of their human resources. Typically, these countries have managed to bring about economic development and we refer to them as **newly industrialising countries** (**NICs**) (see section 6.7). In this chapter, we will consider how far investment in human resources contributes towards improving people's quality of life and we will examine the role of industry in economic development.

6.2 Employment in the formal and informal sectors

People may work in one of two different sectors of the economy. In the **formal sector**, jobs are officially recognised by the state, they are perfomed for a wage and they are relatively secure with the hours and working conditions clearly established (Fig. 6.1). Contrastingly, in the **informal sector** people are self-employed and do not receive a permanent wage (Fig. 6.2). While in developed countries an example of informal work is textiles homeworking (e.g. making garments at home for retailers), in developing countries it tends to be characterised by employment in family businesses, as unpaid family work on agricultural small-holdings or as an urban labour force (Fig. 6.3).

The nature of employment in the informal sectors in most developing economies is such that many people are actually **underemployed**. This usually occurs when work is temporary or seasonal and applies to informal work in

Figure 6.1 Employment in the formal sector: metropolitan police give assistance, London, UK

Figure 6.2 Employment in the informal sector: resurfacing mud walls, Kano, Nigeria. Approximately 40–70 per cent of the urban labour force of the developing world work 'informally'.

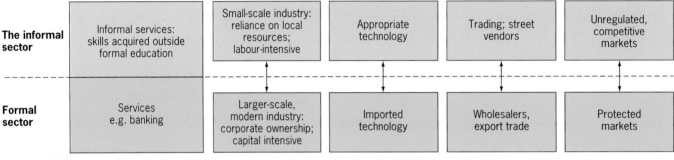

The informal sector	Informal services: skills acquired outside formal education	Small-scale industry: reliance on local resources; labour-intensive	Appropriate technology	Trading; street vendors	Unregulated, competitive markets
Formal sector	Services e.g. banking	Larger-scale, modern industry: corporate ownership; capital intensive	Imported technology	Wholesalers, export trade	Protected markets

Figure 6.3 Differences between the formal and informal sectors

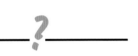

1 Use Figures 6.1–6.3.
a Identify some of the main features of • formal and • informal work.
b With Figure 6.3 to help, make a comparison between the two types of work in both • developed and • developing countries.

2 With reference to Figure 6.4, compare and comment on the relative percentages of people working in the formal and informal sectors in different parts of the world.

3 Use Figure 6.5. In groups, discuss the reasons why large numbers of people employed informally, or who are underemployed, can hinder national economic development.

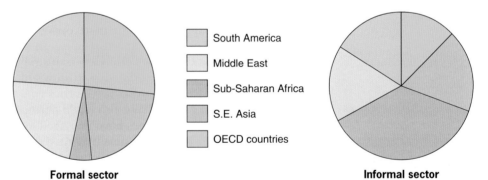

South America
Middle East
Sub-Saharan Africa
S.E. Asia
OECD countries

Formal sector   **Informal sector**

Figure 6.4 Average percentage of world workforce employed in formal and informal sectors (*Source: The Economist: Book of Vital World Statistics*, 1992)

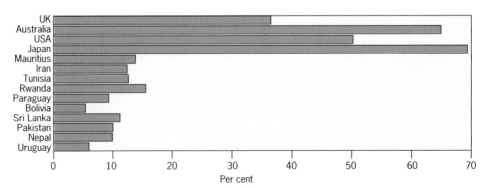

Figure 6.5 Income tax as a percentage of total current revenue, 1992 (*Source: World Bank Report*, 1994)

Figure 6.6 The unemployment time bomb (*Source: International Labour Office*)

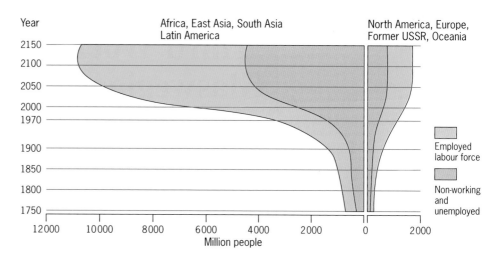

both urban and rural areas (see Fig. 6.9). For example, street vendors in many large cities, such as Bombay in India, depend on tourists to boost their income. Their wages will therefore be substantially higher during the 'tourist season' than at other times. In rural areas, landless labourers may only be employed during harvest and so lack that income during the rest of the year.

6.3 Unemployment

Unemployment is a serious world problem with a growing number of people who are out of work or who are facing the threat of being made redundant (Fig. 6.6). In fact, a combination of large numbers of people employed informally, those underemployed and the unemployed make it difficult for authorities to collect accurate labour statistics (see section 3.3). This is true for both developing as well as developed countries (Fig. 6.7).

Impact of unemployment

It is important to understand that unemployment has different consequences for people in both developing and developed countries (Fig. 6.9). In most developed countries, the state often provides for unemployed people through social security schemes (Fig. 6.8). Such schemes are generally non-existent in the developing countries, though, so the unemployed here may have to depend on the support of extended families.

The 'pull', or attraction, of employment opportunities in cities means there is a particularly strong rural-to-urban migration in developing countries (see section 4.5). In fact, these cities tend to have a concentration of both employment and social service provision while the rural areas 'push' people away with their lack of such services. The result is the highest rates of urban growth in the world (Table 6.1, see Fig. 4.17).

Jobless figures not trusted

The Government's official unemployment figures are not trusted or believed, an inquiry by a panel of Britain's most senior statisticians has concluded. 'It is clear to us that the general public, many politicians, the media and various pressure groups do not trust the unemployment figures or find them convincing.'

'The CC [claimant count] is not trusted, is not based on any agreed concept of unemployment, is inconsistent over time due to changes in the claimant system, and cannot be used for international comparisons. We conclude that the CC should cease to be the basis for the monthly headline figure and internationally recognised definition.'

Figure 6.7 Counting the jobless (*Source: Rosie Waterhouse, The Independent, 5 April 1995*)

4a From Figure 6.6, estimate how many people in the world will be unemployed by 2150.
b Using information from previous chapters, suggest why unemployment is likely to slow down after 2050.

5 Read Figure 6.7 and refer to section 3.3. Give reasons why it is difficult for both developed and developing countries to obtain accurate statistics on • numbers of people employed/unemployed, • the size of the potential workforce.

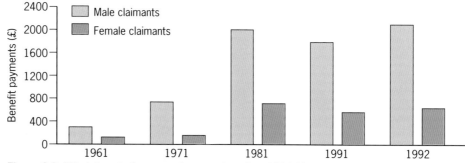

Figure 6.8 UK claimants for unemployment benefits, 1994 (*Source: HMSO*)

Figure 6.9 Life in Strathclyde's slums ... a world away from India (*Source:* Ian Bell, *The Observer*, 12 Feb. 1995)

Table 6.1 Urbanisation (*Source:* Selmes et al., 1995)

Country	Urban population (% 1987)	Rate of urbanisation (% increase, 1950–87)
Egypt	48	16
Ghana	32	17
Zaire	38	19
Kenya	22	16
Pakistan	31	13
India	27	9
China	38	17
Thailand	21	10
USA	74	10
Mexico	71	28
Jamaica	51	21
Peru	69	33
Argentina	85	20
UK	92	8
France	74	18
Poland	61	22
Italy	68	14
Romania	49	23
Australia	85	10

6 Study the opinions in Figure 6.9.

a Explain why the researchers suggest that unemployment in Glasgow is worse than living in a poor Indian village.

b In your opinion, for long-term unemployment situations, how would life dependent on state benefits compare with life where you are dependent on a large family for support?

'Third World' label drives Glaswegians to despair

IT IS not a choice most of us will ever face. Which to prefer: a mud hut in southern India's Nilgiri Hills or a home in a Glasgow slum. Two Indian researchers raised the question at the UN World Summit on Social Development, which ends in Copenhagen today.

Stan and Mari Thekaekara said that Glasgow's Easterhouse was 'soulless' and 'demoralised', its abandoned apartments reeking of decay and menace. The penniless tribesmen of the Nilgiri Hills outside Mysore were better off than the unemployed of Easterhouse. 'We had never in India met a man who had been unemployed for 20 years. We have seasonal unemployment, but not for 20 years of purposeless, meaningless existence,' they said.

Easterhouse has a reputation for joblessness, violence, drugs and rotting houses, and its health record is among the worst in Europe.

Yet when newspapers reported that Easterhouse was facing a 'meaningless future' worse than anything confronting India's peasants, locals felt no shock of recognition.

Is life, as one newspaper put it, really 'better in a mud hut than a Glasgow slum'? Have Britain's poor joined the Third – or is it Fourth World?

'My reaction is disbelief,' says Alex Hamilton, project leader with the community-based Easterhouse Project. 'How they could possibly make such a comparison is totally beyond me.'

Lazar Savarimuthli, of the Bangalore-based India Social Institute, is another sceptic. He concedes that India's poor take the initiative, but it is also true that illiteracy rates are high in the sub-continent, that many children do not attend school and there is nothing romantic about 'putting your hand in shit' to survive. 'Don't,' he advises, 'idolise India's poverty.'

David Black, a worker with the Glasgow Healthy City Project, sponsored by the World Health Organisation, argues that you cannot compare radically different cultures: 'The quality of life for the poorest in Glasgow is still better than the quality of life for the poorest in India.'

But what, equally, does 'quality of life' mean to the long-term unemployed or to those for whom drugs offer the only cash economy? The Thekaekaras confessed surprise at the 'surface wealth' of Easterhouse, but claimed that in India lack of jobs was only seasonal, that people in the hills south of Mysore took the initiative, that hope thrived.

You could say more: 13 people have died this year already in Glasgow because of drugs, on council estates suicide rates and early deaths soar above those in middle-class areas, opportunities are few and standards of health are a national disgrace.

What the Indian researchers illustrate, perhaps, is a gulf in perceptions as great as any gulf in wealth. Stan Thekaekara spoke of India's poor 'scavenging in garbage heaps of junk' and found that preferable to the supposed apathy of Easterhouse. Are we insulted or unsurprised? And whoever said Easterhouse was unique in Britain?

6.4 Reasons for unemployment in developing countries

The reasons for large-scale unemployment in the developing countries are varied. Although neo-Malthusians (see section 5.2) blame the high rates of population growth for unemployment and poverty in these locations, rapid population growth is not the only cause of these problems.

One major cause of unemployment in developing countries is **structural adjustment programmes** (**SAPs**) (see section 2.3). Alongside existing unemployment trends, there has been increasing joblessness in the formal sectors since the World Bank and International Monetary Fund (IMF) introduced SAPs. One of the conditions of World Bank and IMF loans to developing countries is that they reduce government (public) spending and adopt privatisation policies (see Fig. 2.12). In practice, such privatisation causes governments to give up control or ownership of companies and corporations and so lose valuable income. The knock-on result of this is that governments then have to remove subsidies on essential services such as health, education and transport etc. The introduction of SAPs will, according to the World Bank, promote a **free-market economy**.

Since governments in the developing countries have always been the largest employers of labour in the formal sector, the adoption of these SAPs has led to massive job losses in countries such as Ghana, Nigeria, Brazil and Bolivia. In Ghana in particular, 28 000 jobs were lost in one year because of the structural adjustment programme imposed by the IMF.

Overall, unemployment has worsened in both developed and developing countries since the 1970s. World recession has hit manufacturing industry and so primary and secondary workers are particularly affected. This is also due to an increase in mechanisation as well as a growth of the tertiary sector.

6.5 Management of human resources in developing countries

Specific policies aimed at developing human resources include improving health care, education and training in vocational skills. However, before any improvement can be made in these areas, the promotion of better health and education is of paramount importance. This helps to reduce poverty and so bring about economic and social development (Fig. 6.10, see sections 3.7, 5.3). However, the financial resources needed to improve education and health care have generally declined in many developing countries over the last 20 years (Table 6.2).

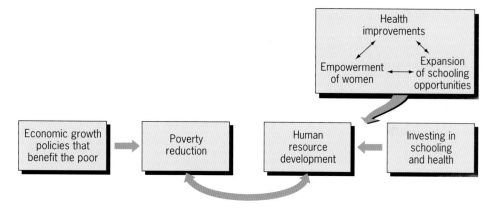

Figure 6.10 Mutually reinforcing cycles: reduction of poverty and development of human resources (*Source: World Development Report,* 1993)

Table 6.2 Government expenditure on health and education (1972–92) (*Source: World Development Report*, 1992 and 1994)

Country	% of total expenditure on education		% of total expenditure on health	
	1972	1992	1972	1992
Malawi	15.8	10.4	5.5	7.8
India	2.3	2.1	1.5	1.6
Sri Lanka	13.0	10.1	6.4	4.8
Chile	14.5	13.3	10.0	11.1
Mexico	16.4	13.9	4.5	1.9
Brazil	8.3	3.7	6.7	6.9
Kenya	21.9	20.1	7.9	5.4
Tunisia	30.5	17.5	7.4	6.6
UK	2.6	13.2	12.2	13.8
South Korea	15.8	16.2	1.2	1.2

7a For each country listed in Table 6.2, draw two bars on one graph to show the direction and amount of change in government expenditure on health and education from 1972 to 1992.
b Comment on the trend shown by your graph.

Education
The share of world **GNP** spent on education rose in the mid-1970s and early 1980s. However, by the mid-1990s, spending on education had fallen back to the same level of 5.5 per cent as in 1970 (Fig. 6.11). This reduction in world

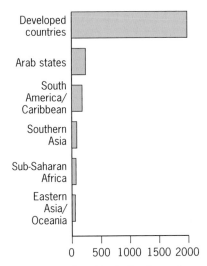

Figure 6.11 The North–South gap in government spending per pupil, in US dollars (*Source: New Internationalist*, October 1993)

?

8 Study Figure 6.12. Compare the differences between enrolment in education and spending for different world regions.

9a Using Figure 6.12, describe the trend in spending in education in sub-Saharan Africa.
b Explain how this has affected enrolment.

10a Referring to Figure 6.14, describe some of the consequences of reduced educational spending on pupils.
b Suggest how such government reductions might influence development in this region.

11a Compare the learning environments experienced by children in the developed and the developing countries as shown in Figures 6.13–6.14.
b What are the positive and negative images being shown in these photographs?
c What quality of life does each image convey?
d Using these images as a basis, make a list of ten factors which are important to you in deciding the quality of life of students.

Figure 6.14 Education in the Ivory Coast: most schools lack any facilities other than a blackboard

spending on education hides an even more dramatic fall in education spending in the developing countries, especially in sub-Saharan Africa (Figs 6.12, 6.14).

Education is also facing limitations in many developed countries because of a reduction in government spending. None the less, the experiences of children in schools here tend to differ greatly from those in developing countries (Fig. 6.13).

Health

Total annual health spending varies enormously between developed and developing countries (Table 6.3). In 1990, the average amount spent on health per person ranged from less than US$10 in several African and Asian countries to more than US$2700 in the USA. Similarly, there were considerable variations in health spending among countries within Africa. For example, Tanzania spent only US$4 per person on health whereas Zimbabwe spent about US$42 in 1990. In Asia, the amounts spent on health in Bangladesh and South Korea were US$7 and US$377 per person respectively during the same period.

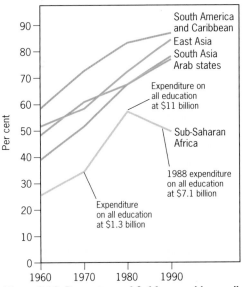

Figure 6.12 Percentage of 6–11-year-olds enrolled in primary school (*Source:* UNESCO, 1993)

Figure 6.13 Education in the UK: most schools have access to the latest technology

Table 6.3 Global health expenditure, 1990 (*Source: World Development Report*, 1993)

Demographic region	Percentage of world population	Total health expenditure (billions $)	Health expenditure as percentage of world total	Public sector health expenditure as percentage of regional total	Percentage of GNP spent on health	Per capita health expenditure ($)
Established market economies	15	1 483	87	60	9.2	1 860
Formerly socialist economies of Europe	7	49	3	71	3.6	142
South America	8	47	3	60	4.0	105
Middle Eastern crescent	10	39	2	58	4.1	77
Other Asian countries and islands	13	42	2	39	4.5	61
India	16	18	1	22	6.0	21
China	22	13	1	59	3.5	11
Sub-Saharan Africa	10	12	1	55	4.5	24
Demographically developing countries	78	170	10	50	4.7	41
World	100	1 702	100	60	8.0	329

> *The extent to which women are free to make decisions affecting their lives may be the key to the future, not only of the poor countries but of the richer ones too. As mothers; producers or suppliers of food, fuel and water; traders and manufacturers; political and community leaders, women are at the centre of the process of change.*
>
> **Dr Nafis Sadik,**
> **(Executive Director of UNPF)**

Figure 6.15 The value of women in the development process (*Source:* UNPF, *The State of World Population,* 1989)

12 Study Table 6.3 and, using a blank base map of the world, choose a suitable cartographic technique to highlight the differences in government health expenditure for all the regions listed.

13 Study Figure 6.16.
a For each of the tasks listed, identify which ones are carried out mostly by women.
b In the light of your findings, discuss how important a woman's role is in supporting a family's existence.

Gender differences

Since the late 1970s, many development experts have recognised that women's active participation in the development process is essential (Fig. 6.15). We now know that women perform approximately two-thirds of the world's work for just 10 per cent of the world's income. In recent studies of 17 developing countries, women's work hours exceeded men's by 30 per cent. Even data from 12 developed countries found that women in formal employment worked about 20 per cent longer hours than men.

Although women participate and are involved in all major economic activities (Table 6.4), some institutional, social, psychological and cultural obstacles still limit or tend to undermine their role in development. This is reflected by the percentage of economically active women shown in Table 6.4 which is a measure of formal jobs. As such, the statistic underplays the many millions of women and men who work in informal jobs (see section 6.2).

Despite the fact that women carry the greater share of work in most subsistence economies (Fig. 6.16), their contribution is lost because of the formal definition of work which looks at economic or monetary value. As a

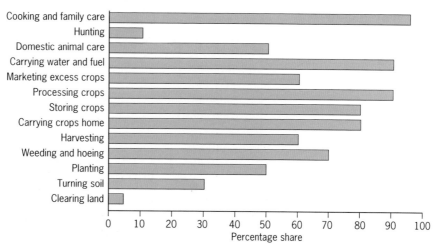

Figure 6.16 Women's percentage share of food system tasks in Africa (*Source:* Barrett and Browne, 1991)

Table 6.4 Women's economic activities in selected countries (*Source: The world's women*, UN Press, 1991)

Region	Country	Women as percentage of economically active population (1990)	Occupational groups (females per 100 males) 1980s			
			Administrative and managerial workers	Clerical/sales service workers	Production and transport	Agriculture
Developed economies	Australia	38	42	138	28	30
	USA	41	61	183	23	19
	France	40	10	164	18	48
	Portugal	37	17	108	34	101
	UK	39	29	225	18	18
Africa	Cameroon	33	6	26	9	82
	Egypt	10	16	23	6	26
	Zambia	28	12	44	6	26
	Gambia	40	17	57	16	98
	Zimbabwe	34	17	57	16	98
South America and Caribbean	Costa Rica	22	29	95	25	5
	Ecuador	19	18	79	13	8
	Mexico	27	18	98	21	5
	Paraguay	21	58	98	21	5
	Venezuela	28	17	86	11	4
Asia	Bangladesh	7	2	29	20	1
	China	43	12	71	55	88
	India	25	2	11	15	31
	Sri Lanka	27	7	35	31	51
	Turkey	34	3	14	9	109

result, non-paid work and services provided by women in many societies remain unacknowledged. Jobs such as cooking, cleaning, caring for the family, harvesting and fetching water are not included in any economic definition of waged work, leaving women unrecognised in most employment statistics (Fig. 6.17).

Because of the important role of women for both social and economic functions, particularly in developing countries, governments realise it is necessary to develop the skills and potential of women. This will then bring about further social and economic development (Fig. 6.18). Development experts accept that the physical and economic subjugation of women in the past has held back development in certain countries. In addition, the cultural

14 Study Table 6.4 and compare the regional variations in: • women as a percentage of the economically active population and • the ratio of females to males in each occupational group.

15a Draw a similar time chart to Figure 6.17 to show the work of a British woman.
b Compare the two charts and assess the differences in the women's lifestyles.

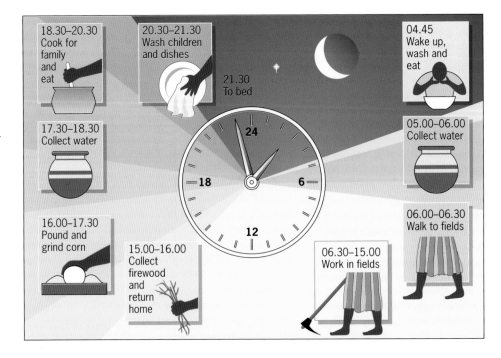

Figure 6.17 A day in the life of a typical rural African woman (*Source:* Maggie Murray and Buchi Emecheta, *Our Own Freedom*, Sheba Feminist Publishers)

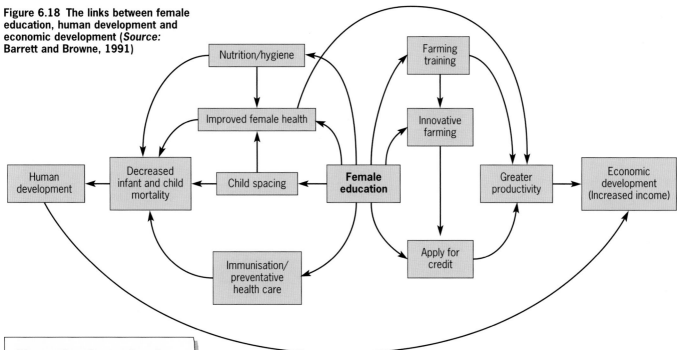

Figure 6.18 The links between female education, human development and economic development (*Source:* Barrett and Browne, 1991)

Break the chain

The World Bank has said the chain of poor maternal health has to be broken by special emphasis being placed on adolescent girls, to stop the cycle of early childbearing, poor health and nutrition, and poverty.

About 500000 women world wide die as a result of too many pregnancies, too close together and too young.

The World Bank confirms the situation is worst in developing countries where 'women's disproportionate poverty, low social status and reproductive role expose them to high health risks, resulting in needless and largely preventable suffering and premature death'.

Citing statistics which show that one thousand women die in childbirth each day, Ann Tinker, the organisation's senior health adviser, said the World Bank plans to push for greater investment in 'a holistic approach to women's health', which includes issues such as gender discrimination in nutrition and health care during childhood, early pregnancy and adolescence, and violence against women.

Figure 6.19 Maternal health

16 Use Figure 6.18 to explain the links between education, health and development.

17 Read Figure 6.19 and assess how frequent pregnancies affect women's health and their contribution to economic development.

pressure to have many children (see section 3.7) has serious health consequences for women (Fig. 6.19), so more and more national and international organisations are addressing the issue of women in development. Examples of such organisations are the United Nations Development Fund for Women (UNIFEM), the United Nations International Research and Training Institute for the Advancement of Women (INSTRAW) and Women in Development Expert Group (WID).

Women and education

If access to education and the acquisition of skills are essential for finding secure and waged employment, women are at a distinct disadvantage when compared with men. As seen in Chapter 3, for social and cultural reasons females usually have lower school enrolment and higher drop-out rates in the poor nations of Asia and Africa (Fig. 6.20). Social pressures cause women to have children and become principal carer and provider at an early age. An estimated 90 million girls in the world have no education at all and of the 960 million illiterate people in the world, two-thirds are women.

Cultural influences

Apart from unequal access to education, some cultures, religions and traditional customs in the developing world are very repressive to women (see section 3.7). Even in some developed countries, women still do not have equal status with men. In certain Muslim and Hindu societies, such as Pakistan and India, purdah is practised. This is the custom of keeping women in seclusion with clothing that conceals them completely when they go out. This custom often prevents women from taking an active part in social, economic and political activities outside their homes.

Similarly, certain religions, such as Hinduism, actively discriminate against women. Because of their belief, some parents prefer baby boys to girls (see section 5.6). This sometimes results in female infanticide, and widow burning (*suttee*) is still (though very rarely) practised in rural parts of India. Also, as women are generally expected to marry and leave home, their families do not consider the education of female children a priority.

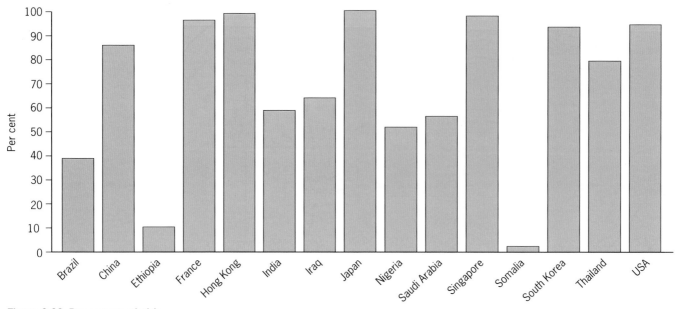

Figure 6.20 Percentage of girls reaching their final year of primary education, 1994 (*Source:* UNICEF, *The Progress of the Nations*, 1994)

18 Assess the impact of increased investment in female education in the developing countries with relation to:
• population growth rates
• life expectancy
• healthcare
• family structure
• generation of income.

19 Use all the information in section 6.5. What are the implications of the global variations in health and education spending on human resource development and the potential to industrialise?

6.6 Development strategies and industrialisation

In both developed and developing countries, there are four major categories of industry, or economic activity (Table 6.5).

Table 6.5 Definitions of employment sectors

Economic sector	Definition	Examples from developing countries
Primary	Exploitation of natural resources; includes people working in agriculture, forestry, mining and fishing	Copper mines of Zaire and Zambia; tin mines of Nigeria; growing jute in Bangladesh; oil palm plantations in Nigeria
Secondary	Manufacturing products from raw materials either for domestic consumption or export. Import-substitution industries produce goods protected by tariffs, quotas and favourable taxes. Governments use these to replace imported manufactured goods, boost domestic industry and reduce foreign exchange deficits	Processing cocoa in Ghana and Sierra Leone for export for chocolate production; textiles in India for export for clothing manufacture; producing bread for domestic consumption in Nigeria
Tertiary	Jobs where people provide services to other people and industries	Transport; retailing; financial services
Quarternary	Jobs where people supply information or expertise	Hi-tech; information services; education

The influence of industrialised countries
In the nineteenth century, many countries in Europe and North America experienced rapid industrialisation and urbanisation. Successful industrialisation led to economic growth and prosperity for these now developed countries.

In response to this, many developing countries in the late twentieth century see industry as the basis for their economic development. However, while in many developed countries the industry and service sectors contribute a significant proportion to their GDPs (Table 6.6), the proportions are very different in many developing countries (Table 6.7). The 24 countries that make up the Organisation for Economic Co-operation and Development (OECD), otherwise known as the 'rich man's club', produce three-quarters of the world's industrial output.

20 Use Tables 6.6 and 6.7.
a Choose a suitable statistical technique to measure the relationship between GDP per capita and the percentage contribution from agriculture in both developed and developing countries.
b Comment on your results and suggest reasons for any differences.

21 You are a researcher for the World Bank and have to give a general report on the links between world industrial sectors and economic development.
a Compare the percentage contributions made by:
• agriculture, • manufacturing industry and • services to the GDPs of both developed and developing countries.
b Using triangular graph paper, plot the figures from both tables to show the relative contributions of the different sectors to the total GDPs of both developed and developing countries.
c Write your assessment of world economic development using contrasting countries. Draw conclusions from your comparisons made in **a** and **b**.

Table 6.6 Percentage contribution of agriculture, industry and services to gross domestic product in selected (OECD) countries, 1992 (*Source: *World Bank Report*, 1994; †*The World Factbook*)

Country	GDP (million US$)	GDP per capita† (US$)	Percentage contribution of agriculture	Percentage contribution of industry	Percentage contribution of services*
Australia	294 760	16 200	3	30	67
Austria	185 235	20 985	3	36	61
Belgium	218 836	17 300	2	30	68
Denmark	123 546	17 700	4	27	69
Finland	93 869	16 200	5	30	64
France	1 319 883	18 300	3	29	68
Germany	1 789 261	16 700	2	39	60
Ireland	43 294	11 200	10	10	80
Italy	1 222 962	16 700	3	32	65
Japan	3 670 979	19 000	2	42	56
Netherlands	320 290	16 600	4	29	67
Norway	112 906	17 100	3	35	62
Sweden	220 834	17 200	2	32	66
Turkey	99 696	3 400	15	30	55
UK (1993)	819 038	14 145	2	33	65

Table 6.7 Percentage contribution of agriculture, industry and services to gross domestic product in selected developing countries, 1992 (*Source: *World Bank Report*, 1994; †*The World Factbook*)

Country	GDP (million US$)	GDP per capita† (US$)	Percentage contribution of agriculture	Percentage contribution of industry	Percentage contribution of services*
Algeria	35 674	2 130	10	47	38
Bangladesh	23 783	200	9	17	49
Botswana	3 700	2 800	4	52	43
Cameroon	10 397	1 040	22	30	49
Ethiopia	6 257	130	8	13	39
Gabon	5 913	3 090	5	46	45
Ghana	6 884	400	9	16	35
India	214 598	380	17	27	40
Morocco	28 401	1 060	19	33	52
Namibia	2 106	1 400	6	26	62
Panama	6 001	2 040	8	14	76
Sierra Leone	634	330	5	16	46
Somalia	879	210	5	9	26
Sudan	—	450	9	17	50
Tunisia	13 854	1 320	17	31	51
Uganda	2 998	300	4	11	32

Rostow's model of economic development

Based on the experiences of the rich industrialised nations, economists during the 1950s and the 1960s developed a number of general theories of economic growth. An American, W W Rostow, published his model in 1960 and this is now called a 'linear-stages' theory of development (Fig. 6.21). We can use it to analyse the experiences of a number of countries at different stages of development (Fig. 6.22).

Rostow's model is particularly concerned with the stages countries go through to achieve economic growth and these are dependent on capital. Rostow proposes that countries can develop if they save 5–10 per cent of their national income and invest these savings in manufacturing industry.

The model gives investment as the key to economic growth. With increasing investment in industry, a country will move from a subsistence-based economy

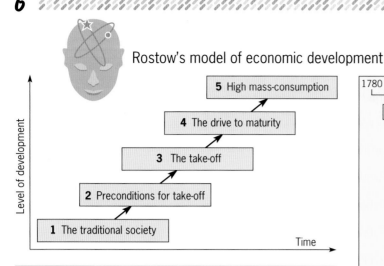

Rostow's model of economic development

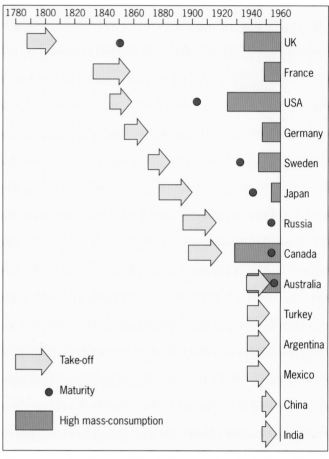

Stage 1: A subsistence economy using limited technology. The society is self sufficient and relatively isolated.

Stage 2: Outside influences lead to the development of industries based around local resources. Agriculture is more commercialised and becomes mechanised. Improvements in infrastructure encourage trade. Urbanisation begins. Investment in manufacturing industry is 5–10% of GDP.

Stage 3: An important stage lasting 20–30 years during which the country accumulates wealth by trade. Investment in technology for manufacturing to produce goods for exports, thus generating wealth for the next stage.

Stage 4: Economic growth should by now be self-sustaining. This spreads to all parts of the country because of the multiplier effect. More complex transport systems develop and technology continues to improve. Some early infant industries decline. A broad industrial base leads to the creation of wealth which can be invested in social and welfare provision.

Stage 5: Rapid expansion of tertiary activities and high employment in services result in a decline in manufacturing employment. Social and welfare facilities continue to expand. Mature industries thrive using high level technology to produce consumer durables.

Figure 6.21 Rostow's linear stages model of economic growth

Figure 6.22 Application of Rostow's model in selected countries (*After:* Horsfall, *Manufacturing Industry*, Blackwell, 1977)

22 Use Figure 6.21 to compare and contrast the time lags between the take-off and high mass consumption periods for each country in Figure 6.22.

(stage 1) to an economy dominated by the production of consumer goods and tertiary and quarternary industries (stages 4–5).

Rostow's model implies that developing countries need to follow the stages of development experienced by the western industrialised nations (see Fig. 3.24). The model also assumes that developed countries can sell technology to the developing countries to stimulate industrial output in these poorer areas. An increase in wealth, brought about by the use of modern technology, will therefore make it possible for developing countries to invest increasing amounts of their income in manufacturing industry. According to the model, this will enable developing countries to 'take off' economically.

Weaknesses of Rostow's model
Critics of Rostow suggest that the model is too simplistic. They dispute its assumption that the experiences of developed countries are appropriate for all developing countries.

Resources
Countries which were among the first to industrialise, such as the UK, had access to enormous amounts of natural resources both at home and in their colonies. However, developing countries of the twentieth century have access to relatively fewer natural resources. Contrary to Rostow, therefore, it is unlikely that the past experiences of developed countries will, or can, be followed by all the developing countries.

23 Discuss the extent to which Rostow's model applies to the developing countries today. Refer to specific examples in your answer.

24 Could a Stage 6 be added to Rostow's five stages? If so, what would the features of such a stage be? Give reasons for your answer.

Markets

The UK also had huge world markets to supply during its early stages of industrial development. Although the economies of other European countries and those of North America used tariffs to protect themselves from UK-made goods, and so also prospered, the UK still had the huge market of her colonies. The income from these markets made investments in industry possible, leading to further economic growth. The UK was therefore able to pass through to the take-off stage. The developing countries today do not have such market opportunities either at home or abroad. Their domestic markets tend to be limited in terms of purchasing power, while the conditions of world trade restrict developing countries from competing favourably on world markets (see Chapter 8). This is because of high **tariffs** imposed by developed countries on the import of finished goods. Consequently, developing countries are forced to export materials in only a raw or semi-finished state. Overall, therefore, these problems mean that the capital necessary for investment, as stressed by Rostow, is simply not available.

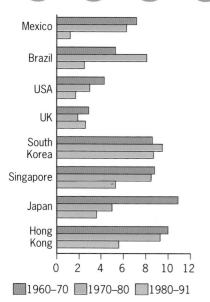

1960–70 □1970–80 □1980–91

Figure 6.23 Percentage growth rate of real GDP in selected countries, 1960–91 (Source: World Bank, 1982–93)

6.7 The emergence of newly industrialising countries

There are a number of countries in Asia and South America that show a reasonable level of industrialisation. These are known as the newly industrialising countries (NICs) and have experienced rapid growth in their manufacturing output and exports over recent decades. Their economies have expanded much faster than the economies of developed countries in terms of real GDP growth (Fig. 6.23).

We may refer to countries such as Brazil and Mexico as newly industrialising, but the Asian NICs are, in many ways, the most economically successful. This group includes, among others, South Korea, Taiwan, Thailand, Malaysia, Hong Kong and Singapore (Table 6.8).

Table 6.8 General indicators for selected NICs, 1994 (Sources: World Population Data Sheet 1994, Population reference Bureau, Inc. Washington D.C. Human Development Report, United Nations Development Programme (UNDP), 1993)

Country	Population (millions)	Population growth rate %	% under 15 years	% over 65 years	Average life expectancy at birth	GNP per capita	Human Development Index (HDI)[†]
Brazil	155.3	1.7	35	5	64	2 770	0.730
Hong Kong	5.8	0.7	21	9	78	15 380	0.913
Malaysia	19.5	2.3	36	4	71	2 790	0.790
Mexico	91.8	2.2	35	4	70	3 470	0.805
Singapore	2.9	1.2	23	6	74	15 750	0.849
South Korea	44.5	1.0	24	5	71	6 790	0.872
Taiwan	21.1	1.0	26	7	74	*	*
Thailand	59.4	1.4	29	5	67	1 840	0.715

* No data available for Taiwan † HDI is 1990 data

The rise of Hong Kong, Singapore, Taiwan and South Korea
The reasons for the success of these Asian NICs (otherwise known as the 'Little Tigers') vary from country to country (Fig. 6.24).

The importance of human resources
Due to a combination of large-scale immigration and high population growth rates, each of the four countries has a large workforce. During the 1950s and 1960s, the NICs specialised in traditional, labour-intensive industries, such as textiles, clothing, footwear and leather products, making the best use of their

25 Study Table 6.8.
a Rank the countries listed in order of GNP per capita.
b Using the other indicators of development, comment on the relationship between level of GNP and standard of living.
c Compare the standard of living in these NICs with that of selected African countries in Table 1.6.

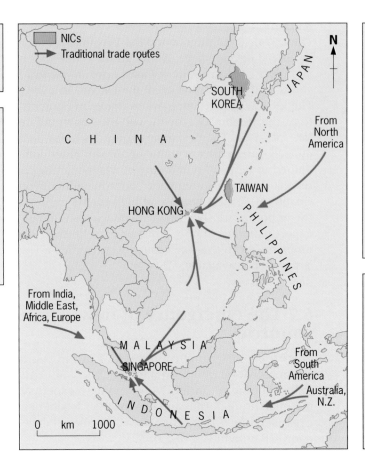

General problems
- Lack a raw material base
- Lack wealthy domestic markets

General advantages
- Relatively well–educated workforce
- Adoption of export–oriented policies
- Beneficial interventionist policies of own governments
- Influence of Japan and the USA in establishing industries and in technology transfer
- Hong Kong used as China's back door

Historical advantages
- Convergence of trade routes
- Influence of British Empire's worldwide trading network on Hong Kong and Singapore
- Hong Kong and Singapore developed as entrepôts, i.e. ports without duties
- Industry, transport links, trade and education of Taiwan and South Korea influenced by Japanese colonial rule and domination until 1945; adoption of Japanese work ethic
- Substantial economic and technical aid and investment given by USA to Taiwan and South Korea, 1951–65

Historical disadvantages
- Immigration since WW2 from China into Hong Kong and Singapore
- Korea devastated and divided after 1950–53 Korean war
- Taiwan received huge numbers of Chinese refugees after 1949 changing the island's demography and politics
- Singapore's withdrawal from the Federation of Malaysia (1965) meant loss of access to raw materials

Figure 6.24 South-East Asia's newly industrialising countries

Figure 6.25 Changing structure of exports from selected NICs, 1960–92 (*Source:* World Bank)

workforce. During the 1960s and 1970s the NIC governments used this cheap labour as a major resource in their development plans. One obvious result of cheap labour was the relocation of transnational corporations (TNCs), particularly those from Japan, to the NICs. The TNCs then gained the economic advantages of low labour costs, while people in the NICs were employed and the countries invested in the industrial process. Since then, the NICs have developed more capital-intensive mature industries, such as electronics, and now export a wider range of products. (Fig. 6.25).

Historical human influences
With both the colonial and industrial influence of Japan came the adoption of the 'Japanese work ethic'. This is the belief in the virtue of hard work, allegiance to employers and the importance of harmony in the workplace.

We can also see the influence of other countries through political factors. Many capitalist entrepreneurs fled from Communist China and set up businesses in places such as Taiwan and Hong Kong. Similarly, many Chinese from Malaysia migrated to Singapore also seeking greater business opportunities (see section 4.7).

Education
The levels of education in these four NICs are relatively high, certainly higher than in most African countries (see Figs 6.20, 6.12). A common feature of the NICs is that their governments have always shown a commitment to improving the quality of education for their people. In fact, everybody in Taiwan, Singapore, Hong Kong and South Korea has access to primary and secondary school facilities. Even female enrolment in education is high (Table 6.9). Literacy rates are high, and the numbers of people receiving higher education are increasing.

26 Study Figure 6.25 and describe the changing structure of exports for each country for the period 1960–92.

27 Explain why the use of human resources has allowed the Asian group of NICs to develop their industries successfully.

28a Assess the influence of Japan in the emergence of the Asian NICs.
b In which ways has Japan benefited from economic ties with these NICs?

29a Draw a diagram to illustrate the linkages which might develop between industries in a typical NIC.
b Describe how these linkages might influence the growth or decline of the economy.

30 Analyse the four Asian NICs and identify common factors in their economic success.

Table 6.9 Female enrolment in education (% of total number in educational age group), 1988–90 and female literacy rates, 1989 (*Sources: Human Development Report*, United Nations Development Programme, 1993; *Infrastructure for Development*, World Development Report, World Bank, 1994)

Region	Country	Primary	Secondary	Tertiary	Female literacy rates (age 15–24)
NICs	Philippines	98	75	28	92
	Thailand	88	32	16	96
	Malaysia	93	58	7	83
	South Korea	100	86	28	*
	Singapore	100	71	*	96
Africa	Ethiopia	24	12	1	*
	Malawi	52	3	1	31
	Nigeria	62	17	2	31
	Sudan	43	17	2	14
	Mali	14	4	1	14
	Kenya	93	19	1	49

NB: In most countries primary age group is 6–11 years, secondary age group 12–16 and tertiary age is over 16 years.

Industrial changes

With such human influences from abroad and a workforce which is being increasingly educated, the NICs have successfully improved both the skills and productivity of their people. This enables the NICs to use their human resources to the utmost and so develop new areas of **comparative advantage**, that is, provide cost advantages for the production of certain products. For example, the NICs traditionally enjoyed comparative advantages in the textiles and footwear industries because of their cheap labour. However, as living standards have risen in the NICs, labour is no longer as cheap and such products are manufactured more cheaply elsewhere. Countries like India and Bangladesh have developed their own textile industries using even cheaper labour. The NICs have therefore had to diversify their industrial base because of the increased competition and reduction of potential markets.

In response, the NICs shifted to less labour-intensive, more skill-intensive and more technologically advanced industries (Fig. 6.26). These include electronics, machinery, motor vehicles and chemicals.

As the range of skills of the workforce improves, including management techniques, the production process becomes more efficient and technologically more advanced goods will be developed. This trend conforms with the product life theory, which suggests that countries at different stages of development will produce different kinds of products, which will eventually be replaced as technology progresses.

Figure 6.26 Hi-tech industry: working on circuit boards, Taipei, Taiwan

South Korea: a miracle of economic development

Before the Korean War (1950–3) Korea was one country. The political differences, expressed in the war, meant that in 1953 Korea was divided into two countries of similar size. The Communist-controlled North Korea was backed by China and the former USSR and is located in the northern half of the Korean peninsula. The capitalist Republic of South Korea is separated from North Korea along the 38th parallel (Fig. 6.27). Unlike its northern neighbour, South Korea was supported by the USA and Japan and has since adopted an extremely successful export-oriented economic policy.

Early stages of economic growth

After the Korean war, the USA gave enormous amounts of economic and military aid to South Korea. This was in the form of cheap loans, technical expertise and military equipment. This external support gave South Koreans the basis for economic development. They used the funds to provide extensive education services, improve their infrastructure and create some **import-substitution** industries. However, the gathering pace of development during the 1960s was brought about by the determination of the South Korean people themselves.

After 1960, the country entered the take-off stage (see Fig. 6.21). Its growth rate (real GDP) averaged 10 per cent per annum during 1960–80, exceeding even Japanese growth (Table 6.10). Rapid expansion in manufacturing output led to a 34 per cent growth in exports during the 1960s and a 23 per cent growth rate during the 1970s (Table 6.11). Such growth could not be sustained for ever, but South Korea was able to transform itself from a poor-income country to a middle-income one in a relatively short time.

Import substitution and export-led growth in the 1960s

During the 1950s, the South Korean government protected any new or infant industries by tariffs and quotas. New domestic industries were to provide for the needs of the home market as much as possible. This is referred to as inward-looking policy and is known as import substitution.

Figure 6.27 South Korea

The government encouraged labour-intensive industries to produce manufactured goods for export and so create much-needed employment. These goods included textiles, clothing, footwear and leather products. South Korea enjoyed a comparative advantage in the promotion of such labour-intensive activities because wage rates were low and the resulting goods could then be sold at competitive prices.

State intervention, or government policy, was therefore aimed at stimulating the growth of exports. Devaluation of the currency in 1962 meant that exports were even more competitive because it reduced their price on world markets. In addition, the government offered tax incentives and loans to businesses. The creation of free trade zones also encouraged foreign businesses to invest in South Korea. Such investors as AEG of Germany and Kawasaki of Japan, were then allowed to take their profits back to their own countries.

Table 6.10 South Korea

Year	GNP per capita (US$)
1977	820
1982	2 010
1991	6 330

Table 6.11 Steel and car production in South Korea

	1970	1980	1982	1984	1986	1988	1990
Steel production (million tonnes)	0.5	10.2	11.8	13	14.6	19.1	23.1
Car production (thousands)	—	57	98	167	458	868	968

Change of policy during the 1970s and 1980s

The South Korean government's policy was to create a heavy-industrial base. Such industries as iron and steel, shipbuilding, machinery and petrochemicals were intended to provide a foundation for further economic development.

Although South Korea has few raw materials and by the 1970s was receiving little foreign aid, the country was able to expand its industry because of large internal savings. As in the previous decade, the government provided cheap loans and subsidies to investors, and so attracted many local and foreign businesses. Often huge plants, especially in shipbuilding and iron and steel, were chosen for government industrial support (Fig. 6.28). South Korea's principal trading partners are Japan, the USA, Singapore, Hong Kong, Germany, Malaysia, Australia, the UK and Canada.

With some technical support from Japan and the United States, South Korea developed new high-technology industries and increased exports in shipbuilding, machinery, steel and electronics (Table 6.12). It would have been difficult for a country such as South Korea, as well as other NICs, to have invested enough without transnational capital.

Table 6.12 South Korea: value of exports

Year	Value of exports (US$)
1971	88 million
1981	2 .2 billion
1992	76 billion

Strengthening the economy

In 1980 different parts of South Korea's economy became linked. For example, petrochemicals produce synthetic fibres for the textile industries. They also provide the basis for the manufacturing of fertilisers and drugs.

Towards the end of the 1980s, and during the beginning of the 1990s, the South Korean government concentrated investment in light industry. This was

Figure 6.28 Hyundai shipyard: South Korea's shipbuilding industry has grown spectacularly. In 1974, it ranked 70th in the world; in 1981 it was 2nd after only Japan. Hyundai has one of the world's largest shipyards at over 500 000m^2, with 45 ships under construction at once using modern equipment, cheap raw materials and a cheap, highly disciplined labour force.

partly in response to a more hostile international market, protectionist policies and slower growth in world trade. The policy improved South Korean goods and concentrated on the production of more expensive consumer items such as electronics and high quality textiles. While during the early 1980s, the bulk of production was in consumer electronics such as televisions and videos, South Korea has since diversified into more advanced areas such as semi-conductors, including large integrated circuits, electronic industrial plant, computers and telecommunications.

31 Use Figure 6.27 to give the geographical advantages and disadvantages of South Korea for industrial development.

32 Explain how South Korea's change of economic policy affected the value of exports (Table 6.12).

33 Describe the extent to which the South Korean experience fits Rostow's model of industrial development.

6.8 Transnational corporations and economic dependency

Transnational corporations (TNCs) are very large firms with branches, or subsidiary companies, in more than one country. Since World War 2 there has been a considerable increase in the number of TNCs as they have taken over smaller firms. More recently, their numbers are falling as individual TNCs have merged with others. As a result, these bigger organisations hold even more economic power and influence. The main advantage of TNCs is the large scale of their operations which enables them to run efficiently and reduce operational

With so many commodity producers and so few buyers the price will tend to stay low

Cereals
5 companies
77%

Bananas
3 companies
80%

Cocoa
3 companies
83%

Tea
3 companies
85%

Tobacco
4 companies
87%

Figure 6.29 Percentage market share of transnational companies in world primary commodity trade (*Source:* Christian Aid, *A Raw Deal*, 1992)

costs. TNCs have the capital to establish large plants which lower unit costs and this allows them to make savings known as **economies of scale**. Reduced costs from mass production lead to increased profits and so TNCs can invest heavily in research, marketing, advertising and general development. This concentrated investment increases competition in the global markets.

Companies such as Nestlé, Hitachi and Unilever each have turnovers of approximately UK£20 billion per annum. In 1992, this exceeded the total value of the exports of all but five of the world's developing countries. In the mid-1990s, just 500 TNCs controlled 70 per cent of world trade, 80 per cent of world investment and 30 per cent of the global GDP.

Developing countries and TNCs

TNCs have a very powerful influence on developing countries and their economies. In many cases, the corporations control most, if not all, activities involved with a product from producing the raw material, through to processing, packaging, transport, advertising and sales. TNCs now tend to dominate the world's primary production (Fig. 6.29). Unilever, with its subsidiaries Lipton and Brooke Bond, for example, controls at least 30 per cent of world tea production, processing and trade.

Investment

Many TNCs provide developing countries with necessary investment and the provision of skills and technology. None the less, the growing influence and economic power of the TNCs in developing countries can create some long-term economic and political problems for their host nations. For example, a TNC may decide to switch production from one country to another, or it may radically change its production processes and operational strategies by, for instance, either increasing production or closing a branch plant. Such decisions are usually made thousands of miles away at the TNC headquarters.

Decision-making

The headquarters and research and development activities of TNCs are most likely to be based in the developed countries of Western Europe, the USA and Japan, where the companies had their origins. These major decision-making regions constitute the global **core**, while the developing countries (where the TNCs locate their routine production activities) are the **peripheral** regions (Fig. 6.30, see section 1.4).

?

34 Describe the stages of income generation and regional economic growth which follow the establishment of a TNC in:
• a developed country and
• a developing country.

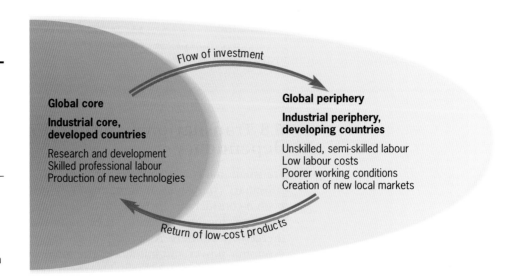

Global core

Industrial core, developed countries

Research and development
Skilled professional labour
Production of new technologies

Flow of investment

Global periphery

Industrial periphery, developing countries

Unskilled, semi-skilled labour
Low labour costs
Poorer working conditions
Creation of new local markets

Return of low-cost products

Figure 6.30 The international division of labour

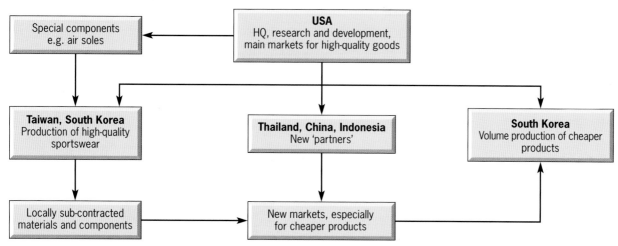

Figure 6.31 The structure of a typical TNC: Nike

Nike worldwide

An example of a TNC with different operations spread through numerous countries is Nike (Fig. 6.31). Nike operates in more than 80 countries worldwide. The company has three major headquarters in Hong Kong (covering Asia), the Netherlands (covering Europe) and the USA (covering the world). Sections of the operation's functions are divided globally, with design taking place in America, Asia and Europe. Manufacturing of key technical components occurs in America while subcontractors in Asia manufacture whole shoes.

Nike views its Far Eastern subcontractors as partners who are responsible for the quality of goods leaving their own factories. In addition to delegating responsibility to local factories in this way, Nike also involves the local companies in decision-making and some research and development. Company policy also tries to provide some security for factories, workers, and their country of location. Nike does this by guaranteeing with the factories that their orders for new products will not vary more than 20 per cent a month.

Overdependency

There are three main ways in which TNCs may affect the future of developing countries:

1 TNC economic domination can discourage local investment and damage indigenous enterprise.
2 Dependency on the investment and employment provided by a TNC may result in the host country losing control of its own economy, e.g. as the TNC makes decisions for its own profit and not the long-term economic prosperity of the host country.
3 The operations of TNCs may affect the welfare of the local community and the protection of the natural environment.

We can see the worst effects of TNCs in the case of the American-owned TNC, Union Carbide in India. The factory, which produced pesticides, was located 5km from the densely populated Bhopal in Madhya Pradesh. In December 1984, 45 tonnes of methycyanate gas leaked from the factory and drifted over a 7km area. An estimated 2 500 people died and over 200 000 were injured from cyanide-related poisoning. The Indian government filed for compensation from Union Carbide but with the closure of the company, victims are still waiting to receive compensation (Fig. 6.32).

Free trade zones

To attract TNCs to locate within developing countries, many of them are establishing free trade zones (Fig. 6.33).

Figure 6.32 TNC damage: Bhopal residents demonstrate against Union Carbide, 1984

Table 6.13 Advantages and disadvantages of TNCs in the host countries

Advantages to the country	Disadvantages
• Provides secure employment (in the local area) and a guaranteed income.	• Capital intensive nature of modern industry results in relatively small numbers being employed.
• Improves levels of education and skills.	• Wages usually low.
• Brings investment into the country and boosts exports to help the balance of payments (increased GDP).	• Profits usually go oversees.
• Increased personal income can lead to increased demand for consumer goods and the growth of new industries.	• GNP grows at a slower rate than that of the parent company's, widening the gap between developed and developing countries.
• Widens the economic base of the country.	• Decisions are made outside the country and the company could decide to withdraw at any time.
• Improvements in roads and other parts of the infrastructure.	• Exploitation of the workforce.
• Brings new technology to a developing country.	• Insufficient attention paid to health and safety factors or protection of the environment.

TNC activities tend to be highly mechanised and capital intensive so the growing labour force is not supplied with sufficient jobs.

Tax reductions or annual tax-free periods

Few planning controls and few import controls. Governments hope that the presence of a TNC will then start a multiplier effect and inward investment.

Cheap energy supplies

Grants for machinery and buildings; grants for training workforce

Women: 80–90% of light-assembly wokers in free trade zones are women. World-wide, women receive lower wages than men so some companies selectively employ single women. In the Philippines' Bataan Export Processing Zone, the Mattel toy company offered prizes to workers who underwent sterilisation thus avoiding maternity payments.

Trade unions are usually banned

Figure 6.33 The elements of free trade zones

35 Study Table 6.13 and consider whether the advantages of TNCs outweigh their disadvantages for the host countries.

36 Write an article for a current affairs magazine, such as *New Internationalist*, stating your own opinion towards the presence of TNCs in many developing countries. Give reasons and examples to back up your statements.

37 Design your own model of economic development along similar lines to that of Rostow's model (see section 6.6). Include the 'human' side of the industrialisation process, such as health and education, whch Rostow's model omits.

Since the early 1970s, the United Nations has been discussing a code of conduct for transnationals to establish rights and duties for both TNCs and the host countries. However, such an international agreement has proved impossible to make, primarily because of the TNCs' economic power and desire to increase their own profits. Even on a national level, when companies are threatened by regulations, they can simply close their operations and shift to another country in search of increasing profits.

Summary
- Development of human resources is essential for successful industrialisation.
- Investment in health and education is an important strategy for developing a country's human resources.
- In the developing countries, most people are employed in the informal sector.
- The weak industrial base of many developing countries means that fewer people are employed in the formal sector.
- Structural adjustment programmes introduced in many developing countries by the World Bank and IMF have led to growing levels of unemployment.
- The important role women play in social and economic activities should not be overlooked in any development strategies.
- Industrialisation has been regarded as essential to economic development since World War 2.
- Newly industrialising countries have managed to industrialise successfully by the efficient management of their human resources.
- Transnational corporations play a vital, but sometimes controversial role, in the industrial development of many countries.

7 Natural resources and development

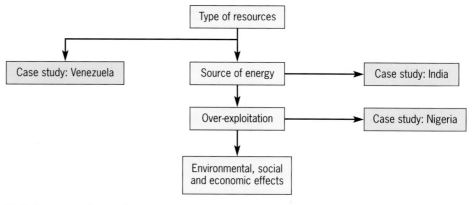

7.1 Introduction

The availability of natural resources is critical for economic development. Equally important are the uses to which resources are put and the need to manage non-renewable resources.

In this chapter, we identify the different types of natural resources and their uneven distribution. We also look at the different rates of consumption between **developed** and **developing countries** and the implications of this for all countries. We can then assess the wide gap between the wealth of the North and the poverty of the South, according to their access to and use of resources. In the light of this, we will consider the issue of **sustainability** and the growing problem of environmental pollution.

7.2 The types, nature and use of resources

A resource is something which people use to survive, to generate wealth or simply enjoy. Clean air, water and food are all basic resources which we sometimes take for granted. In fact, the earth has a vast range of natural resources which are usually divided into two categories: renewable and non-renewable (Fig. 7.1).

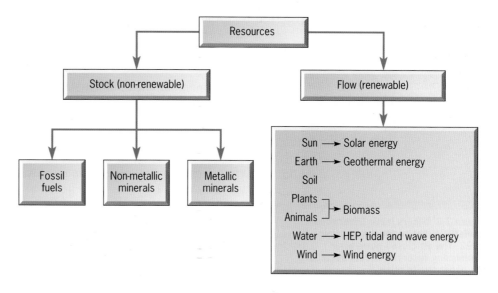

Figure 7.1 Classification of resources

Figure 7.2 Depleting renewable resources: unloading cod at Petty Harbour, the Grand Banks of Newfoundland, Canada, once the world's richest fishery. Scientists 'managing' the Banks set catch limits to allow stocks to recover but the cod catch fell from 810 000 tonnes in 1968 to 150 000 tonnes in 1977 to estimates of existing stock at 120 000 in 1992. In 1993, fishing at Grand Banks was banned altogether because there were barely enough cod to spawn.

Renewable resources

We can use a renewable resource over and over again. Soil, water, plants and animals are all renewable (**non-finite**) resources. For example, farmers use the same fields to grow crops year after year. So, in this sense, the land is renewable. Nutrients taken from the soil by plants, are returned as the plants die and decompose. The soil therefore regenerates naturally, provided the land is not used for the same crop for too many years.

However, a resource is only renewable if the rate at which it is used, the rate of depletion, does not exceed the rate at which it can regenerate itself. If a renewable resource is used faster than it can be regenerated, it may be used up or become extinct. Fish, like other animals, are a natural resource. They can be harvested regularly, but if too many are caught and faster than they can reproduce, they may die out (Fig. 7.2).

Resources that, in theory, are renewable are called **flows**, because they are in constant supply. However, as some of these resources are used more quickly than they are being replaced, environmentalists see the need for sustainability. This ensures the use of renewable resources at a rate which allows them to regenerate themselves naturally and successfully.

Non-renewable resources

Non-renewable resources are **finite** as they are limited in quantity and cannot be used more than once. They are also called **stocks**, the opposite of flows.

Minerals are the earth's non-renewable resources. These are naturally occurring elements and compounds, usually divided into four groups:

• Metals: copper, bauxite and iron.
• Industrial minerals: lime, soda ash and the by-products of coal and oil.
• Construction materials: sand and gravel.
• Energy minerals: coal, oil and natural gas (fossil fuels) and uranium (the raw material used to produce nuclear energy).

When we refer to non-renewable resources, the term resource means the quantity of a mineral known, or believed to exist, on the surface or in the earth's crust. Mineral resources are 'dynamic', that is, their quantities change as people discover new deposits. However, we call that part of a resource which we know about, and which is available for exploitation, the **reserve** (Fig. 7.3).

The life expectancy of a mineral is calculated on its reserves and the current rate of exploitation (Table 7.1). In particular, satellite imagery, also called

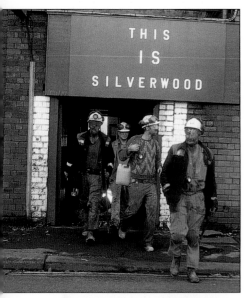

Figure 7.3 Miners leave Silverwood Colliery, Yorkshire for the last time, 1992. The pit closed down when diminishing reserves of coal became too expensive to mine.

Figure 7.4 Landsat satellite image of rock formations in central Utah, USA. The grey/brown oval-shaped feature to the right of centre is the San Rafael Swell, a plateau formed from an eroded dome formation. This is edged at left and top right by shale (blue), with thin golden brown lines indicating sandstone layers. Between this and the deep brown-coloured mountains to the left of centre is a band of the pale blue shales over which alluvial fans (red) have been deposited. The golden yellow area at bottom right is part of the San Rafael Desert. Important uranium deposits are known at the bottom end of the Swell.

Table 7.1 Estimated reserves of minerals (*Source:* Sorensen, 1989)

Mineral	Years
Lead	50
Copper	120
Tin	150
Platinum group	340
Nickel	1 500

1 Explain the factors that may influence the life expectancy of a mineral resource (Table 7.1).

2 Discuss the effects of varying 'life spans' of mineral reserves on the economies of those countries dependent on such minerals.

3a For each of the resources illustrated in Table 7.2, draw a pie chart to illustrate the percentage consumed by: • the developed and • the developing countries.
b Comment on the differences between the two pie charts.
c Work in groups. Refer to Malthusian theory (section 5.2) and discuss the implications of a `Malthusian resource crisis' for both developed and developing countries.

remote sensing, can reveal an area's geology, often uncovering specific structures that might contain valuable resources. For example, earth observation satellites, such as *Landsat,* have helped discover copper deposits in Pakistan, copper, gold and molybdenum in Mexico, alluvial tin in the Amazon and uranium in the USA and Australia (Fig. 7.4).

Calculations of mineral reserves are, though, made more difficult as scientists discover new reserves through improved research techniques. In addition, more efficient use, recycling possibilities and the discovery of cheaper alternatives, such as ethanol (alcohol fuel for cars made from sugar cane) and orimulsion (liquid coal to generate electricity), all affect the accuracy of attempts to determine the life span of minerals.

Resource use
The distribution of the world's natural resources varies globally, regionally and nationally. Similarly, the use of resources differs, but this depends on how much people need and value them. Population growth and the demands of increasingly high standards of living are two factors increasing the exploitation of natural resources.

On average, far more resources are consumed by the rich, developed nations in the North than the developing countries in the poor South (Table 7.2). Although three-quarters of the world's population lives in the developing countries, these people consume only one-sixth of the world's resources.

Table 7.2 Consumption of resources (*Source:* Parikh et al., *Consumption Patterns*, Indira Gandhi Institute of Development Research, 1991)

		Developed	Developing	Ratio
Agricultural products	– Cereals	717	247	2.9
	– Milk	320	39	8.2
	– Meat	61	11	5.5
Wood products	– Roundwood	388	399	1.1
	– Sawnwood	213	19	11.2
	– Paper	148	11	13.5
Fertilisers		70	15	4.7
Cement		451	130	3.5
Iron and steel		469	36	13.0
Aluminium		16	1	16.0
Cars (vehicles per capita)		0.28	0.01	28.0

Units: kg or m² of land required per capita

?

4 Using an atlas, trace the distribution of each of the three main categories of forest. Identify the regions where most of the three forest types are located. (The atlas may include sub-groups of these three categories. Include these in your answer.)

7.3 The distribution and use of forests

There are three main categories of forest type: tropical rainforest, temperate coniferous forest and deciduous woodland forest. Tropical rainforests are much richer in species than the other two types while the temperate vegetation is faster growing. However, many of the tropical tree species take hundreds of years to mature. The rainforest **ecosystem**, or interdependence of species, is fragile and easily disturbed, so this type of forest is more permanently destroyed than the other two.

The importance of tropical rainforests
Tropical rainforests are the richest source of life on earth (Fig. 7.5). They play a vital part in the earth's natural cycles of air, soil and water through photosynthesis, absorbing carbon dioxide and giving out the oxygen which we breathe.

Food Virtually everything we eat for breakfast (including Rice Krispies, Cornflakes and Coco Pops!) originally came from the rainforests – even eggs. The domestic chicken has been bred from the red jungle fowl of Indian forests. At least 1650 known tropical forest plants have potential as vegetable crops.

Drugs 70% of the 3000 plants identified by the US National Cancer Institute as having anti-cancer properties come from the rainforest. Thanks to the alkaloids yielded by the rosy periwinkle, a child suffering from leukaemia now has an 80% likelihood of survival. One in four household chemicals or medicines contain compounds derived from rainforest species.

Energy 1 200 hectares of the fast-growing 'ipilipil' tree could generate the fuel equivalent of 1 million barrels of oil annually. Just 6 Philippine 'petroleum nut' trees can produce 300 litres of oil annually for cooking or lighting – plantations could greatly relieve the fuelwood crisis in the developing world.

Subsistence farming Rainforests provide food and firewood for local inhabitants.

Commercial agriculture Over one-quarter of the cleared Amazon rainforest is now used for large-scale cattle ranching. Demand for cheap supplies of animal fodder in developed countries encourages cash crops grown on rainforest land, e.g. Thailand exports cassava to the EU.

Logging International timber companies fell many tropical trees to find one or two hardwoods for furniture and veneers. Many plantations are also established

Biodiversity Tropical forests have over half of the world's species in just 7% of land area with highest co-evolution: 155 000 of the known 255 000 plants; 80% of insects and 90% of primates. One hectare had 41 000 tree canopy insects including 12 000 beetles. Tropical forests are 5 to 20 times richer in trees than temperate forests.

Tourism Rainforests are fast becoming alternative exotic holiday destinations.

Figure 7.5 Tropical rainforests
(*After*: Friends of the Earth)

Effects of tropical deforestation
At present, an area of rainforest the size of England, Scotland and Wales is cut down every year (Fig. 7.6). Already this depletion has had serious social, economic and environmental consequences locally, regionally and globally (Fig. 7.7). Intensive cash-crop production in many cleared rainforests has robbed the soil of its nutrients and led to severe land degradation. Similarly, timber and mining concessions, granted to multinationals, mean that much forest is cleared for logging, mines and roads. Landowners and commercial farmers have cleared vast belts of rainforest for large-scale farm production. In the process, they have evicted many smallholders who have then been forced to migrate to the over-crowded cities. Other small-scale farmers have been forced to move on to marginal land with poorer soils.

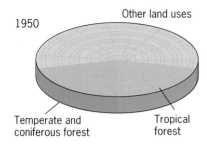

1950

Other land uses

Temperate and
coniferous forest

Tropical
forest

1975

2000

Figure 7.6 Shrinking forests

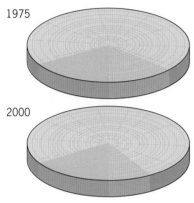

Depletion of temperate forest reserves

Thousands of years ago, much of the earth was covered by forest, but since people started to cultivate the land, they have used up forest reserves. For example, the United States has lost one third of its forest cover and 85 per cent of its primary forest (excluding Alaska). Europe has virtually no primary forest left, with its remaining forests being managed plantations of just a few commercial tree species. China has lost three-quarters of its forest while most of the world's remaining temperate forest areas are in Canada and Russia. Temperate-zone forests are now mostly stable in area, though many of the soil nutrients in them are declining, together with the wood quality and the growth rate.

The pressure on temperate-zone forests

Temperate forests are under threat from growing environmental pollution. Air pollution from industry, energy generation and transport has increased the concentration of sulphur dioxide and oxides of nitrogen in the atmosphere to create acid rain. This, in turn, leads to the slow death of vast areas of forest as trees lose their vegetation and growth is retarded. Also, as soils become more acidic the forests become less able to regenerate themselves.

To satisfy the demand for increasing amounts of softwood, which is used to produce paper, many governments in developed countries are actively encouraging afforestation programmes (replanting trees). For example, the British government has increased the forested area of Britain from 5 per cent to 9 per cent by giving tax incentives to those who plant and maintain forested areas, and by supporting the work of the Forestry Commission.

The link between deforestation and development

Some development experts suggest that there is a close link between deforestation and growing levels of debt in many developing countries (see section 2.4). The pressure on many developing countries to increase their **GNP**s as quickly as possible, to help pay back their debts, has forced them to exploit their natural resources, including forests, for export (Fig. 7.8).

Some of those developing countries with large debts and large areas of tropical rainforest also have high deforestation rates. In fact, the value of tropical timber from developing countries has increased enormously during the last few decades, rising from US$500 million per annum in 1960 to an estimated US$20 000 million per annum in 1994. In spite of this huge increase in the value of tropical rainforest products, a high percentage of the export earnings for many developing countries is still used to service their debts and gain valued foreign currency.

Figure 7.7 Settlers clearing rainforest to grow crops and grass. Locally: the soil soon loses its quality and settlers are forced to abandon the land. Nationally: loss of rainforest may upset the water cycle in northern Brazil and so influence rainfall and human activities over a much wider area.

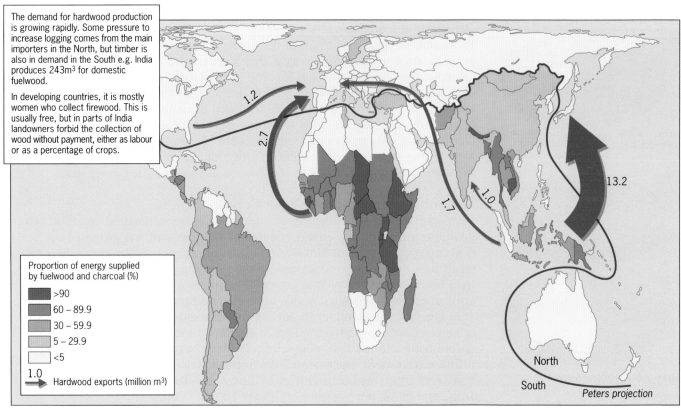

The demand for hardwood production is growing rapidly. Some pressure to increase logging comes from the main importers in the North, but timber is also in demand in the South e.g. India produces 243m³ for domestic fuelwood.

In developing countries, it is mostly women who collect firewood. This is usually free, but in parts of India landowners forbid the collection of wood without payment, either as labour or as a percentage of crops.

Proportion of energy supplied by fuelwood and charcoal (%)

- >90
- 60 – 89.9
- 30 – 59.9
- 5 – 29.9
- <5

1.0
→ Hardwood exports (million m³)

North
South
Peters projection

Figure 7.8 Where the wood goes

5 You are researching wood energy sources for the Food and Agriculture Organisation.
a Use Figure 7.8 to describe regional variations in the proportions of energy supplied by fuelwood and charcoal.
b Write an outline plan suggesting how people dependent on fuelwood could manage this resource.
c Assume that your research team succeeds in developing a sustainable plan for fuelwood management. Assess the long-term benefits of your plan.

6 Which of the environmental consequences of deforestation is likely to have the greatest long-term effects on the global ecosystem?

Fuelwood
Natural vegetation, especially wood, is the oldest resource to be exploited by people. In fact, in 1995 wood is still the single most important source of energy for many developing countries (Fig. 7.8). It accounts for up to 60 per cent of energy consumption in Africa, and for a global energy average of about 6 per cent. However, in many parts of the world, the exploitation of firewood far exceeds its regeneration. As a result, the depletion of fuelwood in developing countries is as serious an energy crisis as the dwindling of fossil fuel reserves for developed countries.

7.4 The distribution and use of minerals

Minerals are naturally occurring inorganic substances. A mineral resource, or deposit, exists when there is a concentration of minerals which would be economically profitable for people to mine (Fig. 7.9).

Non-fuel minerals
The distribution of minerals is spread unevenly throughout the world. Some countries have a lot of valuable minerals which, with metals, they are dependent on for over 50 per cent of their exports. For example, Zambia is a major world supplier of copper and cobalt. These two minerals earn at least 85 per cent of the country's annual foreign exchange, along with lead, zinc, gold, tin and coal. Although Zaire is the world's largest producer of cobalt and industrial diamonds, copper is its most valuable exported mineral giving 55 per cent of Zaire's export earnings. It also exports uranium, tin, gold, silver, zinc, manganese, tungsten and cadmium.

An ore is a metal-bearing rock which occurs naturally in the earth's crust. Table 7.3 lists the economically most important metallic ores. Different rocks have varying degrees of concentration of metal. Where there is a particularly low percentage of metal in the ore, it becomes uneconomic to mine the rock for its metal content. The cut-off grade is the lowest concentration of metal

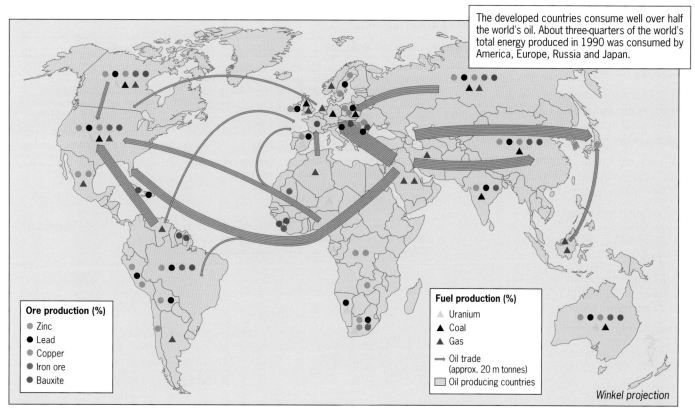

The developed countries consume well over half the world's oil. About three-quarters of the world's total energy produced in 1990 was consumed by America, Europe, Russia and Japan.

Ore production (%)
- Zinc
- Lead
- Copper
- Iron ore
- Bauxite

Fuel production (%)
- Uranium
- Coal
- Gas
- Oil trade (approx. 20 m tonnes)
- Oil producing countries

Winkel projection

Figure 7.9 World ore and fuel production

7 Study Table 7.3. Using an economic atlas, identify the countries with the largest deposits of those minerals listed.

8a Find out how much the earnings from these minerals contribute to each country's GDP.
b Which of these countries are developing?
c Discuss the economic results for a developing country which gains large export earnings from mineral deposits.

9a List some of the economically important uses of the minerals in Table 7.3.
b Identify four or five household items which contain some of the metals listed in Table 7.3.
c Suggest reasons why those countries depending heavily on mineral exports have low GDPs.

10 How much are developed countries dependent on mineral exporting countries for the production of consumer goods?

necessary to make the ore worth mining. If more efficient methods of extracting minerals were invented or if the price of a mineral rises, then the cut-off grade may go down.

Table 7.3 Economically important minerals (*Source:* Meadows, Meadows, Randers, *Beyond the Limits*, Earthscan, 1992)

Element	Percentage of the earth's crust	Cut-off grade as a percentage of the resource
Mercury	0.0000089	0.1
Tungsten	0.00011	0.45
Lead	0.0012	4
Chromium	0.011	23
Tin	0.00017	0.35
Silver	0.0000075	0.01
Gold	0.00000035	0.00035
Molybdenum	0.00013	0.1
Zinc	0.0094	3.5
Manganese	0.13	25
Nickel	0.0089	0.9
Cobalt	0.0025	0.2
Phosphorus	0.12	8.8
Copper	0.0063	0.35
Titanium	0.64	10
Iron	5.820	20
Aluminium	8.3	18.5

Fuels

The Industrial Revolution, which took place in the developed countries from 1750 to the late 1800s, was based largely on the supply of non-renewable sources of energy. Even today, industrialised countries consume large and increasing quantities of non-renewable fossil fuels such as oil, coal and gas (Table 7.4, Fig. 7.9).

7

11 Study Figure 7.9 and describe the major oil-source regions and the major oil-receiving regions.

12 What does the world's flow of oil tell you about the varying levels of industrial activities in different regions of the world?

13 To what extent is the Middle East strategically important to the world's energy supply (Fig. 7.10)?

14 In what ways could: • the supply of oil and • the prices of oil, be affected by political instability in this region?

15 Comment on the distribution of uranium deposits in relation to the **North/South divide**.

Table 7.4 Fuel resources

Resource	Locational examples	Uses	Problems
Oil	Middle East: more than half the world's oil reserves are in Saudi Arabia, Iraq, Kuwait and Abu Dhabi USA: 6 per cent	Petrol, aviation fuel, diesel oil, chemical industries, gases, asphalt, domestic heat	Oil spillage e.g. Exxon Valdez, 1989; Ogoni Land, Nigeria; effluents affect vegetation, marine life; cause of international conflict, e.g. Gulf War, 1991
Natural gas	Canada, North Sea, former USSR	Chemical industries, fuels	Transported by pipeline; impact on natural environment; leakage.
Uranium	Australia, Africa, North America; Canada is the world's leading producer since it exploited a rich vein averaging 2% uranium at Key Lake in Saskatchewan	Nuclear power for electricity	Threat of radiation leaks, e.g. Chernobyl, April 1986
Coal	USA, Canada, W & E Europe, former USSR, Australasia and China	Thermal power for electricity, coal by-products used in chemical industry	Emissions of SO_2 contributes to acid rain

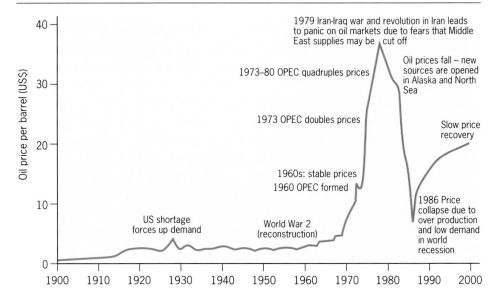

Figure 7.10 Oil prices in the twentieth century

Exploitation of natural resources in Venezuela

Venezuela is one of the wealthiest nations in South America with one of the world's fastest growing economies (Table 7.5). It owes its wealth to the mineral and energy resources of many kinds throughout the country (Figs 7.11–7.12). However, although Venezuela has vast mineral resources, non-oil mining contributes less than one per cent towards the country's GDP.

Coal

Venezuela has huge reserves of coal, estimated at over 2 billion tonnes, much of which are in the Guasare open-cast mine in the western state of Zulia. There are plans to invest in a port-and-rail infrastructure to transport the coal, which should help make it possible to increase production to 20 million tonnes per annum by the end of the 1990s. In eastern Venezuela, the Fila Maestra

mine, which produced 0.3 million tonnes in 1992, is part-owned by the Japanese **transnational corporation** (**TNC**) Mitsubishi. Most of Venezuela's coal is exported with 1.85 million tonnes sold to the EU, Scandinavia, the USA and the Caribbean in 1991.

16 Use Table 7.5 to make some comparisons of Venezuela with other South American countries and the UK.

17a Use Table 7.5 and Figure 7.11 to identify problems faced by Venezuela.
b Suggest how Venezuela's use of resources can help with these problems.

Table 7.5 Venezuela: basic and comparative data, 1993 (*Source:* IMF, World Bank)

Country	Area (000km²)	Population (millions)	Population growth (%)	Urban population (%)	Life expectancy	Infant mortality, 1993 (per 1000 births)	GNP per capita (US$)	Inflation, av. 1985–93 (%)
Venezuela	912	20.7	2.5	84	70	20.2	2 840	35.2
Colombia	1 139	35.6	1.8	68	69	33	1 400	25.6
Argentina	2 768	32.31	1.3	86	68	25.6	6 050	—
UK	242	58.4	0.2	92	76	6.6	17 970	5.7

Deforestation rate
1% net annual
Mining/quarrying
Diamonds: 219 000 carats
Iron ore: 11 770 000 metric tons
Phosphate rock: 100 000 metric tons
Gold: 4 670 kilograms
Oil industry
• production peaked in 1970
• nationalised in 1975
• reserves of heavy and medium crudes estimated at 64 billion barrels (largest in the western hemisphere)
• 1993 accounts for: 23% GDP; 74% export earnings; 61% central government revenues (1993)

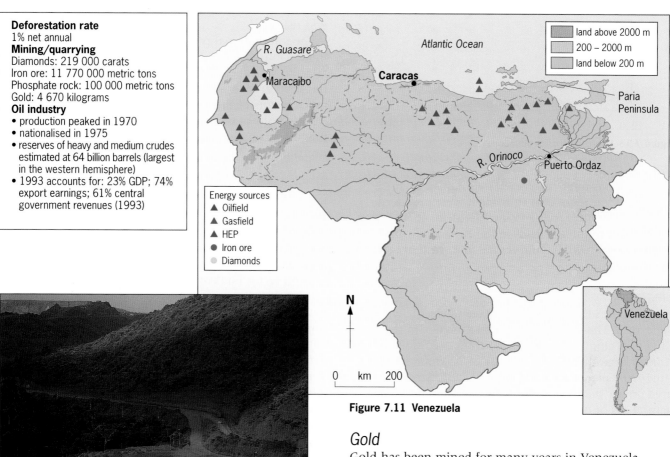

Figure 7.11 Venezuela

Figure 7.12 Iron ore mining, Cerro Rico, Venezuela

Bauxite

The Venezuelan government owns a bauxite mine in south-east Venezuela. Aluminium is the country's second most important export commodity after oil and the largest alumina factory in South America is located at Puerto Ordaz on the River Orinoco. In 1990, 0.6 million tonnes of aluminium were produced and the government plans to increase this output to 2 million by the year 2000. Cheap hydro-electric power (HEP) has enabled Venezuela to become the world's lowest-cost producer of aluminium. This is because the production of aluminium from bauxite requires vast amounts of electricity.

Gold

Gold has been mined for many years in Venezuela, although much of the output is produced illegally by unofficial or 'wildcat' miners known as *garimpeiros*. The use of mercury for the extraction of gold has led to serious environmental degradation in many parts of eastern Venezuela.

Oil

Thirteen per cent of Venezuela's GDP comes from oil exports. Venezuela is in fact the world's ninth largest producer of oil and was a founder member of OPEC (Organisation of Petroleum Exporting Countries) in 1960 (see Fig. 7.10). The country's oil industry was nationalised in 1975. However, Venezuela's 1992 oil production levels were lower than those of the early 1970s because of quotas imposed by OPEC to avoid a fall in the price of oil on world markets (Fig. 7.13). None the less, new oil discoveries continue to be made and export revenues reached US$10.1 billion in 1990.

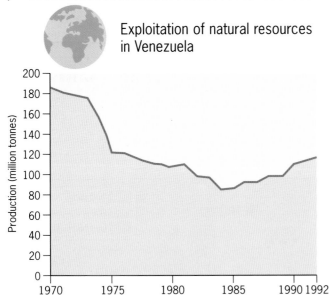

Exploitation of natural resources in Venezuela

Figure 7.13 Venezuela: oil production

Natural gas

Venezuela has huge reserves of natural gas. In 1992, 31 million tonnes of coal equivalent were produced. The government is trying to increase demand by laying pipelines from the gas fields in the Paria Peninsula to the industrial towns in the central and western parts of the country.

Electricity

HEP produces the largest percentage of electricity in Venezuela. The Guri hydro-electric complex in the Guyana region (south of Cuidad Guayana) is one of world's largest and has a capacity of 1000 megawatts. Other HEP plants are under construction. Small oil-fired power stations are also being converted to burn natural gas or orimulsion (a new 'liquid coal' developed jointly by British Petroleum and Venezuela's national oil company).

Economic outlook

For most of the 20th century the economy of Venezuela has been based on the exploitation of petroleum and petroleum products. Before then, the country's economy was based on agricultural exports, in particular coffee and cocoa. Investment of the proceeds of the oil industry gave Venezuela high rates of growth and rising standards of living in those years when demand for oil was steady and the international price was rising.

The international recession of 1979–81 led to a slump in demand for oil and collapse in prices which seriously affected Venezuela's economy. Since then the country has tried to diversify its economic base by encouraging other sectors of the economy, for example exploiting rich deposits of other minerals and by developing manufacturing industries and services, including tourism (Figs 7.14–7.15).

In 1995, Venezuela's economic policy is concentrated on dealing with the combined effects of recession, the large budget deficit and high inflation (Table 7.6). Economic growth contracted by 3.3 per cent in 1994, compared with just –0.4 in 1993. In fact, it was only a strong performance by the oil sector which prevented Venezuela's economy from worsening further, as the non-oil sector had contracted by 5.3 per cent.

In spite of the increasing revenue from oil, the external debt problem in Venezuela remains. It was hoped that huge reserves of oil would guard against deficits, but the drop in oil prices in the late 1970s and early 1980s, caused Venezuela to fall into debt. In 1993, Venezuela's debt had grown to US$35.5 billion, that is 70 per cent of the country's GDP. Interest payments in that year amounted to 20 per cent of the total export revenue. Venezuela's economic growth and future thus depends very heavily on a stable international oil price.

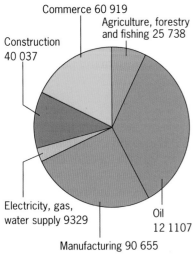

Figure 7.14 Venezuela: structure of GDP by sector (billion Bolivars), 1993 (*Source*: Banco Central)

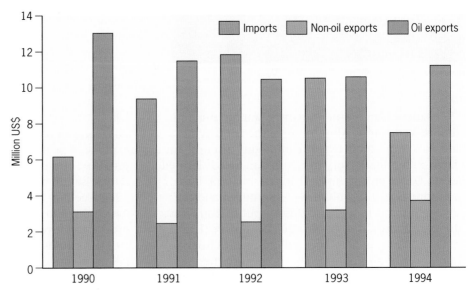

Figure 7.15 Venezuela: external trade (*Source*: IMF)

18 You are a fund manager looking to invest in a South American country. Use all the information in this section to decide whether or not to move into Venezuela. Give reasons for your decision.

Table 7.6 Venezuela: growth indicators (*Source:* IMF; Dun & Bradstreet's International Risk & Payment Review)

	1989	1990	1991	1992	1993	1994
Real GDP growth (%)	8.3	4.5	10.4	7.3	-0.4	-3.3
Oil production (%)	6.8	5.3	10.3	–0.3	3.4	5.7
Inflation (%)	—	—	31	31.9	45.9	70.8
Unemployment (% of workforce)	—	—	8.9	7.9	6.6	8.7

Exploitation and poison leave the North Sea fighting for survival

THE North Sea is in danger of becoming an empty sea, its previous abundance threatened by the twin problems of pollution and over-exploitation of fish stocks.

Ten years of failure to stop the rape of the sea by European Community's common fisheries policy and the accumulation of heavy metals, chemicals and excess nutrients are alarming many North Sea states.

Overfishing is reducing dramatically catches of species like cod and haddock, and wiping out breeding stocks.

Cod catches landed in Britain have dropped from 366 674 tonnes in 1970 to 148 024 in 1980 and 74 000 tonnes in 1990. The figures for haddock have dropped from 179 527 tonnes to 52 115 over the same period.

The question is how to reconcile the desire of the EC public for more and more fish, the wish of thousands of fishermen to continue their way of life, and the fact that soon there will be too few fish in the North Sea, English Channel and Irish Sea to make it worthwhile casting a net.

Figure 7.17 Disaster facing the seas and jobs (*Source:* Paul Brown, *The Guardian*, 17 August 1992)

19 Given the trend in population growth (see section 3.4), suggest how the world's resource use shown in Figure 7.16 is likely to change.

20 What are the likely social, economic and political effects of fish declines on the populations whose livelihood depends on fishing (Fig. 7.17)?

7.5 Over-exploitation of resources

Resource consumption patterns show that the developed countries use an unequal share of the earth's resources (see Table 7.2). As the developing countries also try to industrialise, following the rich North's example, they too cling to the idea that economic growth is the key to employment, social mobility and technological advance. Consequently, as the supply of natural resources lessens, both the developed and the developing countries must consider how best to conserve these resources. At the same time, they will continue trying to raise the standard of living for their populations although the world's increasing population means that more resources are used (Fig. 7.16).

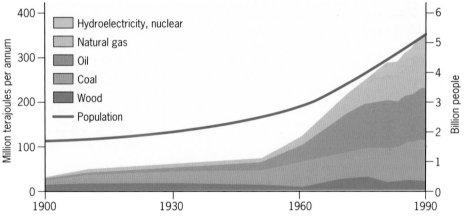

Figure 7.16 World resource consumption and population growth

Environmental, social and economic effects
The high rate of exploitation and depletion of the earth's natural resources has serious social and economic implications for both the developed and developing countries.

Declining fisheries
Both pollution and over-harvesting of the world's fishery resources have resulted in a steep decline in fish catches and the near extinction of some species of fish (Fig. 7.17, see Fig. 7.2). For example, of the 30 species that once supported commercial fisheries in the Black Sea, only five remain by the mid-1990s. The Black Sea is a dumping ground for chemical and organic pollutants from countries around its shores. As a result of pollution and over-harvesting during the last decade, the total fish catch in the Black Sea has fallen from 700 000 to 100 000 tonnes. Similarly, we can see declining fish resources in other world fishing regions, such as in the north-west Atlantic where the catch has fallen by 42 per cent in twenty years and in the north-west Pacific where it fell by 10 per cent between 1988 and 1992.

Burning fossil fuels
When fossil fuels burn, waste gases are released. Large quantities of these gases can be toxic and this therefore affects both our health and pollutes the environment.

Global warming and the greenhouse effect

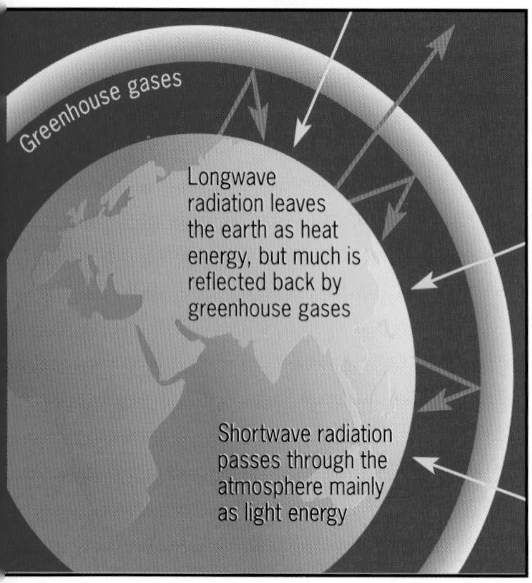

One of the main waste gases emitted by burning fossil fuels is carbon dioxide (CO_2). CO_2 is also one of several greenhouse gases (Table 7.7). These are important for trapping some of the sun's heat in our atmosphere and so maintaining temperatures (Fig. 7.18). Without this **greenhouse effect**, temperatures on earth would fall at least 30°C and so life could not exist. However, an accumulation of greenhouse gases is also harmful to life. This is because the more gases there are in the atmosphere, the more heat is trapped at the earth's surface. Scientists blame the large-scale consumption of fossil fuels, especially by the developed industrial nations (Fig. 7.19), for the increasing CO_2 in the atmosphere. In turn, scientists consider this CO_2 to be responsible for **global warming**, or raising the temperature of the earth's atmosphere. Although some researchers still question the evidence for global warming, there are indications that temperatures are on the increase (Fig. 7.20).

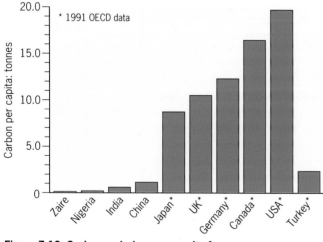

Figure 7.18 The greenhouse effect

Table 7.7 Relative contribution to the greenhouse effect of various greenhouse gases

Greenhouse gas	Source	Approximate relative greenhouse effect per molecule	Current rate of increase (% pa)
Carbon dioxide (CO_2)	Exchanged naturally between the atmosphere, oceans and the living world. The burning of fossil fuels and the loss of tropical rainforests adds to the normal amount.	1	0.5
Methane (CH_4)	Natural gas from rocks, swamps, rice fields and animals.	21	0.9
Nitrous oxide (N_2O)		290	0.25
Chlorofluorocarbons (CFCs) CFC11 } CFC12 }	Aerosols, fridges, blown plastic, packaging.	3 500 7 300	4 4

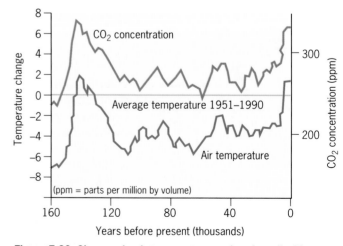

Figure 7.19 Carbon emissions per capita from energy use (*Source:* OECD, 1991, *New Internationalist*, April 1992)

Figure 7.20 Changes in air temperature and carbon dioxide concentrations

21 Work in groups.
a Suggest ways of reducing gas emissions.
b Which of your suggestions: • can individuals do, • need government involvement?

22 You have been approached by the United Nations Environment Programme (UNEP) to join an international group examining the greenhouse effect. Your task is to write a report on the greenhouse effect for presentation at a UN conference. Your report should comment on the following:
• evidence for the greenhouse effect.
• the implications of the greenhouse effect.
• the political options for limiting social and economic damage.

Figure 7.21 Tree damaged by acid rain, Bavaria, Germany

Acid rain

Burning coal also produces sulphur dioxide (SO_2), or acid gas. In turn, sulphur dioxide combines with water vapour to form **acid rain**. Acid rain upsets the chemical balance of the soil, making it difficult for plants to absorb nutrients (Fig. 7.21), while the chemicals in acid rain are also dangerous to marine life.

Cars and aircraft run on oil-based products that emit nitrogen oxides (NO_x), gases which contribute to the formation of acid rain. Hydrocarbons, either from car exhausts or from industrial activities, usually react with ultra-violet radiation from the sun to produce photochemical smog near the ground. The resultant poor air quality irritates the eyes and lungs and, for some people, causes asthma.

Ozone

Ozone (O_3) in the ozone layer filters out ultra-violet short-wave radiation from the sun. Since the 1970s, scientists have observed that the ozone layer above both the Arctic and Antarctic has thinned. Many people believe the cause of this depletion is human interference with the atmosphere, particularly by the use of chlorofluorocarbons (CFCs). CFCs release chlorine into the atmosphere and this eventually breaks down ozone. In addition, vehicle and aircraft exhausts react with ultra-violet radiation to produce nitrogen oxides which also destroy ozone. Ultimately, destruction of the ozone layer means that harmful ultra-violet radiation can reach the earth's surface. Some scientists link this radiation to increases in skin cancer and cataracts in humans and a reduction of growth and photosynthesis in plants.

Green economics

As people become more concerned over the global environmental and health problems caused by burning fossil fuels, they have developed measures to reduce greenhouse gases (Table 7.8). In addition, while much of the cause and effects of pollution are seen in the developed North, there is a need for international co-operation. Some pollution-control economists suggest tradable

Table 7.8 Measures to reduce greenhouse gases

Measure	Example
Changing use of fossil fuels	Change from the heavy use of coal to oil and gas
Alternative energy sources	• Renewable energy sources, e.g. HEP, tidal, wave, solar, and wind power, would reduce CO_2 output • Burning methane (a potent greenhouse gas) at landfill waste sites • An increase in nuclear power
Energy pricing and efficiency	• Increasing the fuel efficiency of buildings • Increasing the fuel efficiency of transport • Global energy pricing strategy that involves pricing fuels to reflect their environmental costs
Control of deforestation	• Provision of constructive advice on forest management
Programmes to replant trees (afforestation)	• Alternative uses like tourism could help to conserve these resources

23a Give a Malthusian explanation for the environmental problem of acid rain and the theoretical catastrophe of global warming.
b Write an environmentalist's response to these issues to prevent them getting worse.
(For **a** and **b**, see section 5.2.)

- Each country prepares a budget of greenhouse gas emissions to set against the size of its population and its carbon 'sinks', i.e. vegetation, soil and the earth's total cleaning capacity.

- Each country's share of the oceanic and atmospheric sinks is calculated.

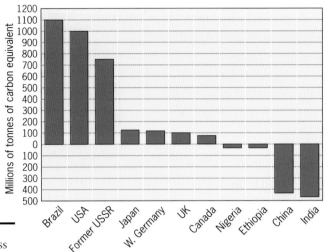

- Each country's permissible emissions are worked out.

- Compensation is paid by those who are over the permitted level to those who are under. Brazil shows highest above quota because of its unique combination of deforestation (reducing the size of its carbon sink), forest burning (increasing its carbon emissions) and heavy industrial pollution,

Figure 7.22 Carbon trading system (*After: New Internationalist*, April 1992)

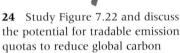

24 Study Figure 7.22 and discuss the potential for tradable emission quotas to reduce global carbon dioxide emissions.

25 What practical problems might arise if the tradable emission quotas system were adopted?

emission quotas for each country (Fig. 7.22). This proposes that total carbon emissions should equal the earth's capacity to absorb them (earth's natural sinks). Countries with unused emissions quotas, mostly in the developing countries, could then sell them to high-level carbon producing nations at fixed rates. This system is part of a global strategy to unite environmentally damaging production methods with national income. The term for such policies is **green economics**.

Petroleum exploration and the environment, Nigeria

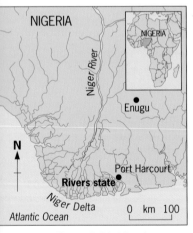

Figure 7.23 Nigeria

Oil was first discovered in Nigeria (Fig. 7.23) in the late 1950s. Ever since, it has been the major source of foreign exchange for this country. Nigerian oil production has fluctuated since the early 1970s reflecting changes in oil prices in the world market (see Fig. 7.10). In the mid-1990s, 95 per cent of Nigeria's foreign earnings were from petroleum. The environmental costs of producing oil have been enormous especially to the local communities.

Shell oil company

Shell, an Anglo-Dutch oil company, is one of the world's largest oil TNCs in the Niger Delta. The company accounts for over 50 per cent of Nigeria's daily oil production. Shell found oil in Rivers state in 1958 and established six oil fields in this highly productive agricultural area. Shell has operated in the area ever since, and has been the target of considerable criticism about the recurrent environmental problems related to drilling.

The Ogonis

The Ogoni region is one of the most densely populated areas in Africa with about 600 people per square kilometre (see section 1.4). The Ogoni people, who have lived in this fertile area for centuries, depended on fishing and farming for their livelihood. In fact, they used to supply most of the food needs of the urban population of Nigeria's south-east.

Effects of oil explorations on the local community

Since 1958, farmers in Ogoni have had to compete with oil companies operating in their area. The powerful influence of Shell and other TNCs in the region has meant that valuable farmland is lost to oil operations. Although traditionally the Ogonis were major food exporters to other parts of Nigeria, they now have to depend on food imports to feed themselves.

Oil spillage and pollution

Oil spillage has been frequent with serious environmental and health consequences for the local community (Fig. 7.24). Between 1976 and 1991, 2976 oil spills amounting to 2.1 million barrels of oil were reported in the Niger Delta area, an average of four spills a week. The Nigerian Ministry of Petroleum attributes most spills to equipment failures and corrosion but the results involve enormous damage to both land and water resources. In 1970, a Shell pipeline carrying crude oil spilled into Ogoni farmland. As a clean-up measure, the leaked fuel was burnt – leaving a semi-solid crust about five metres thick and useless agricultural land. Losses to the local farmers are considerable. In June 1993, a pipe from Shell's Korokoro pumping station burst. Palm oil trees were covered in an oily sheen stopping tappers from collecting any palm oil, chickens and goats died while fish stocks and vegetation were stunted.

Impoverishment and health hazards

While the local economy of the Ogoni people has been devastated by the operations of the oil companies, the people benefit very little from the oil revenue. Although Ogoni land has produced US$30 billion in oil revenue for Shell and the Nigerian government, most Ogonis remain poor. The government has used the oil wealth to develop urban areas such as Lagos, Kaduna, Kano and the new Federal Capital of Abuja (see Fig. 3.1).

Apart from the obvious environmental damage caused by oil spillage, oil exploration also poses serious health hazards to the local community. At Shell's Korokoro flowstation, a large quantity of poisonous gases is constantly released into the atmosphere through gas flaring. There are reports that hydro-carbons are affecting the health of the local population. Oil also bubbles into local water supplies and diarrhoea and vomiting are treated as regular complaints.

The Ogoni response

The people of the Niger Delta area have expressed their anger against the Shell operations in largely peaceful demonstrations, although there have been occasions when the local Ogoni people clashed with the Nigerian military police. In October 1990, the village community at Umuchen, 15 kilometres from Ogoni, organised a peaceful protest against Shell. In the course of this protest, the heavily-armed Nigerian mobile police took

Figure 7.24 Crude oil leak, Korokoro, Niger Delta

part, resulting in the death of 80 villagers and the destruction of about five hundred houses. The Ogoni people of Nigeria are still seeking compensation for the damage caused to them and their environment through oil prospecting (Fig. 7.25).

26 In what ways can local people, such as the Ogonis in the Niger Delta, benefit from the exploitation of natural resources on their land?

27 List, in detail, the possible conflicts of interest over the need to exploit natural resources for national development and the needs of the local communities where such resources are located.

28a As an external investigator, write a report summarising the problems in Rivers state.
b Evaluate the arguments of both the Ogoni people and Shell.
c Give brief suggestions for future development in the area, clearly indicating your priorities.

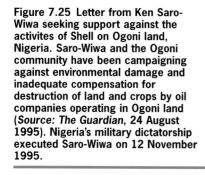
Figure 7.25 Letter from Ken Saro-Wiwa seeking support against the activites of Shell on Ogoni land, Nigeria. Saro-Wiwa and the Ogoni community have been campaigning against environmental damage and inadequate compensation for destruction of land and crops by oil companies operating in Ogoni land (*Source: The Guardian*, 24 August 1995). Nigeria's military dictatorship executed Saro-Wiwa on 12 November 1995.

ALL letters of support are welcome; except that my predicament, and that of the Ogoni people, require just a little more urgency.

At the root of my travails lies Shell, which has exploited, traduced and driven the Ogoni people to extinction in the last three decades. The company has taken over $30 billion out of the Ogoni and has left a completely devastated environment and a trail of human misery.

When I organised the Ogoni people to protest peacefully against Shell's ecological war, the company invited the Nigerian military to intervene. Lethal arms supplied by the British government were used on unarmed Ogoni people while they were sleeping in their beds. Thousands have been murdered, hundreds of thousands driven into the bush and tens of villages flattened.

The World Bank, after studying the Niger delta, has warned that 'an urgent need exists to implement mechanisms to protect the life and health of the region's inhabitants and its ecological systems from further deterioration'. Shell has not faced the consequences of its ecological war on the delta... Help save life and the environment of the Niger delta.

7.6 Alternative energy resources

Because of the problems caused by conventional energy production, people recognise the need for more sustainable methods (Figs 7.26–7.30). These alternative, or renewable, sources of energy tend to use natural resource flows, rather than stock resources (see Fig. 7.1).

Hydro-electric power (HEP)
Water under high pressure is used to drive a turbine linked to an electricity-producing generator. HEP produces one quarter of the total energy generated worldwide and is growing in importance: Norway receives 99 per cent of its electricity from HEP, Zaire 97 per cent and Brazil 96 per cent.

Transport costs, from the production areas mostly in mountains, are high e.g. about 70% of China's HEP capacity is in the south-west, but less than 10% is harnessed because of the cost of transporting it to more populated areas. However, China is building the large-scale Three Gorges HEP Project on the Yangtse River. Financed by the USA and Canada, it has the world's largest volume concrete dam. Elsewhere, parts of China depend on small-scale HEP plants with capacities of between one kilowatt and one megawatt. These supply just over 2% of China's energy needs.

Solar power
The sun's rays are concentrated by reflectors (heliostats), heating fluid which drives a turbine for generating electricity or for heating. Because plants need the sun to grow, fuelwood, agricultural waste and animal dung, collectively known as **biomass**, are also classified as solar energy.

Wave and tidal power
After tides rise behind the barrage (13.5 m at Rance), water is gradually released turning turbines to generate electricity. This is a cheap form of generating electricity but building costs are high.

29 You work for the Department of Energy.
a Gather information about the varieties of renewable energy in order to assess their development in the UK (Figures 7.26–7.30)
b For each renewable energy source, list the possibilities and limitations of its development.
c Would you recommend the Department of Energy to invest in renewable resources? If so, which three should be encouraged? Give your reasons.

Figure 7.26 Itaipu plant on the Paraná River, between Brazil and Paraguay, has the largest HEP-generating capacity in the world of 12 600 megawatts

Geothermal power
Geothermal energy is derived from steam trapped deep in the earth which, when brought to the surface, drives a turbine. Theoretically, this source of subterranean energy is limitless, but in most habitable areas of the earth the hot rocks lie so deep that drilling is too expensive.

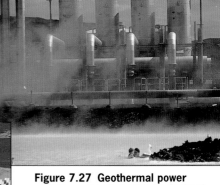

Figure 7.27 Geothermal power complex using hot springs, Iceland

Figure 7.28 Basin of solar generating screens, California, USA

Figure 7.29 Tidal barrage across the Rance estuary, France (1966)

Figure 7.30 Wind turbines, Netherlands

Wind power
Wind pushes three spinning rotor blades which drive a turbine to generate electricity. The electrical energy produced from a turbine is proportional to the windspeed. Thus, a 10m/s wind will produce 8 times more electricity than a 5m/s wind.

Energy resources mix in India

Commercial energy consumption

In India (Fig. 7.31), industry is by far the largest consumer of commercial forms of energy, with transport
being the second largest. Commercial energy sources
include coal, gas, oil, hydro-electric and nuclear. Coal is
the main source of commercial energy and India is, in
fact, one of the world's leading coal producers. Oil and
gas supply just under half the country's commercial
needs, while HEP is also important, although only 20
per cent of the country's potential has been tapped.

India also has large reserves of thorium. Thorium is a
fuel similar to uranium and is used in nuclear reactors.
Partly because of this, India is one of the relatively few
developing countries which has its own nuclear power
industry (Fig. 7.32). Approximately three per cent of
India's electricity comes from nuclear power and there
are ambitious plans for a ten-fold expansion by the end
of the century.

Traditional sources of energy

Over 40 per cent of the total energy used in India
comes from non-commercial, renewable sources. Non-
commercial energy is mostly used in rural areas where
72 per cent of the population lives. A majority of these
people depend on fuelwood, agricultural waste and
animal dung (biomass fuel, see Fig. 7.28).

Inadequate electricity facilities in many villages and
limited use of kerosene for cooking, mean that biomass
provides the cooking fuel for many rural households. A
large programme of rural electrification has brought
electricity to two out of three of India's 500 000
villages, but only about eight per cent of rural homes
are connected to the electricity grid. The electricity in

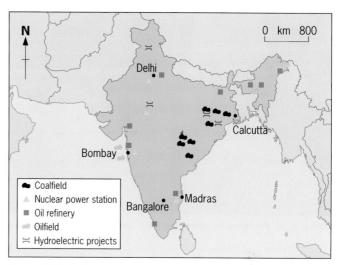

Figure 7.31 India

these areas is used mainly for irrigation pumps to bring
water to farmland.

Forests cover nearly a quarter of India, but there is an
acute shortage of fuelwood in many areas (Fig. 7.33,
see Fig. 7.8). The amount of fuelwood burned annually
far exceeds India's afforestation programme (Fig. 7.33).

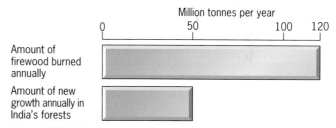

**Figure 7.33 India: supply and demand for fuelwood (*Source:
M Raw, Resources and Environment, Unwin Hyman, 1989*)**

This results in soil erosion and a shortage of fuelwood,
so people are forced to burn animal dung which could
otherwise fertilise the crops and so increase food
production. Ultimately, this creates a **poverty trap**, the
effects of which are difficult to reverse once set in
motion.

The problem of energy shortage in rural areas in
India, as in many developing countries, can only be
solved through the expansion of the non-commercial
sector. The greatest demand for energy in Indian rural
areas is for cooking. However, the traditional stove, the
chullah, is extremely inefficient, although it burns
firewood, agricultural waste and dung. The introduction
of improved *chullahs* is already proving effective and it
is hoped that eventually the new-version chullah will
help save up to 17 million tonnes of firewood a year
(Fig. 7.34).

**Figure 7.32 Commercial energy: nuclear power station, Bombay,
where the production of nuclear energy is important for India's
industrialisation**

Energy resources mix in India

Figure 7.34 The local hope for India's energy future?

Biogas

Another solution is the production of biogas. This is made by placing animal dung, other farm wastes and vegetation in sealed concrete and steel containers. The sun's heat then helps bacteria to decompose these natural materials rapidly and, during the process, methane gas is produced. The methane is stored and used for cooking and lighting, either by individuals or by whole communities. In addition, farmers can use residue from the sealed containers as fertiliser. The Indian government is keen to promote such community energy projects which also help improve the output of small-scale farmers. In light of the global fuelwood crisis (see Fig. 7.6) such schemes can also help to save valuable wood.

Trombe walls

A more 'alternative' approach to saving energy is at Leh, in Northern India. Trombe walls absorb heat by day and let it out at night by working on the same principle as a conservatory. A thermally blackened wall is placed behind glass on the south-facing side of a dwelling. The air in the living space is then warmed by natural or forced convection through a system of ducts. Heat loss may be minimised at night or there may be vents to allow for cooling on hot days. Alternatively, the trombe wall can be filled with water and the structure relocated on the roof provided that the load can be supported by the building.

30 As an expert for the United Nations Development Programme (UNDP) you have to recommend alternative strategies for energy production to the Indian government.
a Assess the advantages and disadvantages of: • high-tech commercial energy production (Fig. 7.32); • low-tech small-scale production (Fig. 7.34).
b Compare the different approaches and for each suggest: • who is likely to benefit; • the sustainability of the strategy.

31 Considering the estimated reserves and current consumption rates of non-renewable resources (see Tables 7.1–7.3), how might countries benefit in the long term from the use of renewable flows of energy?

Summary

- Resources are vital for successful economic development.

- The types of resources are broadly categorised into renewable and non-renewable.

- Renewable resources, known as flows, are capable of being used over and over again. Non-renewable resources, known as stocks, are finite.

- The depletion of the tropical rainforests has serious social, environmental and economic consequences, not only for local areas but for the whole world.

- High rates of deforestation in the developing countries have led to a large-scale fuelwood crisis as many people depend on this primary source of energy.

- Although the distribution of the world's natural resources varies widely, the developed countries consume the most.

- Exploitation of renewable resources must not go beyond their ability to regenerate. If it does, then the use of the resource is considered non-sustainable.

- The high use of non-renewable resources means a global reduction of stocks.

- Heavy reliance on fossil fuels has resulted in serious environmental pollution. This has serious consequences for both developed and developing countries.

- Alternative, sustainable supplies of energy are being developed in response to the loss of non-renewable resources.

8 *World trade and commodities*

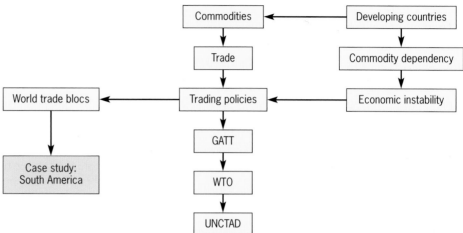

8.1 Introduction

Trade is the exchange of goods and services. In this chapter we examine world trade with special reference to commodities. Commodities are goods for sale, either raw materials or manufactured goods. However, the term is most commonly used for raw materials, like coal, cotton, tin and bananas, as it will be in this chapter. Trade is the major force behind economic relations between nations, with some countries benefiting more than others (Fig. 8.1). This follows the concept of **comparative advantage** (see section 6.7). We discuss the reasons why many developing countries receive low returns from international trade and examine the issue of dependency on exports of primary commodities.

8.2 The history of trade between developed and developing countries

There has been trade of commodities and manufactured goods between nations for thousands of years. One early example is the Egyptians who, four thousand years ago, exported gold and wine to the area we know as Syria, in exchange for wood and pottery. During the colonial period, from the 16th to the 19th centuries, the 'triangular trade' between Europe, Africa and the Americas flourished (see Fig. 2.5).

The natural resources of the world are unevenly distributed (see Figs 7.8, 7.9). For instance, Europe has few **reserves** of minerals compared with Africa, and it does not have the climate to grow cotton or coffee. Over the past five hundred years, the more powerful nations have imported raw materials as cheaply as possible to manufacture into goods for export. In return, they sold their finished goods back to the colonies – as expensively as possible. This pattern fits the economic theory of **mercantilism**. Mercantilism relates to trade during the seventeenth and eighteenth centuries. It suggests that the wealth of a nation is dependent on gaining natural resources through foreign trade.

This pattern of world trade persists today and results in a division between the industrialised **developed countries** of the North, and the **developing countries** of the South (See Fig. 1.1). In addition, some developing countries have industrialised to become **newly industrialising countries** (**NIC**s, see

Figure 8.1 Trading floor of the New York Stock Exchange. The Stock Exchange is a financial market where investments in industrial and commercial corporations are bought and sold. Commodity trading, which occurs at a separate commodity exchange, is the buying and selling of natural products.

135

section 6.7). However, most developing countries today lack the basic skills, infrastructure, technology and finance to establish a significant industrial base. At the same time, many of their commodities are still in demand by the developed countries. This dependence of developed and developing countries on one another ultimately causes problems for both, although mostly for the developing countries.

8.3 Problems for developing countries dependent on commodity exports

The main problem for countries which depend on the export of primary commodities (Fig. 8.2) is economic instability. This is especially so for countries which depend on the export of just one primary product (Fig. 8.3). Even a small change in the price of the commodity exported can affect a country's economy drastically. For example, world demand for copper fell heavily as factory-made fibre optics replaced copper telephone wires. As a result, the price of copper also fell and Zambia's national income was greatly reduced.

?

1a Study Figure 8.2 and describe the regional variations in commodity dependence throughout Africa.

b Select four countries in Africa which depend heavily on commodity exports (other than those listed in Fig. 8.3). Find out which commodities are associated with each country.

2a On a base map of Africa, shade the countries you selected in **1b** and those in Figure 8.3 which depend heavily on a single export commodity.

b Find out to where each of these products is mostly exported.

c Find out what other commodities each of these countries produce on a commercial scale.

d Write a paragraph to explain the importance of trade in commodities for Africa.

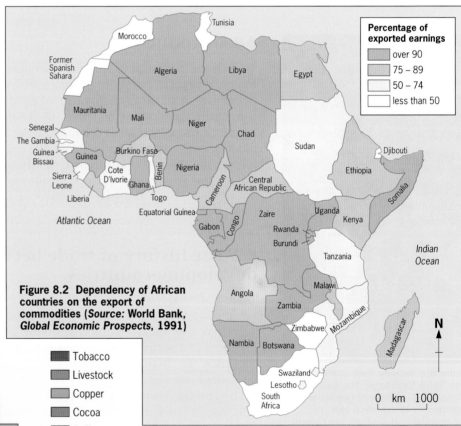

Figure 8.2 Dependency of African countries on the export of commodities (*Source:* World Bank, *Global Economic Prospects*, 1991)

Percentage of exported earnings
- over 90
- 75 – 89
- 50 – 74
- less than 50

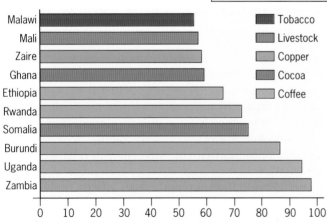

Figure 8.3 Dependency of Sub-Saharan African countries on the export of one commodity as a percentage of their exports (*Source:* Oxfam, *The Trade Trap*, 1992)

Legend:
- Tobacco
- Livestock
- Copper
- Cocoa
- Coffee

Table 8.1 Falling national income among countries that depend on primary commodities, 1960–78

Country	Average annual growth of GNP (%)
Bangladesh	−0.4
Somalia	−0.5
Chad	−1.0
Niger	−1.4
Ghana	−0.5
UK	2.1
USA	2.4

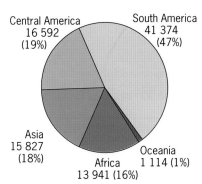

Central America 16 592 (19%)
South America 41 374 (47%)
Asia 15 827 (18%)
Oceania 1 114 (1%)
Africa 13 941 (16%)

Figure 8.4 World coffee production (*Source: New Internationalist*, Sept. 1994)

Table 8.2 The changing price of coffee, 1975–93

1975	144	1982	309	1989	240
1976	315	1983	290	1990	150
1977	517	1984	327	1991	135
1978	359	1985	330	1992	135
1979	382	1985	330	1993	145
1980	344	1986	440	US cents per Kg	
1981	282	1987	258		

Figure 8.5 Brazilian coffee crop destroyed by frost

1970s debt crisis

The debt crisis of the 1970s hit the developing countries hard. At that time, the Middle East countries put up price of oil (see Fig. 7.10). They then invested much of their income in European and US banks. In order to pay interest to their Middle Eastern investors, the banks encouraged developing countries to take out loans. In turn, to raise money to pay their interest, the developing countries had to export more commodities. This, of course, pushed down prices resulting in a reduction in developing countries' income (Table 8.1).

An attempt to maintain and stabilise commodity prices in the 1970s was the International Commodity Agreements (ICAs). However, many of these agreements encouraged nations to increase their production so much that it led to oversupply. For example, too much coffee caused the International Coffee Agreement to collapse in 1989 after the market price of coffee fell from US$1.4 to US$0.70 per pound in just four months. This had an enormous impact on countries which relied heavily on coffee exports. In El Salvador, the value of coffee exports fell from US$700 million in 1988 to US$500 million in 1989.

Oversupply and changing demand

Oversupply affects the price of commodities. For example, many developing countries grow coffee (Fig. 8.4). If there is a good harvest the result is a coffee glut on world markets as supply exceeds demand. This forces prices down. After severe frost in Brazil in 1974 (Fig. 8.5), fungi in Colombia and Mexico in 1976, drought in the Ivory Coast and war in Angola, world coffee stockpiles ran out. Prices rocketed and farmers therefore planted more and more coffee bushes. As these additional bushes contributed to regular production, oversupply took place and so, since the 1980s, coffee prices have gradually dropped off (Table 8.2).

Commodities are also prone to 'boom-bust' cycles. In some years, profits from commodity sales are high, so countries accumulate wealth. However, during 'bust' periods, business slows as demand falls, profits go down, unemployment rises and the economy enters recession. These bust periods may even be the result of fashion, as tastes and styles change. Thus demand for primary products such as cocoa, coffee, sugar and tobacco will fluctuate as people's attitudes to consumption changes. Another set-back is caused by recession in the North. If factories in developed countries close, the producer of their raw materials will no longer have a market. Ultimately, unemployment in the North means increased poverty in the South.

Commodity substitutes

Developed countries now manufacture cheaper, artificial alternatives for certain natural products. The results of this engineering and biotechnology include synthetic cocoa butter, vanilla flavouring and food sweeteners. The long-term effect of such artificial production is to reduce demand for natural goods, which results in a decline in prices. We are all familiar with the substitution of polyester for cotton. In addition, since the early 1980s, US food manufacturers have used maize-based sweeteners instead of sugar. These now make up 60 per cent of the US sweetener market. At the same time, Europeans have increased their sugar-beet production from which they also manufacture sugar products. These changes, and the development of other artificial sweeteners, have led to a fall in the demand for sugar cane from developing countries. Because of the decline in US sugar imports, by 1985 a quarter of a million people were without work on the Philippine island of Negros. This was 1.03 per cent of the labour force of about 24 000 000.

Non-agricultural raw materials have also suffered from synthetic alternatives. Until the mid-1980s, Bolivia's economy was dependent on the export of tin. In the late 1970s, 79 per cent of the country's exports were tin, while it ranked

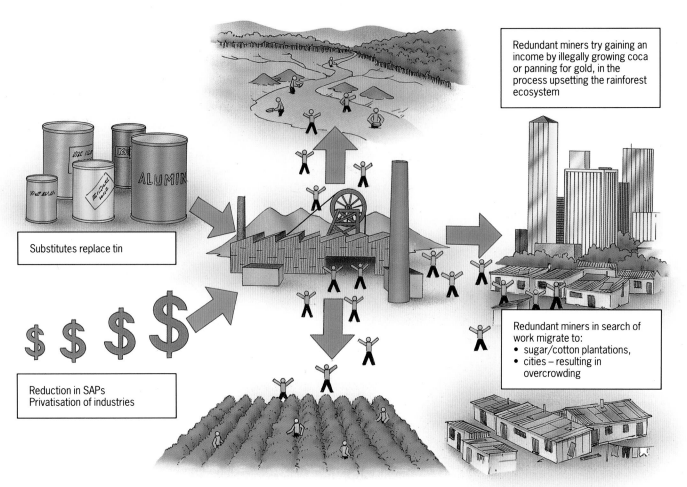

Substitutes replace tin

$ $ $ $

**Reduction in SAPs
Privatisation of industries**

Redundant miners try gaining an
income by illegally growing coca
or panning for gold, in the
process upsetting the rainforest
ecosystem

ALUMIN

Redundant miners in search of
work migrate to:
• sugar/cotton plantations,
• cities – resulting in
  overcrowding

**Figure 8.6 Tin collapse and its
effects in Bolivia**

4 In what ways can the market
collapse of a commodity lead to
poverty in the producing region
(Fig. 8.6)?

5 Discuss the potential problems
of biotechnology on: • countries
that depend on primary
commodities and • on the
consumers of such manufactured
products.

6 Some development experts
have expressed concern over the
effects of biotechnology on the
developing nations, believing it is
'biological colonialism'. Do you
agree? Explain, giving reasons.

ninth in world production (4 per cent). However, technological advances mean
that less tin is used to make tin cans while other types of container have also
been invented. In October 1985 the price of tin fell from UK£8000 to UK£4000
per tonne, halving the Bolivian revenue and leaving thousands of miners
without work (Fig. 8.6).

Weather
All countries dependent on crops are at the mercy of the weather. Tropical
countries, in particular, are threatened by powerful storm systems, such as
hurricanes. These sweep through the Caribbean every year and can devastate
whole crops. Plants are also vulnerable to frost, drought and disease (see Fig.
8.5). Thus, a country dependent on the export of its crops will be damaged
financially if the crop fails. In addition, any farmer who tries changing his crop,
has the expense of changing production systems and waiting for the new plants
to mature. For example, a coffee bush will only be productive after four years'
growth.

Trading policies
Traditionally, it was the developed countries who established and gained most
from international trading policies. We can see the effects of this control in the
form of **tariffs**. Tariffs are taxes added to the cost of goods at different stages of
production. Thus raw materials tend to have much smaller tariffs than
manufactured goods. This means that it is relatively cheap for a manufacturing
country to import the raw materials it needs for production, but it would be
expensive for that country to import the equivalent finished product made from
those raw materials (Figs 8.7–8.8).

7 Use Figures 8.7 and 8.8 to complete a matrix showing the advantages and disadvantages of tariffs for both developed and developing countries.

8a Using Figure 8.9, describe the trends in commodity prices during the 1980s.
b Suggest the impact of such changes on countries supplying commodities.

9 Use the information in section 8.3 to draw an annotated flow diagram summarising the factors which can lead to changes in the price of primary commodities. Your diagram should show factors originating in both developed and developing countries.

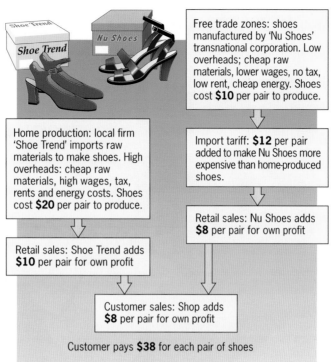

Figure 8.7 How tariffs affect the cost of shoes

Figure 8.8 Tariff escalation: the more processed a product, the higher the tariff (*Source: A Raw Deal*, Christian Aid, 1992)

Fresh pineapples imported to the EU attract a duty of 9%

Canned pineapples imported to the EU attract a duty of 32%

Pineapple juice imported to the EU attracts a duty of 42%

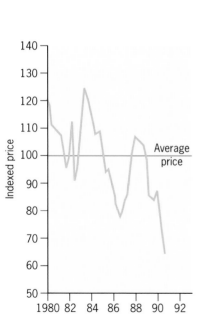

Figure 8.9 Commodity price decline, 1980–92 (*After: The Economist*)

?

10 Use Figure 8.10 to comment on the location of trading blocs. Suggest why few blocs cross the **North-South divide**.

A combination of these problems has led to a long-term, steady decline in the price of commodities (Fig. 8.9). In relation to the price of manufactured goods, this commodity price decline means that in 1975 farmers in Africa could buy a tractor for the equivalent of 8 tonnes of their coffee, but in 1992 a tractor cost them 40 tonnes of coffee.

8.4 World trading blocs

An essential feature of world trade and economic co-operation between nations today is transnational trade organisations or trading blocs (Fig. 8.10). Countries which share geographical, political, historical or economic characteristics often form such blocs to strengthen their trade links.

Types of integration
There are different types of economic and political integration. For co-operation between nations we can use the terms transnational or supranational. In either case, such national relationships are based on either formal or informal agreements. An informal integration is 'loose' and unregulated, for example, a group of developing countries voting along a common line in a UN ballot.

Political collaboration
Some agreements involve political links between nation states, for example, the Organisation of African Unity (OAU), British Commonwealth Association and the North Atlantic Treaty Organisation (NATO). Under these arrangements, the sovereignty of each member state is maintained.

Economic collaboration
The main motive for many agreements between countries is economic. Examples include the European Union (EU), United Nations Organisation and General Agreement on Tariffs and Trade (GATT, see section 8.5).

MERCOSUR: Common Market of the South
Founded: 1995
Aim: To establish an economically integrated zone where goods and services will circulate freely.
Achievements: Common tariff by 2001 on goods imported to member states from non-members.

CARICOM: Caribbean Community and Common Market
Founded: 1973
Aim: To establish free trade and movement of goods among members.

SADCC: Southern African Development Co-ordination Committee
Founded: 1979
Aim: To reduce economic dependence on South Africa.
Achievements: Regional integration of transport and energy supply systems.

EU: European Union
Founded: 1957 (Treaty of Rome)
Aim: Economic integration and co-operation between member states.
Achievements: European citizenship status for all; customers and immigration agreements streamlined to allow European citizens greater freedom to live, work, or study in any member country; border controls relaxed to encourage greater flow of goods between member nations; proposal of single common currency.

NAFTA: North American Free Trade Agreement
Founded: 1992
Aim: To create a free-trade zone and economic integration across North America.
Achievements: Mexico gains from new opportunities to attract new investment and pursue an export-orientated industrialisation policy; Canada, USA benefit from Mexico's supply of cheap, unskilled and semi-skilled labour.

G7: Group of Seven
Founded: 1975
Aim: To co-ordinate economic, financial, trade and security policies; supply of aid.
Achievements: Contributed to formation of WTO; promote competitiveness between members; directs international issues e.g. arms, energy, debt.

ECOWAS: Economic Community of West African States
Founded: 1975
Aim: To promote economic and social integration among independent countries in West Africa.
Achievements: Unity; successfully resists agressive neighbouring states; settles internal conflicts.

ASEAN: Association of South-East Asian Nations
Founded: 1967
Aim: To accelerate economic progress and social and cultural development.
Achievements: Diplomatic co-operation.

LAIA: Latin American Integration Association
Founded: 1980
Aim: To agree preferential tariffs within the group.

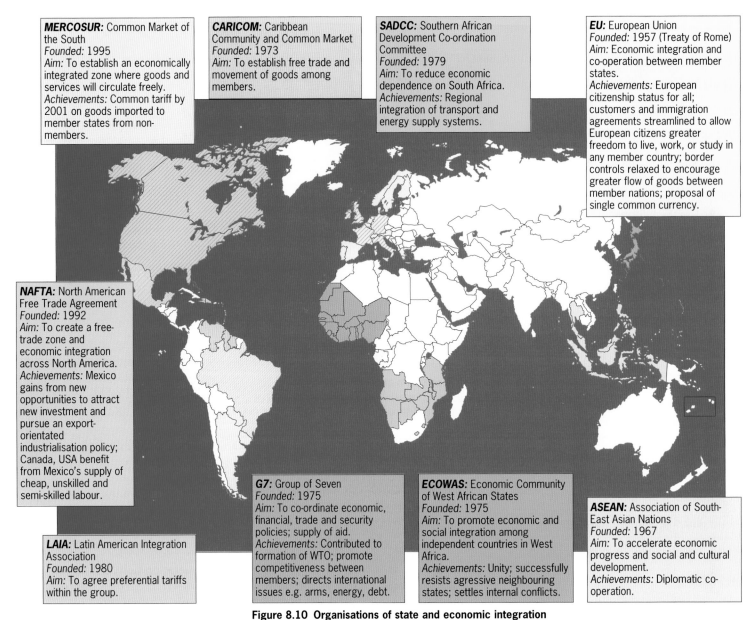

Figure 8.10 Organisations of state and economic integration

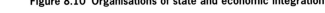

Trade blocs in South and Central America

Bananas are a tropical crop, produced almost exclusively in the developing world. In fact, Asia, followed closely by South America, is the world's main banana-growing region. While many developing countries depend on fruit for much of their export income (Table 8.3), the world fruit markets are dominated by just a few **transnational corporations** (**TNCs**) which control transportation, storage and marketing. Specifically, over 80 per cent of the world's banana trade is operated by only three TNCs: United Brands, the Standard Fruit Company and Del Monte (Fig. 8.11).

People in the developed countries are consuming ever-increasing quantities of bananas. In fact, bananas account for a quarter of the fresh fruit consumed by Americans each year, while trade with the Eastern European countries is also growing. Overall, the world trade in bananas is now worth US$4 billion a year (Fig. 8.12), although there are limited benefits for the countries which grow the fruit. It is usually the large, often transnational, companies which reap the financial rewards.

Banana-exporting countries receive only 11.5 per cent of the price European and USA buyers pay for the fruit (Fig. 8.12). In an attempt to secure their incomes, some countries have formed themselves into protective trade groups.

Figure 8.11 Large-scale banana plantation, Guatemala, owned by transnational corporation, Del Monte

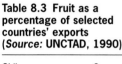

Table 8.3 Fruit as a percentage of selected countries' exports (*Source:* UNCTAD, 1990)

Chile	9
New Zealand	5
Kenya	5
Philippines	5
Turkey	7
Spain	5
Israel	3
St Lucia	54
Guadeloupe	42
Costa Rica	33
Greece	5
Dominica	73
Jamaica	3
Martinque	49
Honduras	46
Belize	25

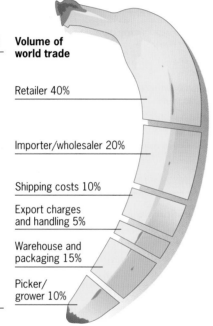

Volume of world trade

Retailer 40%

Importer/wholesaler 20%

Shipping costs 10%

Export charges and handling 5%

Warehouse and packaging 15%

Picker/grower 10%

Figure 8.12 Total value of world trade in bananas, 1995

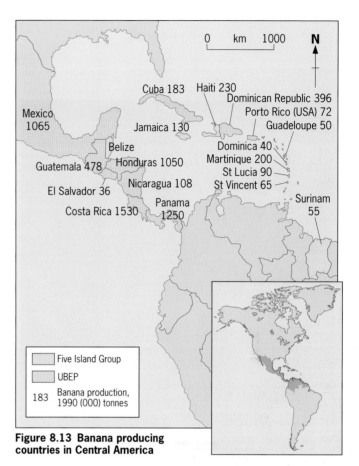

Figure 8.13 Banana producing countries in Central America

UBEP in South America

Between 1970 and 1974, some Central American producers (Fig. 8.13) tried to raise the export taxes paid by the TNCs. However, the corporations resisted strongly, setting off the 'Banana War' of price bargaining and searching for new banana growers. In response to this, the Central American countries gave in to the TNCs and dropped their taxes. Collectively, they lost millions of dollars of revenue from their banana exports each year.

In 1974 a group of South American producers formed the Union of Banana Exporting Countries (UBEP). UBEP's original members were Guatemala, Nicaragua, Colombia, Costa Rica and Panama. These countries were joined later by the Dominican Republic (1976)

and Honduras (1979) and together, inspired by the successes of OPEC (Fig. 7.10), they hope to use their group's power to secure prices and guarantee markets.

Overall, UBEP's share of the world banana market is almost 70 per cent. Were this to increase, UBEP would hold considerable power over the large fruit corporations and consumer nations. In such a position, UBEP could seek the abolition of the 20 per cent European Union (EU) import tariff on Central American bananas. This tariff alone costs Central America around US$1.5 billion every year.

Caribbean co-operation

In the same way that the South American countries grouped together for economic protection, so some Caribbean countries grouped to protect the interests of their banana growers (Fig. 8.14). Historically, these countries were colonies tied into trade agreements to supply particular products for their European colonisers.

Since independence, St. Lucia, the other Windward Islands, Jamaica, Guadeloupe and Martinique have kept close links with their former colonisers, the UK and France. They also formed the Five Islands Group to maintain banana prices, give the growers a steady income and keep jobs on the family-owned fruit farms. In fact, we can see these countries' past colonial ties in the UK's banana purchases (Fig. 8.15). While France

Banana trade blocs in South America

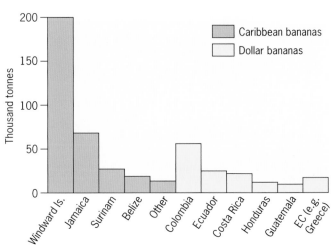

Figure 8.15 UK banana imports, 1991

Table 8.4 Bananas differences

Five Island bananas	Dollar bananas
• higher risk of crop damage from hurricanes	• production areas outside the world's hurricane zones
• mainly grown on family-run small farms	• mainly grown on plantations owned by transnational companies
• family workers sharing wages and profits	• low wages and often poor living conditions, with a ban on trade unions
• high proportion of manual work	• high degree of mechanisation
• softer, browner-skinned bananas, variable in size	• larger bananas, more uniform size, often yellow/green skins

11a Study Figures 8.11 and 8.14 and describe the differences between the farming systems in terms of: • farming inputs • likely income to workers and • job security.
b Suggest what you think are the differing attitudes of the workers and state whether you think TNCs are/would be a benefit to them.

12 Banana sales to the UK make up 70 per cent of Dominica's export earnings. These bananas are usually grown by poor farmers who get only 1.5 per cent of the sale value. Comment on the impact of: • past colonial relations, • TNCs, • tariffs and • trade blocs on both Caribbean and South American growers.

13 Assess the dangers of over-reliance on the commodities exports for the developing countries.

Figure 8.14 Preparing bananas for export, St Lucia, Windward Islands

and the UK buy bananas from their former colonies, other countries, such as Germany, prefer to 'shop' for cheaper bananas. These are known as 'Dollar bananas', while this Caribbean struggle over banana prices became caught up in the South American Banana Wars (Table 8.4).

8.5 General Agreement on Tariffs and Trade

The General Agreement on Tariffs and Trade (GATT) is an international organisation set up in 1947 to encourage open economies and free trade among all nations. GATT was one result of the Bretton Woods conference, held in 1944, to discuss world economic problems following World War 2 (see section 2.3). Together with the World Bank and International Monetary Fund (IMF), GATT was established to help control the world economy and to promote global competition and corporate enterprises. In 1994, over 100 nations were signatories of the agreement.

Table 8.5 GATT and changes to trade with WTO (*Source: Financial Times*, 16 Dec. 1993)

GATT	Changes with WTO	Impact
Industrial tariffs About 5% in rich countries (was 40% in 1940s)	• Tariffs on industrial goods cut by rich countries by more than 33% • 40% of imports enter duty free • Main traders scrap duties on pharmaceuticals, construction equipment, medical equipment, steel, beer, furniture, farm equipment, spirits, wood, paper and toys	• Easier access to world markets for exporters of industrial goods • Lower prices for consumers • Higher-paying jobs as industries become more competitive
Agriculture High subsidies and protected markets in Europe and USA lead to over-production e.g. 1992 OECD grants at $354bn and dumping of surpluses	• Subsidies cut • Farm grants cut 20% • Import barriers converted to tariffs and cut 36% • Japan's and S Korea's closed rice markets opened • Tariffs on tropical products cut 40%	• Lower food prices for consumers • Better sales opportunites for producers • Special treatment for developing countries
Services No international rules covering services, e.g. banking, insurance, transport, tourism, telecommunications, so much protectionism	• Rules for fair trade established • Markets to open between individual countries	• Trade in services boosted
Intellectual property Trade friction with no standard of protection for patents, copyrights or trademarks; much trade in counterfeit goods	• International agreement on patents, copyright and trademarks • Extra time for developing countries to put rules in place	• Boost for foreign investment and technology transfer • Poor countries fear higher prices patents, for drugs and seeds
Textiles and clothing Imports to rich countries restricted; high tariffs; protection raises prices but fails to protect jobs	• Tariffs reduced by both developed and developing countries • Quotas dismantled	• Developing countries able to sell more textiles and clothing abroad • Reduced prices for consumers worldwide

The underlying principle of GATT is that free movement of all goods and capital will ultimately lead to rapid global economic development. Since its creation, GATT has played a major part in world trade and commodity pricing. However, the goal of global development failed to materialise. As we are aware, the economic gap between developed and developing countries has in fact widened (see Fig. 1.1).

GATT and the developing countries

Economists in both developed and developing countries blame the failure of GATT for some problems of developing countries. These include:

• Growing debts (60 per cent of GDP for some countries in 1992), due in part to unfavourable terms of trade under GATT.

• Budget and trade deficits, particularly for countries that rely on a single commodity.

• Discriminatory tariffs: i.e., low tariffs on commodities and high tariffs on semi-finished and finished products which discriminate against developing countries (see Fig. 8.8).

8.6 World Trade Organisation

The World Trade Organisation (WTO) began on 1 January 1995, replacing GATT (Table 8.5). It was formed following the eighth round of multilateral negotiations of GATT and GATT's member states signed the new agreement on 15 April 1994 in Marrakech, Morocco.

The major issues covered by the new WTO are outlined as follows:

• Reduction of tariffs and opening up of markets: e.g. the European agricultural market will be opened up with a 30 per cent cut in farm subsidies; protective barriers against imports of textiles will be reduced.

• General agreement on trade of services: the aim is to open up world markets and promote international financial and insurance services.

?

14 Several **non-governmental organisations** (**NGOs**), such as Christian Aid, Traidcraft and World Development Movement, are campaigning for fairer trade terms in developing countries (see section 11.3). You are the publicity officer for one of these NGOs. Write an article for your magazine outlining the reasons for your charity's work.

15 Discuss the possible effects of a reduction in government subsidies to farmers in the European Union.

16 How would you structure international trade? Do you think it needs to reduce the bias towards the developed countries, or not? Give your reasons.

17 Discuss the ways in which trading has led to increasing economic dependency of the developing countries on the developed nations, since the end of the colonial period.

18 Essay: Attempts to improve the bargaining position of the developing countries and reduce world poverty can only succeed with the support and co-operation of the developed countries. Discuss.

• Trade-Related Intellectual Property Rights (TRIPS): TRIPS protects patents by individuals or companies, giving legal protection against piracy or theft.

WTO and developing countries

The new WTO scheme gives developed countries control over many of the economic policies of developing countries. For example, while TRIPS covers agricultural products, medicines and other primary products, it is still the developed countries who control much of their development and production. Transnational companies who manufacture pharmaceutical products, genetically engineered agricultural seeds and artificial fertilisers will thus enjoy new patent rights, giving them greater control over the goods. This makes competition by local industries illegal.

As a result of WTO, the developing nations which export much of their agricultural produce are now forced to open up their markets. This is in contrast with the developed countries, especially the USA and members of the European Union, who refuse to remove trade barriers against imports from the developing countries.

Many development experts believe that WTO, and its origin agreement GATT, is biased towards the richer nations. WTO considers the corporate business interests of the developed nations while paying little attention to the needs of, and the growing poverty, in many developing nations.

8.7 United Nations Conference on Trade and Development

The United Nations Conference on Trade and Development (UNCTAD) was established in 1964. It was set up in response to the dissatisfaction of the developing countries with GATT. Its major objectives are to address the needs of developing nations in international trade and to look at world trade from wider developmental perspectives.

However, UNCTAD has failed to make any significant improvements in trading relations between developed and developing countries. The Conference has never received much support from the developed countries, so it lacks the power and financial influence to lessen the inequalities of the global economic system.

Summary
- The structure of world trade today has its origins in the colonial period.
- Much of the wealth of the industrialised nations was founded on the supply of commodities from the colonies.
- Most developing countries still depend on the export of commodities.
- While the volume of trade of commodities has increased in the last two decades, the value of such products has declined significantly.
- The dependency on commodity exports by many developing countries makes them vulnerable to outside influences.
- Attempts by some developing countries to stabilise primary commodities prices, by forming trade groups, have largely failed.
- Some countries have organised trading blocs to protect their economies with tariff barriers.
- Many developing countries face discrimination by high tariffs on the import of manufactured goods.
- The international trade organisations have failed to address the disadvantaged position of many developing countries in international trade.

9 *Regional development policies*

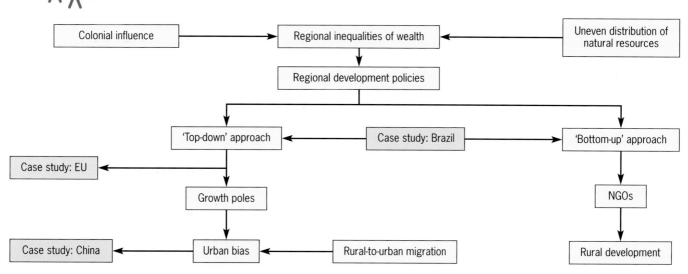

| Colonial influence | → | Regional inequalities of wealth | ← | Uneven distribution of natural resources |

Regional development policies

'Top-down' approach ← Case study: Brazil → 'Bottom-up' approach

Case study: EU

Growth poles

NGOs

Case study: China ← Urban bias ← Rural-to-urban migration

Rural development

Figure 9.1 São Paolo: statue of the *Bandeirantes*, Portuguese pioneers who explored Brazil in their search for gold and diamonds.

9.1 Introduction

Just as we have seen inequalities of wealth on a world scale, so we can see such divisions on a regional scale. Most governments face the challenge of how best to spread wealth and economic opportunity evenly across their country. In this chapter we discuss approaches to addressing this problem in both **developed** and **developing countries**.

9.2 Reasons for regional disparities of wealth

As we have seen, natural resources are never distributed evenly (see Fig. 7.9). Areas rich in natural resources are at an advantage and frequently develop into **core areas**, while the relatively poorer areas remain on the **periphery** (see section 1.4). The terms core and periphery refer to richer and poorer areas of a country respectively. In Friedmann's model (see Fig. 1.17) those in between are 'upward/downward transitional areas' or 'resource frontiers'.

All countries also vary in climate, soils and altitude. These variations can give one area excellent opportunities for agriculture, for example, whilst in another, even **subsistence** farming is difficult.

Additionally, variations in development may have their roots in a country's past. For example, we can partly explain the core and peripheral regions in Brazil by its colonial history. Brazil became a Portuguese colony in 1500. It was governed directly by Portugal until 1822. During this time, the Portuguese exploited the country as a source of commodities for export. Gold, silver, diamonds, timber, sugar and coffee were produced, principally from the south-east of the country and exported to an expanding Europe (Fig. 9.1).

The Portuguese made the south-east of the country their centre for trade and commerce (though they had at first preferred the north-east, where sugar-cane was the primary resource). Ports on the Atlantic coast, such as Rio de Janeiro, Salvador, Fortaleza, Recife and Santos, grew up to export raw materials from Brazil and to import finished products from Europe (see Fig. 9.12). The Portuguese discouraged manufacturing in Brazil throughout the 18th century to prevent competition with their own goods imported from Portugal.

?

1 Describe the possible impact of colonialism on the creation of the rich core and the poor peripheral areas of a country (see also section 2.2).

2 Study Figures 9.2 and 9.3.
a What are the objectives in the creation of growth 'poles'?
b How does the creation of growth poles benefit: • cities, • rural areas?
c Why might large distances between major urban centres and remote peripheral areas make the creation of growth-poles difficult?

3 Using a base map of the UK, identify the major economic growth poles.

9.3 Two approaches to regional development

Regional policies aim to spread economic wealth and development evenly across a country and so reduce differences between regions. There are two approaches to regional policies.

The 'top-down' approach

The government makes decisions about development of regions without the involvement of local people. These 'interventionist' policies tend to concentrate on investment in industry in urban areas, based on the theory that economic growth will spread from large cities to small villages.

Governments therefore often concentrate development resources in **growth poles**, or urban centres. The authorities hope that economic growth will take place and then spread into surrounding areas (Figs 9.2–9.3).

Governments may also designate **growth corridors**, or axes, to encourage industrial investment. Such corridors are usually along major roads which provide good access and so connect large urban centres (Figs 9.4–9.5).

Myrdal's model (see section 1.4) suggests that the spread of development will occur naturally, but most governments favour this interventionist approach.

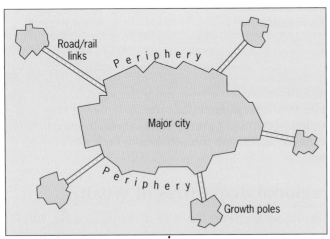

Figure 9.2 Growth poles: an example of top-down planning. Governments direct development funds to specific towns away from a major city. Good road and rail links are an important part of this strategy.

Figure 9.3 Greenfield growth pole in Wales: the UK government gave Sony huge financial incentives to build their new factory on a greenfield site at Pencoed in South Wales, adjacent to the M4 motorway and main railway lines

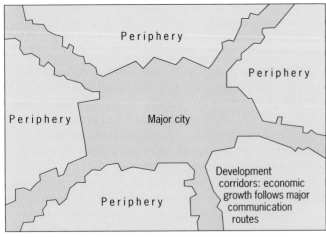

Figure 9.4 Development corridors: an example of top-down planning. Governments direct development funds to development axes along major roads spreading from a core city into the periphery.

Figure 9.5 Development corridor in the south of England: industrial and business park next to the A329 motorway off the M4, Winnersh, Reading

Figure 9.6 Bottom-up approach: women from Saidpur area constructing embankments to prevent flooding, Bangladesh

4a Explain how the development of growth 'corridors' could reduce the size of the periphery and so improve living standards across a region/country (Figs 9.4–9.5).
b Describe why growth corridors may devlop automatically, without government assistance.
c Suggest reasons why some countries, such as the UK, make deliberate attempts to control the spread of growth corridors along major routeways.

5a What methods has your government used to encourage economic growth in depressed areas?
b How could you measure whether such policies have been successful?

6 You are a Christian Aid representative for Uganda. Explain to members of a remote rural village what advantages they might receive from a bottom-up approach to regional planning.

7 Do you think a bottom-up approach would also work for regional planning in developed countries? Give reasons for your answer.

The 'bottom-up' approach

The 'bottom-up' approach is people-centred, concentrating on helping people to help themselves. It involves local people being involved in making decisions about how their region is managed. As such, local communities, especially those in rural areas, are consulted when their government is planning the best method to provide them with food, safe drinking water, shelter, hygiene, health care and education.

Non-governmental organisations (**NGOs**) often give financial aid and technical expertise to help with community-based development strategies (see section 2.7). The projects the NGOs promote are generally small-scale so that groups of people can use relevant technology and local resources. Success of these projects, however, depends on the local people being actively involved and taking control from the beginning, even when outside expertise is involved (see sections 11.2, 11.3).

In bringing development to rural areas, many local projects also provide permanent work and prevent migration to the cities. For example, local people may work to reclaim land by building flood defences and then, once built, the project allows farmers to use their land productively (Fig. 9.6). Without fertile land, farmers could not earn an income, and so would have to leave area, perhaps for a city where they may be unable to find work.

Small-scale local development projects aim to be self-sufficient, but most experts believe that integration with larger-scale national development policies is important. Thus, good transport and communication systems between smaller communities and larger centres are essential.

9.4 Regional development policies in the developed countries

In most developed countries, regional development strategies focus on the promotion of industry and job creation. These policies aim to improve people's standard of living, particularly in areas of economic stagnation and in times of recession. Regional policies in developed countries tend to follow the top-down approach.

European Union regional policy

There are large variations in the levels of economic development within the European Union (EU). Parts of the EU are very prosperous, while others are under-developed (Table 9.1, Figs 9.7–9.9).

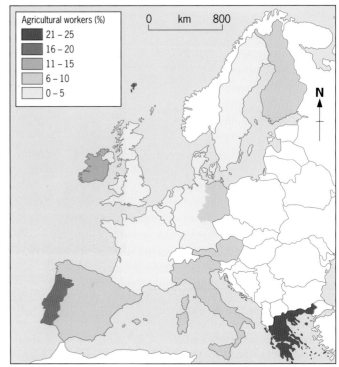

Figure 9.7 Unemployment in Europe as a percentage of the working population, 1993 (*Source:* Eurostat, 1994)

Percentage unemployed
- >16.1
- 12.1 – 16.0
- 8.1 – 12.0
- 4.1 – 8.0
- 0 – 4.0

0 km 800

N

Figure 9.8 Regional variations in agricultural labour force in the European Union, 1989–90 (*Source:* Eurostat, 1994)

Agricultural workers (%)
- 21 – 25
- 16 – 20
- 11 – 15
- 6 – 10
- 0 – 5

0 km 800

N

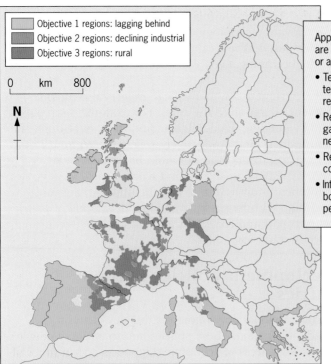

- Objective 1 regions: lagging behind
- Objective 2 regions: declining industrial
- Objective 3 regions: rural

0 km 800

N

Figure 9.9 Regions in the European Union eligible for structural funds (*Source:* Eurostat)

Approximately 9% of Structural Funds are reserved for Community Initiatives or areas with special needs, for example:

- Telematique: promotes advanced telecommunications in Objective 1 regions.
- Regen: promotes the construction of gas and electricity distribution networks in Objective 1 regions.
- Rechar: assists areas suffering from colliery closures
- Interreg: assists areas close to national borders disadvantaged by their peripheral location.

Table 9.1 GNP per capita for European Union countries, 1992

Country	US$
Greece	7 290
Portugal	7 450
Ireland	12 210
Spain	13 970
UK	17 790
Italy	20 460
Netherlands	20 480
Belgium	20 880
Finland	21 970
France	22 260
Austria	22 380
Luxembourg	22 600
Germany	23 030
Denmark	26 000
Sweden	27 010

?

8 Using a base map of Europe, devise a suitable scale and map the data in Table 9.1.

9 Study Figures 9.7 to 9.11. With reference to Figure 1.10, describe some of the main features of the European core and periphery.

Structural Funds amount to less than 0.5% of the total GDP of all the member countries.

A technology park has been created in Malaga and parts of Seville's Expo '92 site are being offered for high-tech research and development.

Regional GDPs vary from 83% higher than the European average in Hamburg to 61% lower than the average in Voreio Algaio in Greece.

The 'high-accessibility' belt between London and Milan has become a **megalopolis** of 80 million people.

The Highlands and Islands of Scotland has one of the most advanced telecommunications networks in Europe. This gives small businesses in the region the ability to link instantly to major centres of commerce and industry.

There is evidence that poorer and less successful cities, dominated by traditional industries, are slipping behind other cities which can attract tertiary and quaternary industries e.g. Greater London has 116 head offices, Helsinki has 12, Copenhagen has 5.

Figure 9.10 Observations about EU regional development policies

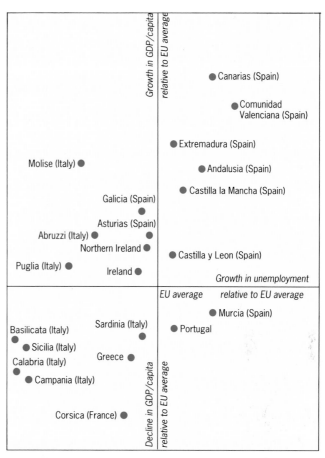

Figure 9.11 Relative changes in unemployment and GDP per capita in Objective One regions during the 1980s (*Source*: Drake, 1994)

One of the aims of the European Commission is to reduce inequalities of wealth and to raise the standard of living in all regions of the EU. A purpose, therefore, of the single market, established in 1993, was to make it easier for industry to invest anywhere in Europe. This was in response to growing fears that the core (see Fig. 1.10) would continue to attract industry at the expense of the periphery, for example Spain and Greece. This would widen the gap between rich and poor areas.

Financial assistance

All disadvantaged regions receive financial assistance from the EU's Structural Funds. There are three main categories of funding:

1 European Regional Development Fund (ERDF) is for disadvantaged regions.

2 European Social Fund (ESF) provides training and employment for the unemployed and, in some areas, helps small and medium-sized businesses to train their workforces.

3 European Agricultural Guidance and Guarantee Fund (EAGGF) supplies monies to the Common Agricultural Policy (CAP). All regions in the EU receive support from EAGGF.

The EU expects that between 1994 and 1999 it will have about UK£90 billion to allocate through these funds. However, not all of the cash will be used in areas defined as disadvantaged. The main objectives of these Funds are:

Objective One The provision of improved infrastructure and new industries in regions with a GDP per capita less than 70 per cent of the EU average and any other region where economic growth is slight. Objective One regions are a priority and will receive approximately 70 per cent of the Structural Funds between 1994 and 1999 (Table 9.2).

Table 9.2 Allocation of Structural Funds by country

Country	Allocation 1989–93	Country	Allocation 1989–93
Spain	£12 000 million	Germany	£5 500 million
Italy	£9 000 million	Ireland	£3 500 million
Portugal	£6 500 million	Belgium	£800 million
Greece	£6 500 million	Netherlands	£700 million
France	£5 500 million	Denmark	£300 million
UK	£5 500 million	Luxembourg	£60 million

Objective Two The promotion of economic development by encouraging economic diversification in regions suffering from decline and high unemployment.

European Union regional policy

Objective Three The promotion of new economic activities, such as small-scale industry or tourism, in rural areas.

Governments and the European Commission decide jointly how much money will be donated to each region, but the region's national government decides how the money is spent. To stop governments cutting their own spending in the disadvantaged regions, any EU grant must be matched by national government funds. This is the principle of additionality. In fact, there is evidence which suggests that the opportunity to obtain EU funds actually encourages national governments to spend more on disadvantaged regions.

European regional development: success or failure?
It is difficult to assess the success or failure of these regional policies (Fig. 9.10). Many of the countries that have joined the EU in recent years have a low GDP per capita, so it is hard to calculate the effect of EU aid after only a short time. Politicians speak of 'convergence', with the reduction in the gap between the rich and poor regions in Europe, but opinion varies.

10   Using Table 9.2, draw a choropleth map to show the allocation of Structural Funds throughout the EU by 1993.

11   Describe how closely the distribution of funds reflects the core/periphery pattern which you described in **9**, and as shown in Figure 1.10.

12a   Referring to Tables 9.1 and 9.2, use Spearman's rank correlation to test the following null hypothesis: There was no relationship between the wealth of a country and the size of the Structural Funds allocation between 1989 and 1993.
b   Comment on your result by stating: • the trend and stength of the relationship; • the significance of your result.

13a   Explain how European policy makes sure that national governments cannot ignore their peripheral areas.
b   Categorise the statements in Figure 9.10 into: • those which believe that convergence is taking place in Europe; • those which do not see convergence occurring.
c   Suggest other ways in which European funds could be used to help peripheral areas.

14   Study Figure 9.11 and identify those regions which appear to have benefited from European assistance in terms of the growth of their GDPs and rates of unemployment.

15   Collect information from daily newspapers concerning the use of EU Structural Funds. Do you think there is evidence of convergence?

9.5 Regional policies in developing countries

Regional policies in developing countries have tended to copy those in the developed, industrialised countries by using top-down strategies. As a result, most investment is in capital-intensive modern industry. However, the demand for labour by these industries can be relatively small. The factories are usually located in urban, core, areas to make the best use of the concentration of facilities, such as financial and insurance services, skilled labour with managerial skills and high-tech methods of production. As a consequence, the more remote, rural areas receive little investment or support.

Regional development in Brazil

Brazil is the fifth most populated country in the world with 159 million people in 1994. It is the largest country in South America, of 8.5 million square kilometres, and has a wide variety of geographical and climatic regions (Fig. 9.12). Brazil is classified as a **newly industrialising country** (NIC) (see section 6.7) and has one of the largest economies in the world. However, the wealth of the country is not distributed evenly (Table 9.3, see Fig. 4.3).

Post-colonial development
In the post-colonial period, after 1822, Brazilian exports, dominated by tobacco and coffee, were produced on plantations mainly in the south-east of the country. The income from the coffee plantations helped fund the first stage of industrialisation in Brazil (Fig. 9.13). As the main industries grew up in the south-east, so the regional imbalances of wealth, previously established by the Portuguese, continued to develop.

Industrial growth
During the 1940s Brazil's dependence on coffee lessened with the development of food and textile industries, mainly in the south-east. The government also

Table 9.3 Brazil: selected indicators of development compared with the USA

Country	Population, 1994 (millions)	Population growth (%)	Urban population (%)	Infant mortality (per 100 births)	GNP per capita, 1992 (US$)	Unemployment 1991 (%)	External debt, 1991 (million US$)
Brazil	155.3	1.7	76	66	2 770	4.3	118
USA	260.8	0.7	75	8.3	23 120	—	—

invested, with foreign companies, in the manufacture of motor vehicles and components, the production of iron, steel and chemicals and engineering industries.

However, Brazil has limited reserves of fossil fuels and has to import three-quarters of its oil requirements. The main oil refineries are close to Rio de Janeiro, Belo Horizonte and the São Paulo area in the south-east (Fig. 9.14). The first regions to supply hydro-electric power (HEP) were also in São Paulo and the Minas Gerais areas. HEP now produces 90 per cent of the country's electrical energy supply. For these two reasons, industry continues to locate in the south-east, although successive governments have tried to reduce the regional inequalities resulting from this concentration of industry. Governments have encouraged transnational corporations to establish plants in areas outside the industrial 'triangle' by stressing the lower labour costs elsewhere. None the less, the superior facilities and infrastructure of the south-east still remain attractive.

Regional policy in Brazil

There have been different approaches to regional policy in Brazil. Some are based on top-down methods, as used in developed countries, and others on the bottom-up approach.

Brazil's own schemes

In 1956 the Brazilians built a new administrative capital, Brasilia (Fig. 9.12). They hoped the new city would integrate the country more fully and focus development resources on the interior. One aspect of

When the Portuguese arrived in Brazil they thought they had found a paradise of untold wealth. They called it El Dorado, the land of gold.

Natural resources include:

- Iron ore
- Gold
- Salt
- Manganese
- Diamonds and gemstones
- Bauxite
- Lead
- Chromium
- Tin
- Copper
- Nickel

Figure 9.12 Brazil: climate, states and communications

Figure 9.13 Brazilians continue development after Portuguese influence diminished: improving the railway network, São Paulo, c.1900

Regional development in Brazil

this was the construction workers who built the new capital. They came from the north-east where unemployment levels were high.

In another effort at integration, governments have tried to attract modern industries to the north-east of the country around Recife and Salvador. Brazil considers these cities to be important growth poles with great economic potential (Fig. 9.14). In addition, engineers have built modern irrigation systems to boost the area's traditional agricultural income which, in the past, has suffered from drought.

Since the world-wide increase in oil prices after the 1973 crisis (see Fig. 7.10), the Brazilians have adopted strategies for conserving energy as well as developing a fuel derived from sugar-cane. This has stimulated growth, especially in the north-east where sugar-cane grows, and has reduced Brazil's dependence on imported oil.

A top-down plan with the World Bank

In 1982 Brazil started the Polonoroeste Project (Fig. 9.15). The World Bank lent Brazil US$443 million for the project.

A bottom-up regional development approach in Brazil

In 1988 four rural workers' unions founded the Agrarian Foundation of Tochantins-Agraguaia (FATA) in the northern province of Pará. With the support of Christian Aid (an NGO), FATA is funding **sustainable** development for the 60 000–70 000 small-scale farmers devoted to growing rice and sugar-cane in the area.

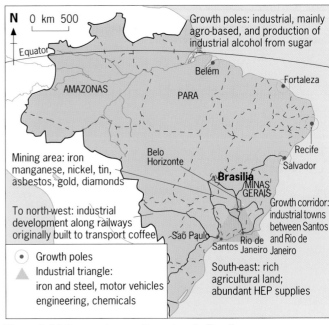

Growth poles: industrial, mainly agro-based, and production of industrial alcohol from sugar

Mining area: iron manganese, nickel, tin, asbestos, gold, diamonds

To north-west: industrial development along railways originally built to transport coffee

Growth corridor: industrial towns between Santos and Rio de Janeiro

South-east: rich agricultural land; abundant HEP supplies

⦿ Growth poles

▲ Industrial triangle: iron and steel, motor vehicles engineering, chemicals

Figure 9.14 Economic growth centres in Brazil

16 Use Figure 9.14 to draw the country's core and peripheral regions on a base map of Brazil. With reference to Friedmann's model (see section 1.4) label the: • core areas; • upward transitional areas; • downward transitional areas; • resource frontiers.

17 Compare and comment on Brazil's regional development policies.

Scheme:
• aimed to ease population pressure in Brazil's crowded south-east.
• aimed to provide land for migrants from the south who had lost their jobs as a result of agricultural mechanisation.
• involved a major national advertising programme to attract Brazilians to this new frontier.
• Involved building a 1500km highway and access roads through the heart of the Amazon Basin.
• Involved landowners buying massive areas of deforested land from migrants and converting them for commercial agriculture e.g. cattle pastures; sugar-cane plantations for Gasohol programme.
• TNCs building new factories e.g. Goodyear; Volkswagen; Nestlé; Nixdorf computer.
• released new resources and minerals e.g. copper, bauxite, zinc; timber, rubber.

Figure 9.15 Aerial view of part of the Polonoroeste Project, Rondonia State, Brazil. This part of the Amazon Basin was virgin rainforest in the early 1970s. By the late 1970s the Brazilian government had designated the area as a resettlement region for people from the drought-prone north-east and urban south. The region, equal to 80% of the size of France, now shows extensive deforestation along roads and rivers.

Problems:
• migrants found the lands to be unsuitable for settlement and agriculture because even after one harvest the delicate Amazon soils became unproductive. Only rainforest agriculture, or shifting cultivation, is sustainable because it allows the rainforest time to restore itself.
• many migrants were therefore forced to sell their land and return to the cities looking for work.
• thousands of people were forced to find waged labour in local factories or on cattle ranches.
• 34 indigenous tribes in the area have been threatened by exposure to disease and the loss of their traditional lifestyles
• hundreds of plant and animal species unique to the rich rainforest ecosystem are at risk of extinction.

Between 12 000 and 15 000 peasant families directly benefit from the project. Collectively, the farmers decide which types of crop they will grow and the scale of production. To help them, FATA has created a small farmers' co-operative where the farmers develop strategies for marketing rice and avoid any costly middle sales person. This means that the farmers receive most of the profit from the sale of their crops. In addition, FATA has built a research and training complex where courses are held on relevant topics for small-scale farmers. The success of

FATA shows that large-scale and export-orientated agriculture is not the only way to improve living standards. This bottom-up approach provides an alternative way forward in which the poor are involved and traditional skills are valued and shared for the benefit of all.

In conclusion, despite government attempts to reduce regional inequalities, the development problems of Brazil persist. We saw the extent of these problems in the scale of Brazilian debt and the poverty felt by the majority of the Brazilian population (see Table 9.3).

9.6 Problems in developing countries

Export-led growth drives many development strategies in the developing countries but it favours metropolitan core regions. For example, large areas of farmland devoted to growing export crops on plantations in Brazil left little land to produce goods for local or national consumption. As a result, subsistence farmers lost their land (see Fig. 4.3), while jobs on the plantations were insecure because of the fluctuations in demand for primary products (see Chapter 8).

In some developing countries, governments enforce national policies for development. These, though, tend to ignore specific regional conditions, local needs and may not be appropriate for the local economy. In response to these problems, therefore, people now view the smaller-scale, 'bottom-up' policies as more appropriate for both local and national needs in the developing countries.

Regional development policies in China

In both developing and developed countries, regional planning tends to have an urban bias (see Figs 9.2–9.5). China is no exception. In 1979, the Chinese government established four small areas along its coast as Special Economic Zones (SEZs). These were open to the rest of the world for trade and investment. By 1984, several other urban areas were declared 'open cities', also to encourage foreign trade (Fig. 9.16).

These 'open' areas are particularly remarkable because China has a communist government which is politically opposed to capitalism and **free trade**. In the past, the government supported all industry, which meant that there was little competition or motive for local management to make a profit. However, the Chinese are now keen to learn new management and manufacturing skills to improve efficiency and make industry more profitable.

There are now 288 open cities, mainly along the coast, with a total population of 160 million people. To encourage foreign trade and investment here, the Chinese government offers a variety of incentives:

• special tax rates at 80 per cent of industrial taxes
• capital, equipment and raw materials imported into China to produce goods for export free from custom duties, VAT and import taxes
• exports, except oil and oil products, free from taxes

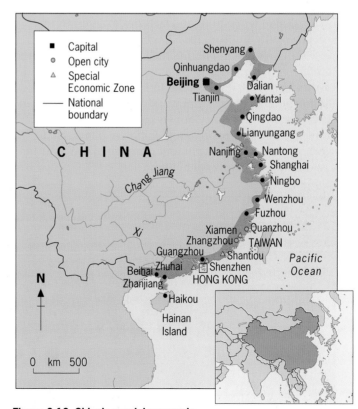

Figure 9.16 China's special economic zones and open cities

Regional development in China

• high-tech industrial investment of US$30 billion subject to only 15 per cent income tax
• local control allows each city to manage its own affairs with little direction from Beijing.

China sees its low-wage-cost workers as its main asset. It hopes this cheap workforce, alongside the incentives of the SEZs, will attract foreign investors to build factories. These factories will then produce goods which China can export for hard currency. In the immediate areas surrounding these prosperous towns, China plans to improve agricultural production to feed the growing city populations and to keep the rural dwellers in work (see Fig. 4.10).

Guangdong province

One of the areas for this new economic activity is the province of Guangdong (Figs 9.17–9.18), with its capital Guangzhou, which aims to copy the commercial success of Hong Kong.

Plans to spread wealth to rural areas

The Chinese government recognises the problems of core areas prospering along a relatively narrow coastal zone (Table 9.4) at the expense of peripheral rural areas (Fig. 9.19). The government has therefore allowed individual ownership of workshops and factories in an effort to spread wealth out from the SEZs into township enterprise schemes. Such schemes include food processing and handicraft industries and are aimed at rural people who cannot find work on the land. In 1987, 23 per cent (88 million people) of the rural workforce were employed in such schemes in areas relatively close to the coastal SEZs. None the less, this government initiative has created work in construction, farm tools, cement manufacturing, coal mining and power generation.

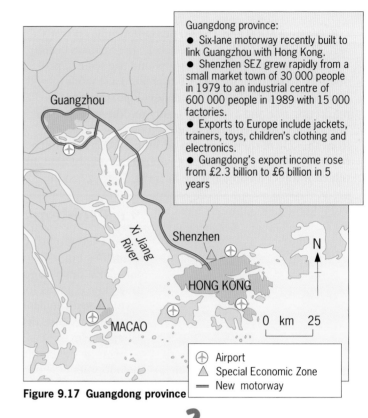

Guangdong province:
● Six-lane motorway recently built to link Guangzhou with Hong Kong.
● Shenzhen SEZ grew rapidly from a small market town of 30 000 people in 1979 to an industrial centre of 600 000 people in 1989 with 15 000 factories.
● Exports to Europe include jackets, trainers, toys, children's clothing and electronics.
● Guangdong's export income rose from £2.3 billion to £6 billion in 5 years

Figure 9.17 Guangdong province

18 With reference to Figures 9.18–9.20, compare the main features of life in the remote parts of rural China with life in the coastal cities.

19 If present regional development policies go unchanged, suggest what problems there might be in the future for the Chinese government and for young people living in the peripheral parts of China.

20 You are a regional policy advisor to the Chinese government. Your brief is to reduce the economic gap between rich coastal and poor rural areas. Write a report outlining your suggestions to spread wealth and opportunity more evenly across the whole of China.

Figure 9.18 Urban China: Central Guangzhou

Figure 9.19 Rural China: village life, Dali, Yunnan Province

Table 9.4 China: average annual income per head, yuan (*Source: The Economist*, 6 June 1992)

District	Yuan
Beijing	2 040
Shanghai	2 334
Xiamen	2 737
Shenzen	4 205
Guangzhou	2 906
Haikou	2 295
Rural China	710

Figure 9.20 China's peasants hold the seeds of discontent (*Source:* Ian Johnson, *The Guardian*, 24 Sept. 1994)

Poverty is absolute for forgotten majority

FAR away from China's boom towns is Hu Banjing, an intense girl aged 12, who lives alone in a small hut with two pigs. Her goal is to be a primary school teacher.

In this remote part of China's rugged south-west, poverty is absolute. Many people wonder how they will feed themselves, and up to 30 per cent of children do not attend school, some because their families cannot afford to clothe them.

Here the average farmer earns just over £46 a year. About 10 million of 33 million people in Guizhou province are classified as poor, meaning they earn less than £12 a year.

This is part of China often overlooked by its government. While many envision a China pulled into the future by its prosperous cities and coastal regions, the hundreds of millions inland may have more impact than the wealthy few.

Indeed the inland's widening gap with the prosperous coast worries China's rulers. With at least 80 million Chinese unable to feed or clothe themselves, the potential for instability is enormous.

Many are not bothering to stick around. About 300 000 people have moved to other parts of China, according to a local official.

This flood of the economically disadvantaged is what concerns Beijing.

When China's overheated economy eventually cools, they will stop sending money back to their poor relatives and return to swell the unemployment lines there. Already, they form part of China's 'floating population' of 50 million who roam the countryside looking for work.

Summary

- Every country, whether developed or developing, has regional variations in wealth.

- Current inequalities in the distribution of wealth of developing countries may result from strategies adopted by former colonial governments.

- Regional development policies aim for a relatively even spread of wealth and development across the whole of a national territory.

- The 'top-down' approach to regional development has governments making decisions with relatively little participation from people in the region.

- 'Top-down' policies tend to concentrate development resources in a few major urban centres (growth poles) with the hope that economic development will 'trickle down', or spread, to neighbouring, economically backward areas.

- Other government interventionist approaches include policies to encourage investment in the run-down areas, mostly rural and semi-rural.

- The 'bottom-up' approach encourages the involvement of local people in the planning and development of projects which will benefit people at the local level.

- In many developing countries, NGOs are actively involved in community-based, bottom-up development strategies.

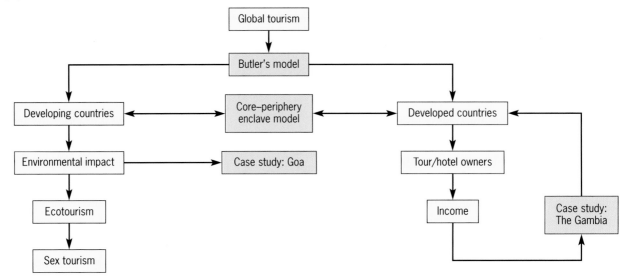

10.1 Introduction

Over the last two decades, tourism has become an important industry in both **developed** and **developing countries**. Every year, an increasing number of people travel as tourists either within their own country or abroad. In this chapter, we examine the economic, social, cultural and environmental impact of this growing industry and its role in development.

10.2 Trends in world tourism

In 1950, about 25 million people travelled abroad as tourists. By the mid-1990s this number had grown to 500 million people (Fig. 10.1). Most of these people travel from one developed country to another, but there is a growing demand for holiday destinations in the developing countries (Fig. 10.2).

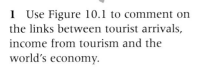

1 Use Figure 10.1 to comment on the links between tourist arrivals, income from tourism and the world's economy.

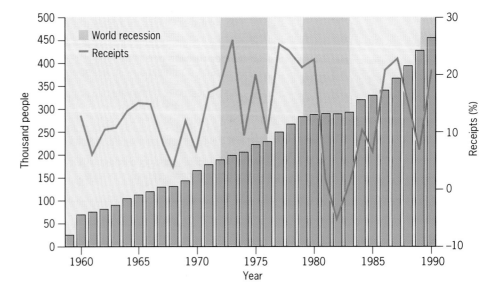

Figure 10.1 World total tourist arrivals and receipts, 1950–90 (*Source*: World Tourism Organisation, 1993)

2a For each world region shown in Figure 10.2, calculate the percentage rise in the number of tourist arrivals between 1980 and 1990.

b Which regions show the highest percentage growth rates?

3 With reference to Figures 10.3 and 10.4, describe the changes in the number of tourists arriving in Africa and South Asia from the different points of departure.

4 Summarise the changes in world tourism patterns since 1950 and suggest reasons for them.

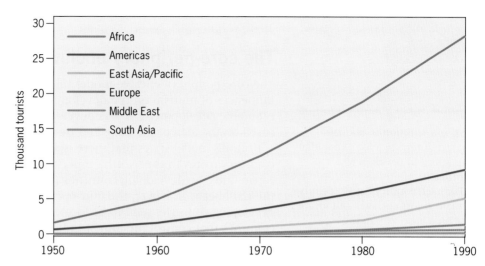

Figure 10.2 Growth in world tourism, 1950–91 (*Source:* WTO, 1991, 1993)

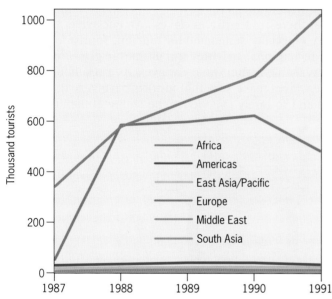

Figure 10.3 International tourist arrivals in Africa (*Source:* WTO, 1993)

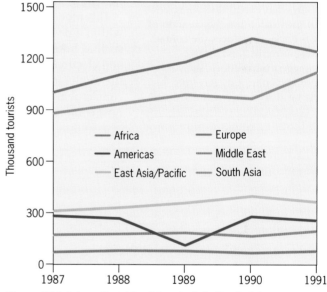

Figure 10.4 International tourist arrivals in South Asia (*Source:* WTO, 1993)

10.3 The role of tourism in development

Many countries now include tourism in their development strategy. It is a valuable source of foreign currency which, in turn, stimulates economic growth. However, there are people, notably environmentalists (see Table 5.1), who are unsure of the benefits of tourism, particularly for developing countries. They feel that the social, cultural and environmental impact of tourism outweighs any economic gain. For example:

• people leave their homes and families to work in tourist resorts

• local culture becomes a spectacle for tourists

• land is taken for building hotels

• less food is grown locally and more is imported

• too much money is spent on tourist facilities

• too little money is spent on improving health, education and housing for the local population.

5a Use a selection of holiday brochures to make a list of popular destinations in developing countries.

b For each country listed, identify the main resort enclaves and locate these on a base map of the country.

c Are there any common features of the enclaves you have identified?

6a To what extent do you agree with the model that the creation of resort enclaves reduces the contact between tourists and locals?

b Suggest what effects such minimal contact may have on:
• the local economy; • the visitors?

The core-periphery enclave model

The core-periphery enclave model (Fig. 10.5) explains the complex social influences of tourism on the developing nations and the role of tourism in economic development. It was developed by Stephen Britton in 1981, and is based on the idea of the **core** and **periphery** (see section 1.4).

Britton's model states that there is a flow of tourists from the developed countries (core) in the 'North', especially Western Europe, North America and Japan, into the developing countries (peripheral) such as The Gambia, India and the Caribbean. However, the tour operators, airlines and owners of hotels in the developing countries tend to be located in the core, so it is those developed countries that control the tourist industry.

Colonial domination and dependency has, to a very large extent, determined which countries are developed and which are developing nations (see section 2.2). Tourism has tended to continue this unequal relationship, with tourists travelling from the core countries to the periphery.

This model also states that there are tourist 'enclaves'. An enclave is an area within a developing country especially designated for tourism. Tourist facilities, such as hotels, restaurants, recreational activities and utilities (e.g. gas, water and electricity) are readily available within these enclaves. As a result, and as the model indicates, these enclaves make sure that tourists have very little contact with local residents and so rarely experience the reality of life in the host community.

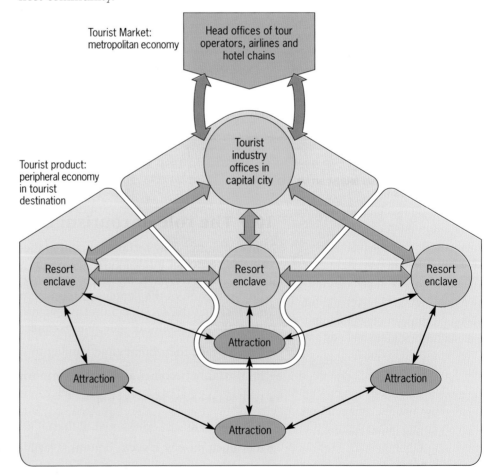

Figure 10.5 Enclave model of tourism (*After:* Britton, 1981)

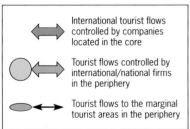

The development of tourism in Goa

Goa is a small state on the west coast of India (Fig. 10.6) with a population of 1.16 million. It was a Portuguese colony for 300 years (1440–1740) although the Portugese influence was restricted to the coastal areas. We can see this particularly well in the 'Old Conquest' area, which is the part of Goa most popular with European tourists (Fig. 10.7). In contrast, Indian tourists tend to visit areas further inland which have Hindu temples, such as Ponda.

The tourist boom began in the 1960s when young people, rejecting conventional society of the developed countries, travelled to Goa. They brought 'hippie' tourism to this part of India and even in 1995 all foreign tourists in Goa are known locally as 'hippies'.

The government's plan for tourism

In the mid-1980s, the Indian Government drew up a Tourist Development Plan designating Goa as a tourist development area (Fig. 10.6). It also decided that the beaches in the states of Kerala, Orissa and Malbahlipuram should be developed for tourism. The plan proposed a wide range of tourist facilities with large five-star hotels as well as smaller, cheaper hotels.

Five-star tourism and environmental concerns

Two pressure groups emerged at this time, though, concerned that an influx of foreign tourists would cause environmental damage unless there was sensitive planning. The Goan Foundation and the Tourist Development Corporation aim to persuade the government to restrict their ambitious plans for tourism in the state of Goa. They are particularly concerned about the following issues.

Building close to the shore line

Many of these new buildings are five-star hotels, owned by foreign companies or companies from other parts of India. Until 1991 no building was allowed within 500 metres of the beaches in Goa. However, the law was then changed permitting hotel companies to build as close as 200 metres to the beaches.

Increasing numbers of high-rise buildings

The most intensive tourist development has been in Calangute (Fig. 10.6). Originally, the legal limit for the height of buildings across all of Goa was two storeys, so that no building should be higher than the palm trees, which are an impressive feature of the Goan coast. However, pressure from hotel developers has meant a change in building regulations so that there are now three- and four-storey hotels along Calangute's main road.

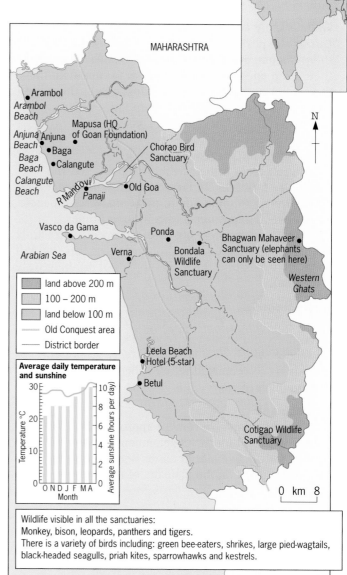

Figure 10.6 Goa

Figure 10.7 Colonial church, Old Conquest area, Goa

The development of tourism in Goa

Water supply and the sewage system

During the peak season, between October and May, there is a massive influx of tourists to Goa. However, there is no adequate sewage system to cope with the increase in numbers of people. Most hotels, therefore, discharge their wastes directly into the sea. Obviously, this has serious environmental consequences threatening the coastal ecosystem.

The hotels in Goa require enormous quantities of fresh water for washing, swimming pools and the irrigation of gardens. In fact, clean drinking water is piped directly to some hotels, while many local people do not even have water on tap in their homes. However, as wells are sunk within the 500-metre limit from the high-tide line, environmentalists fear that salt water may leak into the local supplies of drinking water (Fig. 10.8).

Waste disposal

This is a relatively recent problem. The hotels, restaurants and shops buy food packed in plastic containers which soon litter the streets. At present, there is no co-ordinated refuse collection or waste management in Goa.

Golf courses

In 1993 the Goan government approved the take-over of common land for the development of two golf courses for the five-star hotels at Betul and Verna, in the foothills and on the plateaux of the Western Ghats (Fig. 10.9).

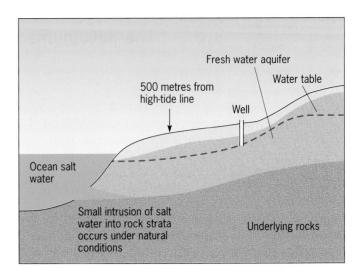

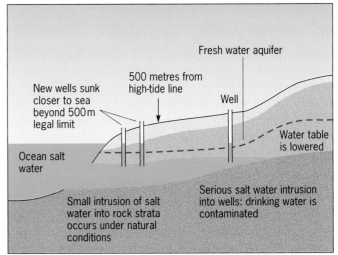

Figure 10.8 The danger of salt in drinking water, Goa

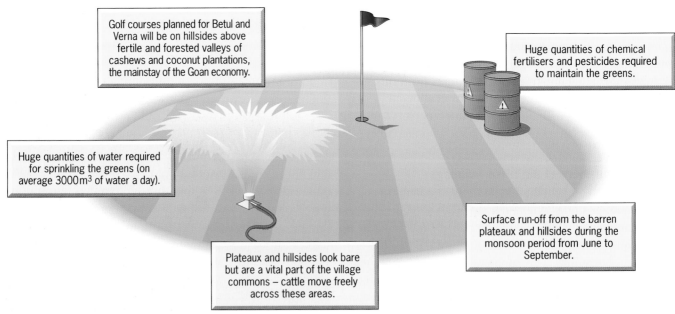

Figure 10.9 The environmental effects of golf courses in Goa

?

7 Use Figure 10.10 and other information in this section to draw a table of the advantages and disadvantages of tourism in Goa under the following headings:
• environment,
• economy,
• social/cultural influences.

8 Relate the enclave model of tourism to the Goan case study by:
a listing the tourist attractions in Goa,
b identifying tourist enclaves within Goa.

9 What do you think are the benefits from tourism to the development of Goa?

THE WORDS and imagery are persuasive: they speak of dream holidays, friendly local people, an unspoilt, palm fringed paradise. But the reality is drug abuse, child prostitution and widespread environmental destruction.

The Indian coastal state of Goa was singled out yesterday as a lesson in how mass tourism to 'exotic' locations has gone badly wrong. According to the pressure group Tourism Concern, Western tour operators are causing much of the damage but are 'washing their hands' of their responsibility.

Goa, which became a Western tourist destination after being discovered by hippies in the 1960s, is now the scene of acid parties, raves and increasing child prostitution.

Tourist buses have been pelted with rotten fish and cow dung, and police mount drives against drug-taking Westerners.

Women protest at their portrayal in tourism literature — at how 'they and events like the local carnival are being commoditised at the expense of their dignity and culture'. Children skip school to peddle drugs to Western tourists, who affront the morality of villagers by sun-bathing in the nude.

Many local groups are also angry at the special treatment tourists receive, according to a Tourism Concern survey. Hotels, many foreign-owned receive subsidised water and electricity. Yet one five-star hotel consumes as much water as five villages and one 'five-star tourist' consumes 28 times more electricity per day than a Goan.

Figure 10.10 Goa's paradise lost (*Source: The Independent*, 27 Jan. 1993)

Effects of tourism on the Goan beaches

The sea and Goa's 105 kilometre coastline are the most valuable source of income to the indigenous Goans. Approximately 50 000 people are dependent on fishing mackerel, sardines, kingfish, pomfret and even shark for a living. Problems arise, though, with tourists using motorised pleasure boats which frighten the fishstock away. As a result, both the income of the local people is reduced while the sea is polluted with oil.

The beaches are also central to the livelihood of many Goans (Fig. 10.11). In fact, fishers often cast their nets directly from the beach. However, they are being denied access to some beaches as these are 'fenced off' and reserved for tourists.

The palm trees, which line the coastal fringes, are also a major source of income. 'Toddy tappers' climb the tall coconut palms and extract the sap to make brown sugar, sweets and 'feni', a potent alcoholic drink. Another local custom is for people to congregate under the palms to shelter from the intense heat at midday. Hotel owners, none the less, continue to cut down the coconut palms and replace them with lawns and buildings, thus destroying the authentic Goan environment (Fig. 10.11).

Figure 10.11 Use of Goa's beaches: Paradise beach (top); Beach market (right)

Butler's model of the evolution of tourist areas

This model examines how tourism develops and changes over time. There are six major stages in Butler's evolution theory of tourism in relation to the developing countries (Fig. 10.12).

Exploration: In which a small number of tourists independently explore a new location. The choice of a destination might come from a desire for personal adventure to explore new natural and cultural territory. At this stage, the economic, social and environmental impacts of tourism are minimal.

Involvement: If early tourists are accepted by the local community then the destination becomes increasingly popular. As more people want to explore the area, arrangements for travel, transport and accommodation are improved. This marks the beginning of local people's involvement in the promotion of tourism.

Development: As local people help to encourage and promote tourism, more outsiders are attracted to the area which leads to a well-defined tourist market. At this stage, tourist firms, mostly from the core countries in the North, take control of the management and organisation of tourism to the area. Package holidays now become commonplace and with them, the loss of local involvement.

Consolidation: Tourism now becomes an important social and economic activity in the country. The extensive development of tourism, through marketing and advertising, affects local communities. Large areas of agricultural land are bought for hotels and other tourist facilities while local people may be forbidden to use beaches reserved for tourists. This causes resentment from local people who do not see how tourism directly benefits them. During this period, the total number of tourists may increase, but the rate of increase in the numbers of tourists begins to decline.

Stagnation: The growing opposition to tourism from the local people and the increasing awareness of the economic, social and environmental problems associated with tourism may prevent the industry from growing further. Fewer new tourists visit, suggesting that the original cultural and physical attractiveness of the destination has gone.

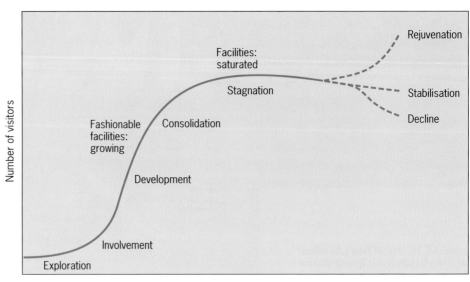

Figure 10.12 Butler's model of the evolution of tourist areas

?

10 Read Figure 10.13.
a According to Butler's model, at which stage of tourism development is South Africa?
b In what ways do you think the government should contribute to the development of tourism here?
c Assess how much the development of tourism in South Africa could stimulate economic and social development in the country as well as in the rest of southern Africa.

11 Design a questionnaire (see Appendix A2) and conduct a survey in your local community to find out:
a who has been on holiday abroad,
b the country(ies) they visited,
c their reasons for choosing such destinations,
d how long they stayed,
e the time of the year they travelled.

12 Based on the information you collect, write a report for a tour operator on holiday destination preferences by people in your community.

Decline: As the destination loses its appeal, tourism will decline. As a result, other destinations become more attractive. Because international tourist firms and operators move out, local involvement may increase for a while. However, as local investors are unable to provide the same services as the foreign tourist companies, the area will eventually lose its tourist industry.

Although the model suggests that the decline stage is reached eventually, it also recognises that it is possible for tourist areas to be rejuvenated. They do this by changing to meet new demand or by sustaining tourist interest. This has happened in Turkey and The Gambia where foreign investment in tourism is creating new resorts and recreating the old ones previously neglected.

South African job hopes ride on tourism

Passport Control at Johannesburg International Airport is overstretched, the new terminals under construction can hardly keep pace, but nobody is complaining. South Africa's tourism boom is well under way and with it the opportunity for enormous economic growth.

After decades in the wilderness, South Africa is not prepared for the onslaught. Hotels are packed, the game reserves are booked up months in advance, and there are not enough flights to meet demand. By the end of June, the number of visitors was already up 52% on the whole of last year, although this rise is expected to tail off by the year-end. For the full year 1 million foreign visitors are expected, against 700 000 in 1994.

But therein lies the new government's dilemma: if the potential of tourism is to be realised and momentum maintained, large-scale investment is vital. This year, tourist's contribution to gross domestic product is set to reach 3.6%, against 2% in 1994, but even that figure is risible against a world average of 7%–10%.

International and local hotel groups are stepping into the breach. Inter-Continental has linked up with Southern Sun to run jointly three five-star hotels in Johannesburg, Cape Town and Durban; Hilton is planning a R200 m (£35 m) hotel in Sandton, Johannesburg, and the Hyatt hotel also in Sandton is virtually complete. Such is the scramble for prime sites that land prices are soaring and the building cost per room has soared from R250 000 to R450 000.

But while most new hotels are in the top price bracket, two- and three-star hotels are in short supply. The next step in

'Tourism this year will account for 3.6% of GDP in South Africa. The world average is more than twice as much'

expanding tourism as a growth market is package holidays but at present they are pitched too high for the mass market. And capacity constraints are being experienced across the board.

Satour sees small hotels and bed-and-breakfast outlets as a big growth area, playing an important role in the government's strategy to integrate tourism into the wider community. In line with the RDP's aim of boosting jobs and rural welfare, game farms for instance, are widening their buying net, taking handicrafts and fresh produce from local villages. This in turn stems the flow of job seekers to the towns and encourages ecologically-sound management, reducing poaching and heightening awareness of tourism's rewards.

Figure 10.13 A new booming industry for South Africa (*Source:* Madeleine Wakemagel, *The Sunday Times*, 8 Oct. 1995) © Times Newspapers Ltd 1995

Tourism and development in The Gambia

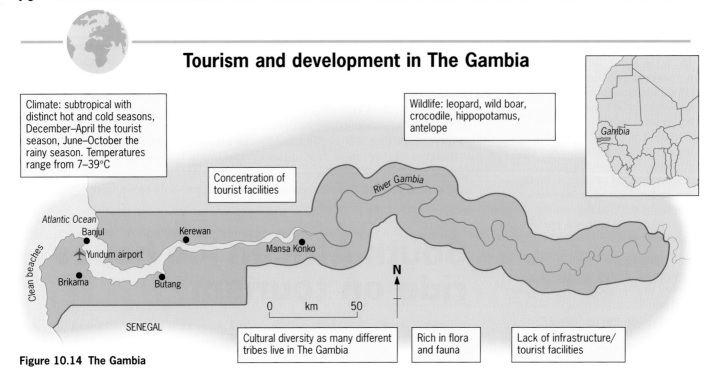

Climate: subtropical with distinct hot and cold seasons, December–April the tourist season, June–October the rainy season. Temperatures range from 7–39°C

Wildlife: leopard, wild boar, crocodile, hippopotamus, antelope

Concentration of tourist facilities

Cultural diversity as many different tribes live in The Gambia

Rich in flora and fauna

Lack of infrastructure/ tourist facilities

Figure 10.14 The Gambia

The climate, environment, flora and fauna, clean beaches and culture of The Gambia in West Africa (Fig. 10.14) attract foreign tourists. The Gambia first emerged as a tourist resort in 1965, but since then its tourist industry has grown considerably (Fig. 10.15) with the support of the United Nations Development Programme (UNDP) and the International Development Agency (IDA). Most tourists come from Northern Europe, with 57 per cent from Britain and 13 per cent from Sweden in 1989–90. In addition, the number of tourists from France, Italy and Germany is growing.

Tourism and foreign investment
Tourism contributes a significant amount to The Gambia's **GNP** (Fig. 10.16). This success is largely due to foreign investment in the industry (Fig. 10.17).

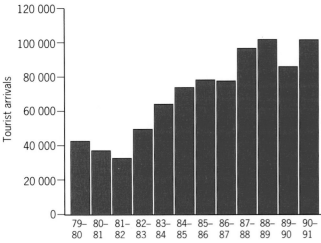

Figure 10.15 Tourist arrivals in The Gambia

For example, the Scandinavian Vingressor Group and the UK Copthorne Hotels (formerly British Caledonian Hotels) play a significant role in hotel development. The government also encourages foreign invesment with incentives of duty-free concessions, tax breaks and preferential land allocations to foreign investors.

However, most tourists in The Gambia book their holidays through a foreign tour operator, use foreign air lines and stay in foreign-owned hotels. In fact, much of the price they pay for their holiday ends up as profit which stays in the developed country where the tour company is based. Some tourism analysts suggest that only 23 per cent of the price of a package holiday to The Gambia reaches the country. Overall, The Gambia is particularly dependent on the British package-holiday market. In 1993–94, of a total of 89 000 air-charter arrivals, 61 000 were from the UK.

Tourism as an employer
Despite foreign operations, tourism does provide employment which benefits the country's economy. In 1989, more than 7000 Gambians, out of a population of one million, **formally** worked in the tourist, or its related, industries. Most of these jobs were direct employment in hotels, restaurants, tour operators and transport. In addition, there are **informal** tourist-related activities, such as manufacturing local handicrafts and supplying fruit and vegetables to hotels. About 3000 people are employed in this indirect way. Unfortunately, though, some hotels close down during the low season from April to October. This means that most workers are **under-employed** (see section 6.2) and are laid off or paid lower wages.

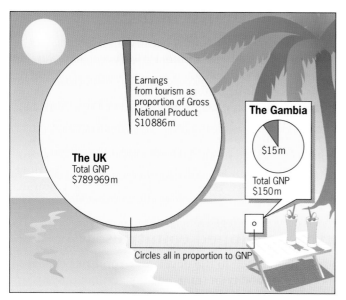

Figure 10.16 Tourism's economic importance to The Gambia (*Source: The Guardian*, 7 May 1991)

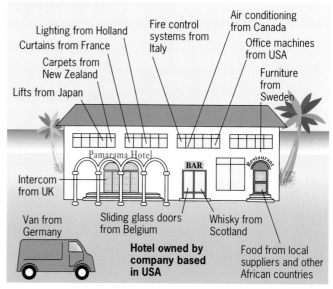

Figure 10.17 How much foreign exchange will this hotel really earn for The Gambia?

Growth of tourism and provision of tourist facilities

Tourists are usually attracted to areas where there are hotels, clean beaches and other tourist facilites. As in many countries, tourism in The Gambia is concentrated where these facilities are available, in a relatively small area near Banjul. Here, there are about 17 standard hotels with 5000 beds.

The impact of tourism on farming and regional development

Such a concentration of facilities results in wide inequalities, with the Banjul area attracting development while the 'up-country' area remains stagnant. Any further development therefore needs to ensure an even geographic distribution of tourist facilities to attract people into less developed parts of the country.

A major problem associated with tourism is that it takes labour away from farming (Fig. 10.18). As a result, the diversion of labour and investment from agriculture into tourism has resulted in an increase of food imports. In 1988, 30 per cent of food consumed in The Gambia was imported at a cost of US$105.2million.

?

13 Use Figure 10.17 to help you estimate how much international tourism expenditure reaches the local people in The Gambia.
b Discuss what might restrict the distribution of tourists' spending to local people.

14a Assess the extent of The Gambia's dependence on international tourism.
b Explain the implications of this for the country's overall economic development.

15 In what ways can a developing country, such as The Gambia, maximise economic advantages from tourism and have greater control over the industry?

Before tourism	**Growth of tourism**	**Decline of tourism**

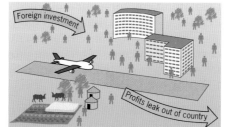

Stage 1
• Available land used for sustainable, subsistence agriculture
• Local communities manage use of land and are self-sufficient

Stage 2
• Tourism developments use prime land
• Agricultural land reduced
• Increasing employment of locals in tourist industry

Stage 3
• Workers dependent on tourist industry are under- employed and unemployed
• Little alternative work in agriculture

Figure 10.18 Effects of tourism on agriculture

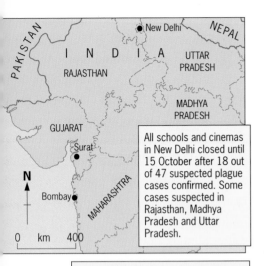

All schools and cinemas in New Delhi closed until 15 October after 18 out of 47 suspected plague cases confirmed. Some cases suspected in Rajasthan, Madhya Pradesh and Uttar Pradesh.

Forty-eight deaths from plague in India: one in Maharashtra, the rest in Surat, Gujarat. Total suspected cases: 1500: 483 in Maharashtra and 871 in Gujarat.

Figure 10.19 Keeping the tourists away (Source: The Guardian, 30 Sept. 1994)

Table 10.1 World's top 10 tourist destinations, 1991 (Source: World Tourist Organisation, 1993)

Rank	Country	Tourist arrivals	World share of arrivals (%)
1	France	55 731	12.25
2	USA	42 723	9.39
3	Spain	35 347	7.77
4	Italy	26 840	5.9
5	Hungary	21 860	4.8
6	Austria	19 092	4.2
7	UK	16 664	3.66
8	Mexico	16 560	3.64
9	Germany	15 648	3.44
10	Canada	14 989	3.29

16 Study Tables 10.1 and 10.2.
a Suggest two reasons why so many of the top-ten countries are European.
b Using a suitable graphical technique, illustrate the world ranking of countries which are the top-ten earners and spenders on tourism.
c Identify those countries which are not *both* top-ten earners and spenders.
d Suggest reasons why the countries identified in **c** are not top tourist spenders.

10.4 Vulnerability of the tourist industry

Tourism is a fluctuating industry. Essentially, this is because of peak and low seasons, which are usually determined by the weather. However, there can also be other factors which affect tourism and its income. These include political instability, inflation, fashion and even the outbreak of disease. Personal safety therefore has a strong influence on people's choice of holiday destination. For example, the failed coup attempt in The Gambia in 1981, and the military takeover there in 1994, meant that people cancelled their package holidays. Similarly, income from tourism slumped in northern India when bubonic plague broke out in 1994 (Fig. 10.19). In fact, many developed countries now issue advice to tourists on personal safety, health and the political situation in certain holiday destinations.

10.5 Tourism in the developed countries

The growth of tourism is not just limited to the developing countries (Tables 10.1 and 10.2). In fact, political instability in some holiday destinations, in countries such as in the former Yugoslavia, The Gambia, Egypt and in the Middle East, means many tourists prefer to visit developed countries – which are probably more peaceful. One clear example of this occurred in the first year after the ceasefire in Northern Ireland. The number of visitors to the province rose by 48 per cent.

Table 10.2 World's top 10 tourist earners and spenders, 1991 (Source: WTO, 1993)

		Tourism earners			Tourism spenders	
Rank	Country	Tourism receipts (US$ million)	World share of receipts (%)	Rank	Tourism expenditure (US$ million)	World share of expenditure (%)
1	USA	45 551	17.45	1	39 418	16.06
2	France	21 300	8.16	6	12 338	5.03
3	Italy	19 668	7.53	5	13 300	5.42
4	Spain	19 004	7.28	14	4 530	1.85
5	Austria	13 956	5.35	9	7 449	3.03
6	UK	12 635	4.84	4	18 850	7.68
7	Germany	10 947	4.19	2	31 650	12.89
8	Switzerland	7 064	2.71	11	5 682	2.31
9	Canada	5 537	2.12	7	10 526	4.29
10	Hong Kong	5 078	1.95	*	*	* *No data

10.6 Ecotourism

Ecotourism, also referred to as 'rural', 'green' or 'alternative' tourism, is based on the natural environment and wildlife of a country. **Sustainability** is the main feature of ecotourism which has grown in popularity partly because of people's concern with our environment and their recognition for the need to conserve it. In addition, ecotourism provides an alternative to the mass tourism of, for example, the Mediterranean resorts. The main factors of ecotourism to ensure its sustainability include:

1 Planning and control of tourism developments – where they will be located and what they look like; transport routes; regional planning.
2 Increasing involvement and control by local and regional communities.
3 Identification of the type of tourism appropriate to local resources and environment.
4 A balance of conservation and development.

A lot of people are attracted by ecotourism because of its remoteness, the small number of people involved and its less sophisticated facilities. If these

17a Explain why some countries are included among the top 10 destinations but not listed as top tourist earners.
b Do you think that tourism has any impact on the economic development of these countries? Give reasons.

18 Research a country or region popular with tourists in either a developed or developing area.
b You are a tourist officer for this region and need to win a government grant for development. The grant is restricted to development that is sustainable. Construct a management plan for your area which combines sustainability with development for locals and tourists.

Figure 10.20
Ecotourists: a rainforest experience on a tributary of the River Amazon, Brazil

features go, then the appeal of ecotourism is lost. Consequently, development must be gradual and limited, although there is an increasing number of tour operators specialising in environmentally sensitive trips to distant and exotic locations (Fig. 10.20).

Ecotourism in Belize

Belize is almost totally undeveloped and only 15 per cent of its land area is cultivated (Fig. 10.21). As a country that recently gained its independence from the British (1981) Belize is now keen to increase its income. In 1992 Belize only had a per capita GNP of US$2200 while 20 per cent of its population of 203 957 were unemployed. The Belize government therefore sees tourism as essential for increasing foreign exchange earnings.

The tourism industry begins

The government of Belize advertises the country as 'friendly and unspoilt', and as 'Belize – so natural' (Fig. 10.22). Although the country is in the early stages of developing its tourist industry, it is keen to avoid the problems associated with mass tourism – pollution; high-rise resorts; crowding; a deteriorating natural environment. Belize therefore promotes small-scale development and tries to foster sustainable tourism.

However, each year increasing numbers of visitors are arriving in Belize. In 1994, tourist arrivals were about 200 000 per annum but the average growth rate stands at 43 per cent. Much of this growth is because of Belize's position close to some of the world's mass tourist resorts. It is only a short trip from the tourist 'crowds' of Miami and New Orleans in the USA, and Cancun in Mexico, to the relative remoteness of Belize.

Sustainable tourism

The government of Belize has designated over 30 per cent of the entire land area as national reserves. As part

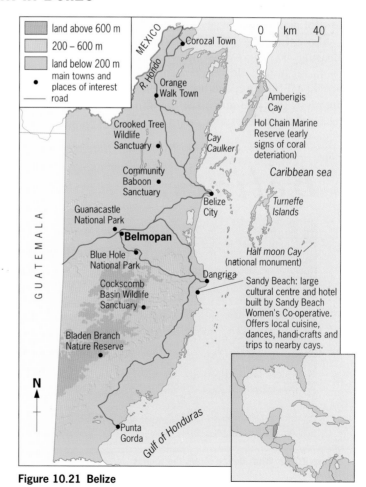

Figure 10.21 Belize

Ecotourism in Belize

of this scheme, farming is banned in the reserves because the government is concerned that both traditional, **subsistence**, 'slash-and-burn' cultivation and more **commercial farming** (see section 5.4) will upset the local ecosystem – and so threaten the country's ecotourism potential.

The government has, though, tried to consider the subsistence farmers living on the reserves. Thus, efforts are being made to incorporate the farmers' needs with the needs of the growing tourist industry. For example, at the Community Baboon Sanctuary, local farmers have agreed to limit their slash-and-burn practices and so protect the habitat of the native howler monkeys. In return, the farmers receive an income from work in tourism as more tourists are attracted to the area.

Development

The challenge for Belize's government is to cope with increasing numbers of tourists while simultaneously protecting the country's fragile ecosystem – including the rare flora and fauna which the tourists want to see. Development, of whatever size, therefore requires careful planning.

Along the coast, development has involved the clearing of mangrove swamps in the north to make room for hotels. However, mangroves perform vital ecological functions without which, the whole coastal area is at risk. Primarily, the mangroves provide rich feeding grounds for fish. Secondly, the swamps protect

against coastal erosion. Other environmental problems will also occur as more building takes place. On the island of Caye Caulker, the recent building of an airstrip has destroyed nesting sites. It has also created a lake of stagnant water which may provide a breeding ground for malaria-carrying mosquitoes.

19   According to Butler's model, at what stage of development is tourism in Belize?

20a   Use Figure 10.22 to decide whether you would like to visit Belize. List those features that: • attract you, • are not interesting to you.
b   Make an assessment of a holiday in Belize according to:
• spending patterns (the proportion you might spend on accomodation, food and drink, souvenirs; who would get your money)
• contact with local people (how and where you would come into contact; whether your contact would help to sustain local communities)
• use of the environment (your impact on the environment; how you would use resources).

21   Write a dialogue between: • Belize's minister for tourism, trying to promote tourism for maximum economic gain, and • the environment minister, trying to minimise the impact of tourism and protect the welfare of local people.
a   Consider the tensions and problems these ministers face including: • how tourism might affect the lives of people living in rural Belize; • how increasing numbers of tourists are putting pressure on the government to develop along more commercial lines.
b   Try to agree on a plan for the future of tourism in Belize.

Belize...

A British colony between 1638 and 1981, Belize is a small country on the edge of the Caribbean Sea. Belize particularly welcomes tourists who seek the attractions of a varied, natural, unspoilt environment. You will experience the wilds of over 2000km^2 untouched mangrove swamps, wetland savanna, mountain pine forests as well as tropical rain forests. In every area there is a vast mix of wildlife including the jaguar, howler monkey, tapir and manatee. At the coast, we can offer you the longest barrier reef in the western hemisphere – second longest in the world!

You can also see tremendous archaeological sites in Belize. Remains of the Mayan civilisation and the Mundo Maya organisation reveal our rich heritage.

Figure 10.22 What Belize offers the tourist

Figure 10.23 Club, Bankok, Thailand

10.7 Sex tourism

South-East Asia is well known for its links between sex and tourism. In fact, United Nations' estimates suggest that there are 700 000 female prostitutes in Thailand alone, the majority of whom are aged between 17 and 24. The sex-tourism trade relies on poorly educated young women who migrate to the cities for work, especially Bangkok. However, as they are unable to find formal employment, many of them work as prostitutes. The influx of foreign military personnel into Thailand during the Vietnam War in the 1960s is an historical reason for the sex industry in Thailand.

Overall, tourism is Thailand's biggest foreign exchange earner with more than three million people visiting Thailand annually. Male visitors outnumber females by more than two to one and sex-related problems are becoming more and more prominent in the country. One example is the increasing number of AIDs cases where approximately 500 000 of Thailand's 59 million people are HIV positive. In the early 1990s the Public Health Committee attempted to force foreign tourists to produce an 'AIDs-free' certificate before entering the country, but the government rejected the idea, fearing the collapse of the tourist trade and loss of valuable income.

However, in 1992 the Thai government tried to improve the country's image and launched a campaign to promote conventional tourist attractions. These included the national parks and the country's heritage, such as the beautiful Buddhist temples in cities such as Bangkok.

22 Essay: Tourism's detrimental effects can far outweigh its short-term benefits in developing countries. Discuss.

Summary

- Tourism is one of the fastest growing industries in many countries throughout the world.
- There are increasing numbers of people travelling both within their own countries and abroad for holidays.
- Many developing countries now promote tourism as a development strategy.
- Although tourism provides substantial foreign exchange for some developing countries, much tourist income 'leaks' back to the developed countries.
- The tourist industry is characterised by seasonal variations and is influenced by changing political and social conditions at both source and destination areas.
- Ecotourism, which is organised around the protection of the natural environment, is an increasingly popular, alternative type of holiday.
- A country's reputation for one type of tourism may change as its government invests in promoting this change.

11 Alternative strategies for development

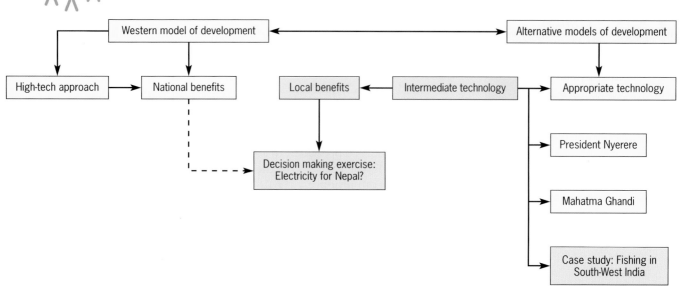

Western model of development

Alternative models of development

High-tech approach → National benefits

Local benefits ← Intermediate technology

Appropriate technology

Decision making exercise: Electricity for Nepal?

President Nyerere

Mahatma Ghandi

Case study: Fishing in South-West India

11.1 Introduction

Most development strategies since 1945 were designed by experts from **developed countries**. We can see the failure of many of these policies in the increasing economic gap between developed and developing nations (see sections 1.1, 1.3). In the first half of this chapter we examine development strategies proposed mostly by people within the **developing countries**. Because these tend to have different aims and structures from many schemes emerging from developed countries (see section 2.3), we call them 'alternative strategies to development'. The chapter's second half then gives information about energy needs in Nepal which you will assess through a decision-making exercise.

11.2 Development is about people

Generally, alternative strategies encourage self help. Local people, who understand their community's needs, work together to help themselves – often, also, with the support of **non-governmental organisations** (**NGOs**) (see section 2.7). Because of this local involvement, such strategies are small scale (compare with section 2.3) and often result in **sustainable development** (see Fig. 7.34). Two past political leaders are famous for their support of alternative development, as illustrated below.

Gandhi's approach

Mahatma Gandhi (1869–1948), the first prime minister of India after independence from British rule in 1947, was a social reformer who encouraged rural development (Fig. 11.1). Before independence, British industrial development policy favoured the location and growth of industry in urban areas and so neglected the rural areas.

Conversely, Gandhi stressed that villages should be the basis of development for society. He called this approach *satyagraha* and through it encouraged rural craft, or cottage, industries. So that every village would become self-sufficient, Gandhi developed 'constructive programmes' which he hoped would lead to balanced development across the whole rural area.

Figure 11.1 Mahatma Gandhi spinning his own cloth, Calcutta, India. In 1925 Gandhi objected to British colonial rule which was epitomised by the cotton industry: raw cotton was exported from India to textile mills in the UK, while finished cloth was then imported back to India. By making his own clothes, Gandhi was boycotting British goods and helping to develop India's village industries.

170

?

1 Assess how Gandhi's village-based strategy of development could improve the quality of life of Indian people living in:
a villages,
b urban areas.

Gandhi was not totally opposed to the development of industry, but he believed that it should be integrated with agriculture. He thought that industries concentrated in cities lead to increased poverty. In addition, if these industries become too highly mechanised, they cannot employ a large labour force. Similarly, if industries are capital intensive, it is the rich who accumulate wealth because they gain the returns on their capital.

In spite of Gandhi's proposals, development planners in India have continued to pursue policies favouring capital intensive industry in, or for, cities (see Fig. 7.32). Rural deprivation and poverty are still widespread in India (see Table 1.5).

Nyerere's Ujamaa concept

President Julius Nyerere of Tanzania believed the poor should be given the freedom to build their own societies as they wished (see Fig. 1.19). 'Growth must come out of our roots, not through the grafting on to those roots of something that is alien to them. It means that our social change will be determined by our own needs, as we see them, and in a direction that we feel to be appropriate for us at any particular time.' (1975)

Nyerere therefore proposed a similar strategy of development to that of Gandhi. Called *Ujamaa* (familyhood) in the Arusha Declaration of 1967, Nyerere's strategy returned to the traditional African way of life where there was no individual ownership of land but it was owned and used by all in the community. In practice this meant that land was not a sellable commodity, so Nyerere was able to establish village co-operatives.

Ujamaa therefore resulted in an economic system that benefited both individuals and households. In conjunction with this, it promoted projects to improve health care, housing, co-operative agriculture and rural crafts. In fact, following Nyerere's reforms, Tanzania boasted one of Africa's best public health services. Additionally, Nyerere believed that African society should rid itself of Western development, which he saw as altering traditional African systems and ultimately creating poverty and misery.

Both Gandhi and Nyerere believed that developing countries themselves should adopt a self-reliant approach. To do so, these countries need to pursue their own appropriate technology and economic principles rather than relying on foreign capital and technology (Fig. 11.2).

Figure 11.2 Imported tractors and trailer being used to harvest sugar cane, Nigeria

2 Using Figure 11.3, suggest the impact of the cassava project in Nigeria (Figs 11.4–11.6) on local:
- productivity,
- income,
- control of development.

11.3 Appropriate technology

Appropriate technology includes any technology that makes the most of each local factor of production, i.e. natural resources, capital or labour, and reduces the use of factors which are scarce. By definition therefore, appropriate technology involves projects which local people are able to manage according to their technological expertise (Fig. 11.3) Appropriate technology for developing countries may, however, progress into *intermediate technology*. This occurs when the technology may be more expensive and efficient than traditional methods, but it is still smaller in scale and more labour-intensive than technology transferred from developed countries (see Fig. 11.2).

Figure 11.3 Advantages of using appropriate technology to meet local needs

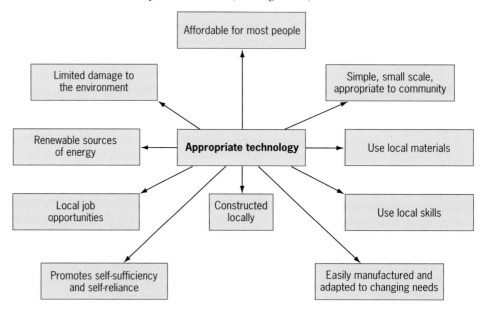

Appropriate technology in Nigeria
Gari is a staple food in Nigeria and other countries in West Africa. It is made from the cassava tuber. The traditional method of processing cassava is to peel it, remove its water and then either grate or pound it by hand. This is an extremely time-consuming operation usually done by women. However, several local initiatives have developed simple, low-tech and cheap machines (Figs 11.4–11.6), saving much of the women's working time (see Fig. 6.17).

Figure 11.6 Cassava-fryer: this new stove has a high burning efficiency and uses much less fuelwood than traditional ovens for drying grated cassava into gari.

Figure 11.5 Cassava water-remover: traditionally, boulders are placed on top of bags of grated or fermented cassava to squeeze the water out. This machine is a much neater and faster process.

Figure 11.4 Cassava peeler with protected sharp cutting blade: traditionally, cassava is peeled using an open knife or cutlass.

Intermediate technology in India
In 1965, the NGO Intermediate Technology Development Group was set up in the UK to promote small-scale appropriate technology. Now called Intermediate Technology (IT), it seeks to increase the income generating abilities of poor people in rural areas of the developing world. IT is therefore a suitable example showing how local needs are identified and low-cost machinery is produced to meet those needs.

Fishing in South-West India

Villages on the southern tip of India's coastline depend on fishing for much of their income. They are, though, some of the poorest communities in India's rural sector. Along the shores of Kerala and Tamil Nadu, fishers traditionally use either a hollowed-out log (dug-out canoe, Fig. 11.7) or a tied-log raft for fishing (kattumaram). The latter is designed to cope with the fierce South-West monsoon surf conditions common off southern Kerala and Tamil Nadu.

Problems

There are two major problems which have reduced fishing capacity in South-West India. Firstly, as deforestation has increased in the area, so large tree trunks and light wood become more and more difficult to find. As a result, the price of traditional fishing boats has spiralled.

Figure 11.8 Construction of plywood boats using stitch-and-glue method

Secondly, from the mid 1970s to the mid-1980s the catches of traditional fishers declined considerably. Many people blamed the destructive practices of trawlers fishing for prawns in coastal waters. To counteract this threat, local fishers organised themselves into unions to campaign for fairer fishing policies. They also turned to technology and added outboard motors to their fishing boats to help them move out of the trawlers' routes and carry more nets.

Developing appropriate technology

Although the fishing communities saw new technology as the best way to improve their catches, their access to information and funds for development were limited. However, since the 1950s, a number of European agencies have worked with the local fishing communities in South-West India on various development projects. These projects provided new technology options but they were inappropriate for the fishers. Eventually, it was only with the participation and consultation of the local fishers that new technology from the European agencies was successfully transferred to meet the communities' needs. Together, both fishers and agencies assessed that these needs were for new boats which were:
• unsinkable, • able to carry engines, • light, • easy to operate from surf-beaten beaches, • built to last about 7–10 years, • more comfortable and with a larger

Figure 11.7 Traditional 3-log fishing boat made from mango wood which can only be used once every 3 days

Fishing in South-West India

carrying capacity than a boat powered by sail and oar,
• within the financial reach of the fishers.

In the early 1980s, the combined efforts of local
fishing communities and external agencies had
developed a suitable new boat (Fig. 11.8–11.9). While
this keeps the centuries-old design of traditional boats,
the building technology, known as 'stitch-and-glue',
was new to the fishing communities. This technique
uses marine plywood and fibreglass, but requires the
same carpentry skills of traditional boat-building. The
result is easily adapted to several craft designs.
Importantly, it is a technology which local industries
can adopt and which uses locally available skills.

Following the successful production of the first boat,
the local fishers and European agencies developed
several other designs. By the end of 1995, there were
about 5 000 plywood boats in operation. Both the new
boat-yards, operated by fishing organisations, as well as
private enterprises were employing local people to build
boats and satisfy demand.

3   With reference to Figures 11.3 and 11.7–11.9, discuss the
effects of small-scale appropriate technology on the
economies of developing countries.

Figure 11.9 Plywood fishing boat under sail

Other alternative strategies

Fair trade, ethics, education, participatory rural development and community
involvement are all key issues in the alternative thinking on development.
Thus, a move away from a wealth-orientated development strategy towards one
in which people are at the centre is now considered socially, ethically and
environmentally desirable (Figs 11.10–11.11, see sections 9.3, 9.5).

4   Use Figures 11.10 and 11.11.
Discuss the benefits of adopting a
human-based industrial
development approach for:
• producers of raw materials,
• firms involved with 'social
accounting',
• the employees of these firms.

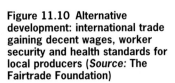

Fairtrade stands for basic human rights for people
working in developing countries who produce goods
for consumption in developed countries.

Figure 11.10 Alternative
development: international trade
gaining decent wages, worker
security and health standards for
local producers (*Source:* The
Fairtrade Foundation)

Cocoa in Belize
The main source of income for many
farmers in Toledo District of Belize is from
cocoa beans. Good cocoa prices during the
1980s meant farmers planted new saplings.
But within a few years prices for their cocoa
on the international market dropped from
50p to 22p per 500g. Farmers were
impoverished: many migrated to the cities;
others left their fruit on the trees – it wasn't
even worth harvesting; the new cocoa
growers' co-operative (TCGA) went into debt.

Maya Gold
March 1994: Green and Blacks
offered to buy cocoa beans from
TCGA. With Fairtrade endorsement for
their new product 'Maya Gold'
chocolate, Green and Blacks paid well
above the market price, at 48p per
500g, and guaranteed to buy all TCGA
could produce for the next three
years. The Belize cocoa farmers now
have the assurance that their work
and investment will be rewarded.

Trade gap: Sadrun earns £28 a month from Action Bag, a supplier to Traidcraft which pioneered social accounting. The Bangladesh worker, who hopes to be elected to the co-operative's management committee, fled her home with her mother during the country's civil war in 1971. Her father and future in-laws were not so lucky. The cash allows her father to eat meat two or three times a month, although she spends most of her income on the education of her four children.

UK firms count the human cost

SOCIAL accounting, by which companies can be assessed against social as well as financial criteria, is about to take off in the UK. At least four major companies are set to publish social accounts detailing how they relate to all their stakeholders – suppliers, employees, customers and shareholders.

Traidcraft, which buys products from more than 100 co-operatives in 26 developing countries and sells them through shops and mail-order catalogues throughout the UK, pioneered social accounting.

According to Richard Evans: 'The prime benefit of social accounting is that it creates a very strong relationship between the stakeholders and the business. For example, last year craft producers noticed that our food side was growing much more

quickly than they were and sought ways to improve their sales.'

Each year Traidcraft focuses on one of its producer countries; this year it was the first and one of the largest suppliers — Bangladesh. This is one of the countries hit by the switch from crafts to foods. Although 21 of the 26 countries saw the value of goods shipped to Traidcraft rise in 1994–95, those from Bangladesh fell by 5 per cent.

Evans visited more than half the 24 producers in the country, all but one of whom expressed confidence in Traidcraft's long-term commitment. The co-operative Action Bag, which makes shopping bags and soft toys, has seen its output double over each of the past two years. But like all suppliers, it demanded more information about the company's marketing

strategies. The social accounts provide at least some of the answers.

The Body Shop and two major financial services groups are social accounting this year.

Allied Dunbar, the insurance giant, is testing the system on its Staff Charity Fund. This will distribute some £35000 to local charities in 1995. According to a spokesman: 'If we are comfortable with that we may extend it to all our community projects, including the Allied Dunbar Charitable Trust, which spends £2m a year.'

Co-operative Bank is preparing a similar social report on its charitable giving, which will amount to some £1m in 1995. According to spokesman Dave Smith: 'We are putting this together in-house. We see our social responsibilities as closely linked to our ethical investment stance.'

Figure 11.11 Alternative development: social accounting (*Source:* Nick Goodway, *The Observer*, 13 Aug. 1995)

11.4 Decision-making exercise: Energy alternatives for Nepal

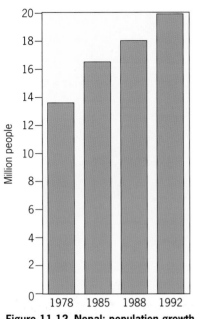

Figure 11.12 Nepal: population growth

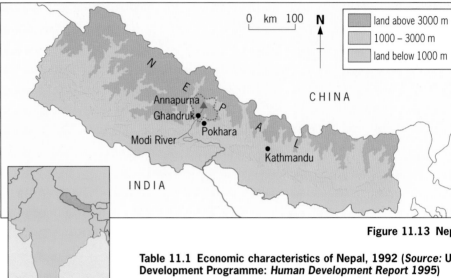

Figure 11.13 Nepal

Table 11.1 Economic characteristics of Nepal, 1992 (*Source:* UN Development Programme: *Human Development Report 1995*)

GDP	US$2.8 billions
Real GDP per capita (PPP*)	US$1170
Total external debt	US$1.8 billions
Debt service ratio (as % of exports of goods and services)	12%
GNP per capita	US$170

*The purchasing power parity (PPP) of a country's currency is the number of units of that currency required to purchase the same goods and services that a US$ will buy in the USA. The real GDP per capita of a country is the GDP converted into US$ on the basis of the purchasing power parity of the country's currency.

Background information

Nepal is a landlocked, mountainous country with no fossil fuels of its own (Figs 11.12–11.13, Table 11.1, see also Fig. 7.9). People use mostly **biomass** fuels (see Fig. 7.28) which include firewood (Table 11.2), dung and other combustible natural materials. These account for 90 per cent of the country's energy consumption (Table 11.3). As a result, women spend about a third of their day collecting firewood for fuel. In fact, cooking uses three-quarters of Nepal's household energy (Fig. 11.14). Another source of energy is the *pani ghatta,* a traditional wooden water wheel, which most villagers use to grind grain.

At present, only 10 per cent of Nepal's 19 million people have access to grid electricity. The government recognises the potential of hydro-electricity and is interested in increasing the supply of electricity via the national grid through medium- and large-scale schemes.

Table 11.2 Forest resources in Nepal (*Source:* UN Environment Programme: *Environment Data Report 1993-4*)

Total forest area	2.1×10^6 ha
Productive forests	1.3×10^6 ha
Fuelwood production	$12\ 795 \times 10^3$ tonnes 1990
Forest cover of Nepal land area	18%

Figure 11.14 Cooking with firewood in a traditional Nepalese kitchen

Table 11.3 Energy potential and consumption in Nepal

- Known exploitable potential of hydro-electricity: 144 000 megawatts (MW)

- Installed capacity: 235 MW

- Traditional fuels consumption, 1971: 96 megajoules (MJ)

- Traditional fuels consumption, 1991: 10 247 MJ

- Commercial energy consumed, 1991: 4 MJ

- Nepal has the potential to generate 30 000 MW of power from its fast flowing rivers from the Himalayas (enough electricity to run Britain's two largest cities, London and Birmingham, with a total population of 8 million).

Figure 11.15. Micro-hydro scheme

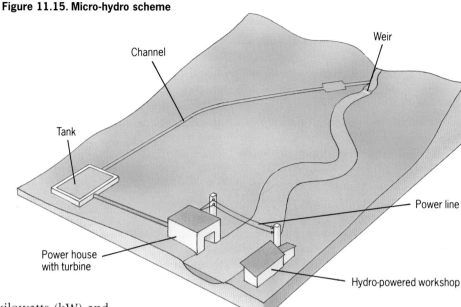

Micro- and mini-hydro schemes

Micro-hydro schemes of up to 100 kilowatts (kW) and mini-hydro schemes from 100 to 1000 kW could provide electricity for up to 50 per cent of Nepal's population (Fig. 11.15). These small-scale schemes operate by using fast-flowing rivers in the mountains, so there is no need for the building of large dams.

In addition to lighting and cooking in homes, people could use this electricity on a commercial basis to mill grain in bakeries and for fruit and vegetable drying.

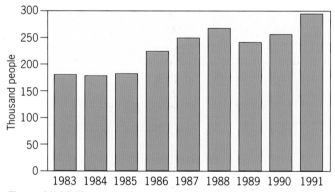

Figure 11.16 Nepal: tourist arrivals

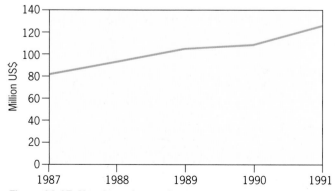

Figure 11.17 Nepal: tourist receipts

Figure 11.18 Ghandruk village, Annapurna region, Nepal

Proposal for large-scale dam at Ghandruk

The Nepalese government plans to construct a huge dam in the Annapurna region of Nepal. Meanwhile, increasing numbers of tourists are visiting Nepal (Figs 11.16–11.17), and the Annapurna region is one of the country's most popular tourist areas. In 1993 alone, 7000 tourists visted the village of Ghandruk (Fig. 11.18). Annapurna is also home to endangered species such as the Asiatic black bear, the clouded leopard and the Annamese macaque.

Ghandruk houses about 270 families living in tightly packed, tall stone buildings perched on a steep hillside overlooking the Modi Khola river. Many villagers served in the British and Indian armies in the past as loyal and fearless Gurkha soldiers. Most villagers' livelihoods used to come from farming, but since the 1970s, trekking tourism has provided them with work.

Decision making exercise:
energy alternatives for Nepal

The energy supply in Ghandruk now falls short of demand. There are increasing pressures on forest resources (Table 11.4) and the amount of cattle dung has diminished with the change from an agriculture-based to a tourism-based economy. In fact, the average tourist uses at least three times as much energy as the Nepali householder.

The energy situation has thus reached a crisis. The government's solution is to drown the Modi Khola valley and install a large hydro scheme. The proposed scheme would produce 10 000 MW of power which would supply 10 per cent of the population in Nepal with grid electricity. The government is keen, therefore, to explore the benefits of this scheme for the area and for the country as a whole. This combines with the government's plans to develop the tourist industry and avoid any dependency by Nepal on imported fuels. In an early report, government advisers listed some of the advantages of the proposed scheme (Table 11.5).

Environmental pressure groups

The King Mahendra Trust for Nature Conservation has set up the Annapurna Conservation Area Project (ACAP) to help communities meet the requirements of tourism and development without damaging the environment. From the start, ACAP has stressed community participation. It is involved in forest-management schemes, reafforestation programmes and a 'kerosene-only' policy for the region near the tourist lodges where fuelwood is severely depleted.

Table 11.4 Deforestation in Nepal, based on all land with about 10% tree crown cover (*Source:* Dr John Soussan, Reading University, 1993)

Year	Million hectares	Area (%)
1965	6.5	45
1980	6.1	43
1985	5.5	37.4

1990s: Deforestation has slowed down, and loss of forest quality is now more of a problem. Deforestation is most noticeable near cities, roads and tourist trekking areas.

Table 11.5 Advantages of large-scale hydroelectric schemes

1 Developers are familiar with the technology.

2 Running costs are low, the fuel is free and constantly available.

3 Hydro-electricity creates no pollution.

4 HEP schemes are long-lasting.

5 Although an area of forest would be lost with the drowning of the valley, in the long term the pressure on forest resources would diminish as grid electricity becomes more widely available.

6 Additional benefits could include: irrigation, aquaculture, opportunities for recreation and tourism, flood control.

ACAP and Development and Consulting Services (a Nepali non-government organisation) are keen to see the development of micro-hydro schemes (see Fig. 11.15). This would generate 50kW of power by diverting a stream which runs past Ghandruk. With this, every house in the village would receive electric light (Fig. 11.19), all the tourist lodges and 20 per cent of families would be able to cook with electricity.

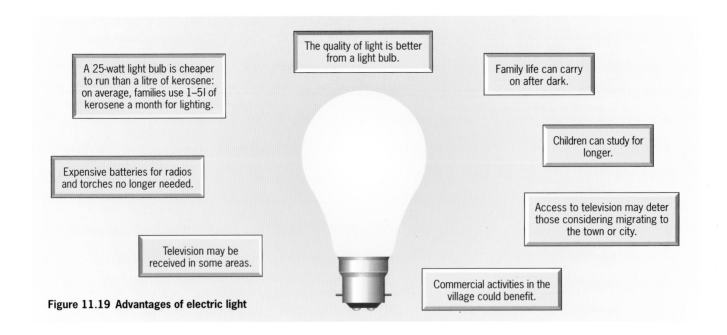

Figure 11.19 Advantages of electric light

Key to success of any hydro-electricity scheme

Electricity has to be cheap and affordable for everyone if local communities are to benefit. Similarly, the project will succeed if people are open to new ideas and willing to change to an electric system. In fact, it is mostly the women who dominate domestic affairs in Nepal, and so they will be the ones to learn how to use the new technology. In addition, local people will become aware of the importance of conservation and development issues by supporting the scheme. For example, cooking with electricity means that fuelwood resources will be sustained, so cheap electric cookers should be an affordable alternative even to the poorest of families.

The aims of any hydro scheme are to benefit the local community and improve people's standard of living. Apart from these, no amount of effort, time or money would be worthwhile (Table 11.6).

Table 11.6 Relative costs of hydro-electricity in Nepal (*Source: Intermediate Technology*, 1994)

- A 50kW micro-hydro would cost rupees 3 590 000 (US$72 000) to build (US$1440 per kW installed).
- Large high-tech hydro-schemes built for the grid cost US$1 billion over 8 years (US$5 000 per kW installed).

?

5 You are assistant to Nepal's government energy adviser. Your task is to prepare a report in which you make recommendations on appropriate energy provision for the Annapurna region.

Although the commercial energy supply in Nepal currently falls short of demand, certain sections of the economy are growing. The demand for energy is therefore increasing. During the general elections in 1991 and 1994 all the major parties included rural electrification as a central issue in their election manifestos. The government is intending to invest heavily in energy production. It is also keen to appear sensitive to environmental considerations because of growing international concern and pressure from environmentalist groups in Nepal.

Your report should include:

a Projected population figures for Nepal for the next 50 years, as well as the likely growth in numbers of tourist arrivals.

b A list of the advantages and disadvantages of both the high-tech and low-tech energy schemes proposed.

c A special report on the environmental and social impacts of each of the schemes.

d A detailed account of exactly who would benefit from each scheme and whether benefits would be long- or short-term.

e Using your report, write your formal recommendations in a letter to the Energy Resource Minister for Nepal.

Summary

- The failures of some large development programmes in many developing countries have prompted a different approach to 'development'.

- Past political leaders have contributed their ideas to 'alternative' development thinking.

- Alternative approaches to development consider local needs and are based on the availability of local resources.

- Such alternative approaches are called development with a 'human face'.

- The technology involved in locally-based strategies is small scale and appropriate to local needs, as well as environmentally more friendly than large-scale, high-tech approaches.

- Small-scale approaches to development can benefit local people and enhance their quality of life.

Appendices

A1 Spearman's rank correlation

This is a statistical technique used to measure the degree of association (correlation) between two sets of variables. Thus it is assumed that there is a relationship between one variable (*x*) and another (*y*). For example, if a country has a high GNP, it is expected that its national energy consumption will also be high. In this case, it is possible to measure the degree of association between GNP and energy consumption by using Spearman's rank correlation method.

The method for calculating the Spearman rank correlation coefficient is as follows:

1 Rank both sets of data (note: highest value is ranked 1).

2 Find the difference between the rank values (*d*).

3 Square each of the differences (*d²*)

4 Find the sum of the squared differences (Σd^2)

5 Multiply the sum of the squared differences by 6 ($6\Sigma d^2$)

6 Divide $6\Sigma d^2$ by ($n^3 - n$), then subtract this total from 1.

Thus the equation for calculating the coefficient is:

$$r_s = 1 - \left[\frac{6\Sigma d^2}{n^3 - n} \right]$$

where *d* = the difference between the ranked values

  d² = square of the difference

  Σd^2 = total of the squared differences

  n = number of paired variables

Once calculated, the value of the coefficient will tell us the strength and direction of the relationship between the two variables. If a perfect positive correlation exists, the coefficient will be +1.0. Conversely, if a perfect negative correlation exists, the coefficient will be –1.0. If there is no relationship whatsoever between the two variables, the coefficient will be 0.

Example

The relationship between Human Development Index (HDI) and literacy rates
(*Source: Human Development Report*, 1995)

Serial no	Country	HDI value	HDI rank	Adult literacy rate	Adult literacy rank	d	d²
1	Mexico	0.842	5	88.6	5	0	0
2	Algeria	0.732	9	57.4	13	4	16
3	Zaire	0.384	15	74.1	10	5	25
4	Niger	0.207	20	12.4	20	0	0
5	Peru	0.709	11	87.3	6	5	25
6	Morocco	0.554	13	40.6	16	3	9
7	Hong Kong	0.905	2	91.2	4	2	4
8	Bangladesh	0.364	16	36.4	17	1	1
9	Rwanda	0.332	17	56.8	14	3	9
10	Kuwait	0.821	7	76.9	9	2	4
11	Jamaica	0.721	10	83.7	8	2	4
12	Canada	0.950	1	99.0	2	0	0
13	S. Korea	0.733	3	97.4	2	1	1
14	Sierra Leone	0.221	19	28.7	19	0	0
15	Togo	0.409	14	47.9	15	1	1
16	Gabon	0.579	12	58.9	12	0	0
17	Afghanistan	0.228	18	28.9	18	0	0

In this example, the Spearman rank correlation coefficient is 0.91. This suggests a strong positive relationship between the HDI and levels of literacy.

Testing the level of significance of the correlation coefficient
Usually, it is necessary to statistically test for the significance of the coefficient. This is to ensure that the nature of the relationship indicated by the coefficient is not due to chance.

The *t*-distribution is normally used for this test of significance. The procedure involves calculating a *t*-value using the formula:

$$t = r_s \sqrt{\frac{n-2}{1-r_s^2}}$$

where n = number of pairs of data

   $(n-2)$ = degrees of freedom

The calculated *t* value obtained from the formula is then compared with the critical value obtained from the *t*-distribution table at the required confidence level and degrees of freedom. If the calculated *t*-value is greater than the table's critical value, it means that the correlation coefficient is statistically significant.

In our example, the calculated *t*-value is 9.31, and the degree of freedom is 18 (i.e. 20 – 2). If we refer to *t*-tables, we find that the critical value at the 0.01 confidence level with degrees of freedom of 18 is 2.88. We can therefore conclude that there is a strong positive association between human development and literacy level and this relationship is statistically significant.

A2 Guide to questionnaires

A questionnaire is a planned collection of questions. It is designed for the purpose of collecting information or particular kinds of data. The basic steps for constructing a questionnaire survey are as follows:

1 State clearly the aims and objectives of the study.

2 Note the critical and essential data required for the study.

3 Know your research methodology and possible alternative strategies of data collection.

4 Understand the central questions you want to ask the respondents. Some questions may be vital for the survey, while others may not be as important.

5 Decide the method of questionnaire administration you will use. This could be respondent's self-administered, researcher's direct interviews of respondents, postal or telephone questionnaires.

6 Understand your target population:
• who they are,
• where they live,
• how and when to contact them,
• when to see them.

7 Think about the possible reactions of respondents to your study. These could be positive, negative, supportive, or argumentative. How people receive your study will determine their co-operation with your questionnaire. Note that some of your respondents could be excited by your questions, some may be unconcerned, while a number may even be cold or aggressive.

8 Decide how many times you want to meet the respondents. Be aware that the first impression is always vital. Most respondents will probably make up their mind on first contact whether or not to support your survey.

9 Determine how large the sample will be, and how best to select the sample. This means you must know the location and distribution of respondents.

The general structure of the questionnaire should consist of:

• a short introductory statement on the survey, or problem, and what the respondents are expected to do,
• respondents socio-economic/demographic background,
• main survey questions,
• other supporting questions.

Sample questionnaire: Holiday experiences in a developing country (survey of British tourists)

This questionnaire is designed to collect information on your most recent holiday experience in a developing country. The survey is intended to examine the social and educational benefits of tourism and to show how tourists' interaction with other cultures can promote better understanding of the world.

This survey is strictly an academic exercise. All information supplied will be used for research and treated in confidence. It is hoped that the study will show how holidays in developing countries can change people's perceptions and attitudes towards such places.

General

1 Estimate the age and sex of the respondent.

	Male	Female
15–25 years	☐	☐
26–40 years	☐	☐
41–60 years	☐	☐
above 60 years	☐	☐

2 To which ethnic group do you belong?

☐ White	☐ Bangladeshi
☐ Black Caribbean	☐ Chinese
☐ Black African	☐ Mixed race
☐ Indian	☐ Other
☐ Pakistani	

3 Name the developing country you have visited

_____

_____

4 What year was your visit? _____

5 How long did you stay? _____

6 What was your major reason for visiting this country?

- ☐ Holiday
- ☐ Work/other business
- ☐ Visiting friends and relatives
- ☐ Religious pilgrimage
- ☐ Education (academic/research)

7 Did you travel alone?   Yes ☐   No ☐

If no, who did you travel with?

- ☐ Family
- ☐ Friend(s)
- ☐ Charity organisation
- ☐ Others

8 What type of accommodation did you use?

- ☐ Hotel
- ☐ Homes of family/friends
- ☐ Caravan/camping
- ☐ Bed and breakfast
- ☐ Youth hostel
- ☐ Self-catering
- ☐ Others (please specify)

9 How would you rate the following facilities in the country?

	Excellent	Good	Average	Poor	Very poor	Don't know
Quality of food	☐	☐	☐	☐	☐	☐
Variety of food	☐	☐	☐	☐	☐	☐
Standard of accommodation	☐	☐	☐	☐	☐	☐
Transport facilities	☐	☐	☐	☐	☐	☐
Leisure facilities	☐	☐	☐	☐	☐	☐

10 Which type of transport did you use most for most travelling within the country?

- ☐ Train
- ☐ Air
- ☐ Car
- ☐ Boat
- ☐ Motorcycle
- ☐ Bicycle
- ☐ Public bus
- ☐ Private coach
- ☐ Others (please specify)

Choice of destination

11 What were your major considerations when choosing your holiday destination country?

- ☐ Recreational facilities
- ☐ Cultural values
- ☐ Health facilities
- ☐ Leisure facilities
- ☐ Religious
- ☐ Good climate and weather conditions
- ☐ Available tourist facilities
- ☐ Safety consideration
- ☐ Scenery
- ☐ Flora and fauna
- ☐ Cost

12 Do you feel you really experienced the country's culture?

Yes ☐   No ☐

General impressions and experiences

13 Did you do any sightseeing while in the country?

Yes ☐   No ☐

If yes, which of these did you visit?

- ☐ Historical monuments/ architecture
- ☐ Art galleries/exhibitions
- ☐ National parks
- ☐ Beaches
- ☐ Landscapes
- ☐ Shrines/holy sites/religious buildings
- ☐ Others (please specify)

14 Were you concerned about any of the following during your stay in the country?

	Yes	No
Personal safety	☐	☐
Political instability	☐	☐
Begging	☐	☐
Prostitution	☐	☐
Pollution	☐	☐
Food poisoning	☐	☐
Safety of property	☐	☐

15 What are your general impressions of the country you visited?

_____

_____

16 Has your visit given you a better understanding of this country and of the people living there?

Yes ☐   No ☐

17 Do you have any plans/desire to visit again?   Yes ☐   No ☐

Thank you for your help in completing this questionnaire.

A3 Age-dependency ratios

Populations can be divided into three groups.

1 Child dependants, i.e. those aged below 16 years. These young people usually depend on their elders for survival. In some countries, though, children are hardly dependent but actually help to provide an income for their families.

2 Economically active, i.e. those 'productive' members of society who work to provide an income and upon whom the rest of society depend. These people are normally aged between 16 and 65. However, many people classified as 'productive' are unable to provide an income, e.g. students, prisoners, physically and mentally disabled, the terminally ill and the long-term unemployed.

3 Aged dependants, i.e. those at 'retirement age' (usually over 65 years) who depend on others, or state funds (as generated by the economically active), for support. Often, the elderly are dependent more on their own savings, or their children, than financial help from the state.

The relationship between these three population divisions varies from country to country. However, for the purposes of analysing the structure of a population, the following dependency ratio is useful:

$$\text{Child dependency ratio} = \frac{population\ 0 - 14 \times 100}{population\ 15 - 64}$$

Example

UK total population = 55.9 million

Population 0–14 = 12.3 million

Population 15–64 = 35.8 million

$$\text{Child dependency ratio} = \frac{12.3 \times 100}{35.8} = 34$$

(i.e., for every person aged 15–64 years, there are 34 children 'dependants'.)

A4 The Lorenz curve

The Lorenz curve is a graph used to show the degree of concentration or diversity of activities within an area (Fig. A4.1). For example, the Lorenz curve may illustrate the concentration or dispersal of immigrants within a city, region or country. It can also illustrate the degree of industrial specialisation or diversification at the same variety of scales.

Example

The purpose of this example is to draw a Lorenz curve based on the data in Tables A4.1 and A4.2. The method for drawing a Lorenz curve is as follows:

a Place your data (column A) in rank order (column B).

b Calculate the total (in this case the total number of tourists visiting both Africa and Asia).

c Convert each value (column A) into a percentage of the total (column C).

d Add these percentages cumulatively (column D).

e To draw the Lorenz curve (Fig. A4.1), plot the rank values (column B) against the cumulative percentages (column D).

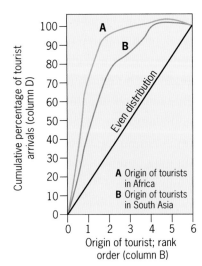

Figure A4.1 Lorenz curve: origin of tourists visiting South Asia and Africa, 1991

Table A4.1: Origin and number of tourists in Africa, 1991
(*Source:* World Tourism Organisation, 1993)

Tourist arrivals from:	Column A Thousand tourists	Column B Rank	Column C Percentage	Column D Cumulative percentage
Africa	10 205	1	64.41	64.41
Europe	4 799	2	30.29	94.70
Americas	451	3	2.85	97.55
East Asia and Pacific	221	4	1.40	98.95
Middle East	118	5	0.75	99.70
South Asia	42	6	0.27	100.00
Total	15 836			

Table A4.2 Origin and number of tourists in South Asia, 1991
(*Source:* World Tourism Organisation, 1993)

Tourist arrivals from:	Column A Thousand tourists	Column B Rank	Column C Percentage	Column D Cumulative percentage
Europe	1 238	1	38.17	38.17
South Asia	1 120	2	34.52	72.69
East Asia and Pacific	363	3	11.18	83.87
Americas	257	4	7.90	91.77
Middle East	191	5	5.88	97.65
Africa	75	6	2.32	100.00
Total	3 244			

Developed countries

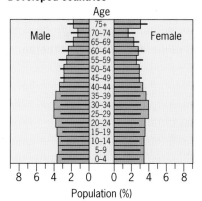

Developing countries

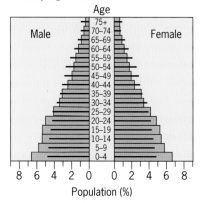

Figure A5.1 Age distribution pyramids (*Source: Philips' Modern School Atlas*, 1992, George Philip in Association with Heinemann Educational, London)

How may the resulting graph be interpreted? If the same number of people were visiting both South Asia and Africa from all the regions listed, the graph would be a straight line (even distribution). The more curved the line, therefore, the greater the degree of concentration. In this case, a high degree of concentration means that the majority of tourists are arriving from relatively few regions of origin. Figure A4.1 shows that South Asia receives a wider range of foreign visitors than Africa.

The Lorenz curve is useful because it reveals a visual impression of concentration. It is especially helpful for comparing several places when their respective Lorenz curves are plotted on one graph (Fig. A4.1). It can also be useful to plot different figures for the same place over several periods in order to illustrate changes over time.

A5 Population pyramids

Age-sex pyramids are bar graphs which illustrate the structure of a population, whether at a regional, national or global scale. A central, vertical, axis is divided into age groups, or cohorts, e.g. 0–4, 5–9, 10–14, 15–19, 20–14 years etc. The horizontal axis represents either the actual number, or the percentage, of people in each of these age groups. The whole graph is then divided into two; males, plotted on the left, and females, plotted on the right.

The typical shape for such population graphs is a pyramid, although this is most usual for developing countries (Fig. A5.1). Developed countries usually have 'mature' population structures which show a more 'balanced' structure. However, the ageing population common to many developed countries gives rise to a more 'top-heavy' pyramid, rather than the wider based pyramid of developing countries.

References

ActionAid (1990), *Common Cause* (Spring edition), ActionAid, Tapstone Road, Somerset.

Agrawal, A N (1994), *Indian Economy, Problems of Development and Planning* (20th Edition), Wishwa Prakashan, a division of Wiley Eastern Ltd., London.

Allen, J E (1992), *UPDATE: Energy resources for a changing world.*, Cambridge University Press.

Archer, M (1991), *Development and health, aspects of applied Geography*, Hodder and Stoughton, London.

Beddis, R (1991), *Third world development and interdependence*, Oxford University Press, London.

Binns, A (1993), 'Nigeria: Africa's Restless Giant', *Teaching Geography*, Vol. 18, No. 2, 1993, pp50.

Central Intelligence Agency (1992), *The World Factbook*, Central Intelligence Agency, Washington, DC.

Coote, B (1992),*The trade trap: poverty and the global commodity markets*, Oxfam Publications, Oxford.

Department for Economic and Social Information and Policy Analysis, Population Division, (1994): *World Population 1994*, United Nations.

Development Education Centre (1990), Where to draw the line? *Studies in political development for 'A' level geography: Senegambia and Brazil*, Development Education Centre (Birmingham) and Longman, Essex.

Drake, G (1994), *Issues in the New Europe*, Hodder and Stoughton, London.

Ecoforum (1993), *Fish curry and rice: a citizens' report on the Goan environment*, The Other India Press, Pune, India.

Food and Agricultural Organisation (1991), *FAO Production Yearbook*, New United Nations.

George, S (1990), *The debt boomerang: how third world debt harms us all*, Pluto Press, London, with the Transnational Institute (TNI), Amsterdam.

George, S (1994), *A fate worse than debt: a radical analysis of the third world debt crisis*, Penguin Group, London.

Hall, R (1989), *UPDATE: World population trends*, Cambridge University Press.

Heppel, B (1990), Pacific sunrise, East Asia's newly industrialising countries, *Geography Review*, March 1990.

HMSO (1994), *Social trends*, HMSO Central Statistics Office, Newport, Gwent.

Instituto del Tercer Mundo (1995), *Third World Guide 1995/96*, Instituto del Tercer Mundo, Uruguay.

Intermediate Technology Group (1994), *Cook electric: the Ghandruk experience*, ITG, Rugby.

Jones, H (1990), *Population geography* (2nd edition), Paul Chapman Publishing Ltd., London.

Knox, P and Agnew J (1994), *The geography of the world economy* (2nd edition), Edward Arnold.

Madden, P (1992), *A raw deal* (2nd edition), Christian Aid, London.

Madeley, J, Sullivan, D and Woodroffe, J (1994), *Who runs the world?*, Christian Aid, London.

Marsden, WE and Marsden, VM (1983), *World in change*. Oliver and Boyd, Edinburgh.

Maslen, P (1990), *Tourism: environment and development perspectives*, WWF, Godalming, Surrey.

Meadows, D, Meadows, D and Randers, J (1992), *Beyond the limits*, Earthscan Publications Ltd., London.

Pearce, D (1992), 'Economics and environment', *Geography Review*, Vol. 6, No. 2, November, 1992, pp27.

Population Concern (1991), *Population: a comprehensive study*, Population Concern, London.

Population Reference Bureau (1994), *Population today: news, numbers and analysis*, Vol. 22, No. 5, May 1994, USA.

Punnett, N (1993), 'Nigeria', *Geofile, No. 216*, Stanley Thornes.

Punnett, N (1994), 'Venezuela', *Geofile, No. 243*, Stanley Thornes.

Raw, M (1989), *Resources and environment*, Unwin Hyman.

Robinson, G (1993), 'The world food problem' *Geography Review*, Vol. 6, No. 4, March 1993.

Royle, S (1995) 'Population and resources in Mauritius', *Geography Review*, Vol. 8, No. 5, May 1995.

Selmes, I (ed.) (1995), *The Geography Collection: World Wide*, Hodder and Stoughton.

The New Internationalist (1988), No. 183, May 1988, New Internationalist Publications, Oxford.

The New Internationalist (1990), No. 214, December 1990, New Internationalist Publications, Oxford.

The New Internationalist (1992), No.230, April 1992, New Internationalist Publications, Oxford.

The New Internationalist (1992), No. 236, October 1992, New Internationalist Publications, Oxford.

The New Internationalist (1992), 'Voluntary aid: the facts', No. 228, February 1992, New Internationalist Publications.

The Population Association of America (1986), *Careers in Population*, The Population Association of America, USA.

United Nations Development Programme (1993), *Human Development Report*, Oxford University Press.

United Nations Development Programme (1995), *Human Development Report*, Oxford University Press.

United Nations Environment Programme (1994), *Environment Data Report 1993–4*, Blackwell.

Wallis, E (1992), 'Global migration trends 1', *Geofile, No. 183*, Stanley Thorne.

Wallis, E (1992), 'Global migration trends 2', *Geofile, No. 184*, Stanley Thornes.

Waugh, D (1990), *Geography: An Integrated Approach*, Nelson.

World Bank (1979), *World Development Report*, Oxford University Press.

World Bank (1980), *World Development Report*, OUP.

World Bank (1985), *World Development Report*, OUP.

World Bank (1992), *World Development Report*, OUP.

World Bank (1993), *World Development Report*, OUP.

World Bank (1994), *World Development Report*, OUP.

World Tourism Organisation (1993), *Year book of tourism statistics*, World Tourism Organisation, Vol. 1, 45th edition.

Glossary

Acid rain An increase in the acidity of precipitation because of pollution e.g. the release of sulphur dioxide and nitrogen oxides from, mostly, power stations and vehicle exhausts.

Actual population change The difference between a population's birth rate and death rate, plus the net effects of migration (see **natural population change**).

Asylum seeker A person in need of refuge in a foreign country. This is usually because of their political or religious beliefs which are against those of the government in the origin country.

Backwash effect Exploitation of the peripheral poor areas in order to sustain economic growth in the rich **core**. This often involves a flow of resources and labour from the **periphery** to the core. The long-term effect of such a flow out of the periphery is polarisation, as poor areas continue to get poorer and rich core areas gain more wealth.

Bilateral aid Financial support given by one government directly to another.

Biomass Living organisms. The rotting waste matter from both plants and animals produces methane which can then be collected and used as fuel.

Bush fallow Farming system where land is left uncultivated for about 3–4 years in order to regain its nutrients, following several years of cropping.

Carrying capacity The **optimum** number of people who can be adequately supported by the productive capacity of the land.

Child dependency ratio The number of children in relation to the number of economically active members of a population (usually expressed as a ratio).

Commercial farming Large scale, modernised food production process run on a capitalist system for profit. This usually involves heavy investment with little emphasis on labour (see **subsistence farming**).

Comparative advantage Cost advantages of a country or region for the production of manufactured goods. Such advantages include abundant resources or human skills.

Core area Central, more prosperous area/region, which tends to attract investment and control functions e.g. headquarters of **TNCs**.

Counter-urbanisation Movement of people move away from conurbations to live in smaller cities, towns or villages, mostly in **developed countries**.

Cumulative causation Theoretical process which leads to the formation of **core** and **periphery** areas. New economic development in the core often stimulates local economy and attracts migrants searching for work. The cumulative effects of movements of people and resources increases wealth in the core.

De-industrialisation The process of declining manufacturing industry e.g. 1970s and 1980s in **developed countries**.

Demographic transition stage A country's rate of population growth or decline, as determined by existing birth and death rates. The 'stage' of population change often relates to economic development.

Demography Study of the statistical characteristics of human populations, e.g. total size, age and sex composition, changes over time with variations in birth and death rates.

Desertification Reduction in agricultural capacity as once fertile land degrades into sterile, dry and unproductive land. This often results from overgrazing, overcropping or deforestation.

Developed countries Economically advanced countries characterised by high standards of living, large industrial and service sectors and high **GNPs**.

Developing countries Countries where the **GDP** is inadequate for generating investment in agriculture and industry. Characterised by low standards of living, large primary sectors and low **GNPs**.

Distance decay effect A decrease in numbers of people moving between places A and B as the distance between A and B increases. This suggests greater interaction between places which are closer together.

Downward spiral Process of declining wealth in **peripheral areas** as people and resources move out of the periphery into the richer **core areas**.

Ecological refugee Migrant forced out of his/her normal place of residence because of natural disaster e.g. earthquake, flood, drought. Also includes industrial accidents e.g. oil spillage, chemical/toxic leaks.

Economic gap Differences in levels of economic prosperity between nations, as measured by indices such as **GNP**.

Economic migrant Person leaving her/his native country to seek better economic opportunities and so settle temporarily in another country.

Economies of scale Cost advantages or savings made as a result of large-scale production.

Ecosystem A natural system that shows the relationships between a community of living things (plants and animals) and their non-living environment.

Emigration   Movement of people away from their native country to settle permanently in another. (Permanent is defined by the United Nations as a period lasting one year or more).

Fertility gap   The difference between the high population growth rates which characterise **developing countries** and the low population growth rates which are typical of the **developed countries**.

Finite resources   Resources limited in supply, e.g. fossil fuels (also termed non-renewable or **stocks**).

First World   The group of countries mostly located in the Northern and Western Hemispheres which have high standards of living.

Flows   Resources which are natural, renewable and in constant supply, e.g. water, air, sun and wind. These resources can be harnessed as renewable energy (compare with **stocks**).

Formal sector   Where people work to receive a regular wage and are assured certain rights, e.g. paid holidays, sickness leave. The government recognises work in the formal sector for tax purposes.

Free market economy   An economic system where methods of production are privately held by individuals and firms. The market then determines the levels of supply and demand.

Free trade   International trade that takes place without trade barriers e.g. **tariffs**, quotas, and so allows the free movement of goods and services between countries.

Global warming   Theoretical process by which the earth's average global temperatures are increasing. This is thought to occur because of the release of **greenhouse** gases by e.g. burning fossil fuels.

Green economics   Economic activities which seek to conserve the environment.

Greenhouse effect   Natural warming of the lower atmosphere as greenhouse gases, e.g. carbon dioxide, sulphur dioxide, nitrous oxide and methane, absorb long-wave radiation emitted from the earth. A build-up of these gases (from pollution) may upset the warming process, causing more heat to be retained in the earth's atmosphere, and so leading to **global warming**.

Gross domestic product (GDP)   The total value of all goods and services produced in a country over a period of one year. It is a measure of the wealth of a country and is often expressed as GDP per capita (i.e., the value of the GDP divided by the population total).

Gross national product (GNP)   The total value of the GDP plus profits from investments abroad.

Growth corridor/pole   An area where governments deliberately encourage investment and resources to stimulate economic development.

Immigration   The entry of individuals into a country other than their own, with the intention to stay for at least 12 months.

Import substitution   The development of local industries and production to replace imported goods, reduce dependency on imports, conserve foreign exchange and improve the balance of payments of a country.

Informal sector   Work done (both paid and unpaid) without the official knowledge of the government and therefore without **formal** control.

Intervening opportunities   Alternative places between two locations, A and B, that are attractive to migrants. These places distract migrants from travelling directly from place A to place B.

Law of diminishing returns   As inputs are added to the production function, a point is reached beyond which yields do not increase but begin to fall.

Marginal land   Land which produces minimal yield and has a low **carrying capacity**. This may be due to poor quality, over-use, or a lack of essential nutrients to support economic agricultural production.

Megalopolis   Large city (200 000–500 000 people) which services surrounding area of up to 3m people, and which grows to merge into another large city.

Mercantilism   Economic theory prevalent in Europe during the 17th and 18th centuries which stresses the importance of trade and commerce as the source of a nation's wealth. Mercantilism depends on wealth and power through exports and the possession of precious commodities e.g. gold, silver.

Multilateral aid   Financial support given through international organisations e.g. World Bank, IMF.

Natural population change   Rate of population change calculated from birth and death rates alone. Additional effects of migration are not included

Neo-colonialism   Control, by an outside power, of a country that is in theory independent – especially through the domination of its economy.

New world   That part of the world discovered since the middle ages. Usually this refers to the Americas (see **old world**).

Newly industrialising country (NIC)   A country that has achieved rapid and successful industrialisation and economic development.

Non-governmental organisation (NGO)   A voluntary, non-political, non-commercial organisation which seeks to help the less privileged members of society.

North-South divide   Term first used in the Brandt report, 1979, to identify the social and economic differences between richer, **developed countries** and poorer, **developing countries**.

Optimum population   The number of people who receive the best standards of living when using available resources and technology.

Old world   That part of the world that was known before the discovery of the Americas, e.g. Europe, Asia and Africa.

Over-population   When a population is so large, in relation to available resources and existing levels of technology, that people do not enjoy decent living standards.

Periphery   Area which is geographically remote from a central **core** area. The periphery often suffers from a lack of resources and wealth and can occur at local, regional, national or global scales (see **cumulative causation**).

Population ceiling   The theoretical maximum number of people who can be supported by the available resources and levels of technology. This is measured according to an area's **carrying capacity**.

Population distribution   The spread of people across the earth.

Population momentum   When current population growth (through increased birth rates) determines future population expansion as new babies reach the child-bearing age.

Reserve   Estimated life-span of a **finite resource** or **stock**.

Shifting cultivation   When farmers clear and burn an area of vegetation to allow them to grow crops for a few years, after which yields decline and they move to a new clearing.

Social forestry   The growing and management of forest resources in a **sustainable** manner.

Spread effects   When benefits from development spread from the **core** to **peripheral** areas. This concept is often associated with the **growth pole** theory.

Stocks   Natural resources which are measurable and limited in supply. The proven quantity of stocks is a **reserve** e.g. coal reserve is the amount of coal known to exist and which remains as yet unexploited.

Structural adjustment programme (**SAP**)   A set of conditions imposed on countries borrowing money from the World Bank. These often result in the government of the borrowing country having to cut national spending.

Subsistence agriculture   Farming system characterised by simple technology, low capital investment and where most produce is used for domestic consumption (compare with **commercial farming**).

Sustainability   Long-term management of the environment in order to maintain its natural resources.

Tariff   A tax or duty charged by a government on imported goods.

Third World   Group of **developing countries** characterised by low incomes and low levels of social and economic development. These countries are mostly located in Africa, Asia and South America.

Trade bloc   Group of countries united to promote common economic interests.

Transnational corporation (**TNC**)   Large company corporation, usually based in a **developed country**, which owns businesses in more than one country.

Under-employment   When people do not have full-time, continuous work and are usually only employed temporarily or seasonally.

Under-population   When there are too few people in a given area to fully exploit existing resources with the available technology. As a result, living standards are low. If numbers increased, living standards should improve.

Urbanisation   The process of more and more people living in towns and cities. It is expected that by the year 2000 over half the world's population will live in urban areas.

War refugee   A person displaced from her/his homeland as a result of war, or political disturbance.

Index

Published by Collins Educational
77–85 Fulham Palace Road
London W6 8JB

An imprint of HarperCollins*Publishers*

©1996 Jane Chrispin and Francis Jegede

First published 1996, reprinted 1997, 1998

ISBN 0 00 3266885

Edited by Anne Montefiore

Designed by Jacky Wedgwood

Design production by Adrienne Lee

Picture research by Caroline Thompson

Computer artwork by Barking Dog Art, Bitmap Graphics, Contour Publishing, Jerry Fowler, Hardlines

Illustrations by Jeremy Gower

Cartoons by Richardson Studio

Printed and Bound by Printing Express Ltd., Hong Kong.

Author dedications

This book is dedicated to our children: Tobi, Evangeline and Eleanor.

We are indebted to many of our colleagues at South East Derbyshire College and the University of Derby, together with our friends who supported us in the course of writing this book. We particularly want to acknowledge the support received from our immediate families and work colleagues especially Dr Irene Brightmer, Geography Lecturer at the University of Derby.

Acknowledgements

Every effort has been made to contact the holders of copyright material, but if any have been inadvertently overlooked the publisher will be pleased to make the necessary arrangements at the first opportunity.

Photographs
The publisher would like to thank the following for permission to reproduce photographs:
Action Aid, Oxfam, Christian Aid 1994, Fig. 2.22;
John Birdsall Photography, Fig. 3.31;
British Library, London/Bridgeman Art Library, Fig. 2.4;
Rob Nelson/Black Star/Colorific, Fig. 5.21;
Prodeepta Das, Fig. 2.11;
Del Monte Fresh Produce (UK) Ltd, Fig. 8.11;
Mary Evans Picture Library, Figs 2.1, 9.13;
John Sylvester/First Light, Fig. 7.2;
Ela Ginalska, Fig. 3.17;
Jurgen Dielenschneider/Holt Studios International, Fig. 3.21;
Hulton Deutsch Collection, Figs 4.2, 11.1;
The Hutchison Library, Figs 3.1, 6.26;
Intermediate Technology/Neil Cooper, Fig. 7.34;
Intermediate Technology/Ian MacWhinnie, Figs 11.7, 11.8;
Intermediate Technology/Paul Calvert, Fig. 11.9;
International Coffee Organization, Fig. 8.5;
Francis Jegede, Figs 11.4, 11.5, 11.6;
London Aerial Photo Library, Figs 1.14, 1.18, 9.3, 9.5;
Stuart Franklin/Magnum Photos Ltd, Fig. 7.12;
Metropolitan Police Service, Fig. 6.1;
James Morris, Fig. 6.2;
H Donnezan/Rapho/Network, Fig. 5.1(top);
B Lewis/Network, Figs 7.3, 9.19;
Christopher Pillitz/Network, Fig. 10.23;
J Hartley/Panos Pictures, Fig. 1.3;
B Tobiasson/Panos Pictures, Fig. 1.4;
C Stowers/Panos Pictures, Fig. 3.16;
B Paton/Panos Pictures, Fig 5.16;
R Johnson/Panos Pictures, Figs 6.32, 10.11;
S Leigh-Lewis/Panos Pictures, Fig. 7.4;
R Giling/Panos Pictures, Fig. 7.32;
P Wolmuth/Panos Pictures, Fig. 8.14;
Popperfoto, Fig. 1.5;
Robert Prosser, Fig. 10.20;
Rex Features, Figs 4.19, 4.29;
Science Photo Library, Figs 2.9, 7.4, 7.29, 7.30, 9.15;
G Smith/Liaison/FSP, Fig. 4.21;
E Bouvet/Gamma Press/FSP, Fig. 4.27;
South American Pictures, Fig. 9.1;
C Pye-Smith/Still Pictures, Fig. 2.10;
J Kaplan/Still Pictures/FoE, Fig. 2.21;
P Harrison/Still Pictures, Figs 3.2, 5.17, 6.14;
C Caldicott/Still Pictures, Fig. 3.18;
M Edwards/Still Pictures, Figs 3.19, 3.28, 5.14;
J Schytte/Still Pictures, Figs 3.20, 9.6, 11.2;
J Maier/Still Pictures, Fig. 4.3;
H Netocny/Still Pictures, Fig.5.1 (bottom);
S Rajkoomar/Still Pictures, Fig. 5.10;
J Etchart/Still Pictures, Fig. 7.26;
Tony Stone Images, Figs 4.15, 5.15, 6.13, 6.28, 7.5, 7.7, 7.21, 7.27, 7.29, 8.1;
Chris Haigh/Tony Stone Images, Fig. 10.7;
Norbert Wu/Tony Stone Images, Fig. 10.22;
Traidcraft, Fig. 11.11;
Tony Waltham Geophotos, Figs 9.18, 11.14, 11.18;
Philip Wolmuth, Fig. 1.2.

Cover picture
Women cycling in Hangzhou, China. *Source:* Tony Stone Images.